Ben Bradlee in his *Washington Post* office

Above
Jack Anderson teaching a Mormon Sunday School class

Opposite
Clark Mollenhoff in stage role as singing politician

Opposite
Carl Rowan at home

Below
Johnny Apple at lunch at Jean-Pierre's

Opposite
Sander Vanocur at home

Above
Helen Thomas in the Oval Office of the White House

Opposite
Soma Golden at home

Below
Scotty Reston

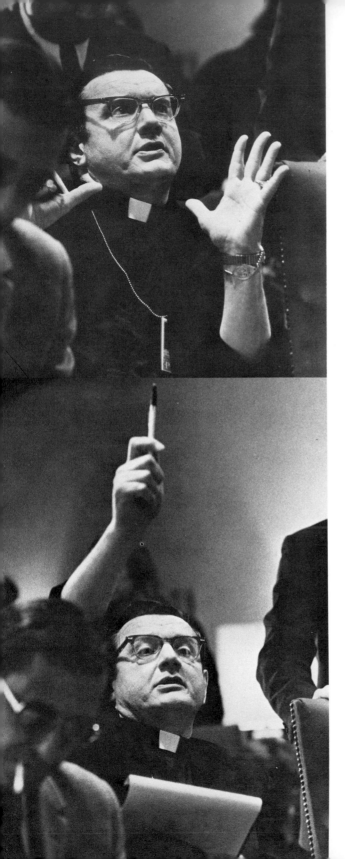

Left
Rev. Lester Kinsolving asking
questions at a White House
press briefing

Opposite
Joe Alsop at home

Opposite
Mike Waters in National Public Radio studio

Below
Susan Stamberg in National Public Radio studio

Above and left
Maxine Cheshire at her office at the
Washington Post

Opposite
Bob Pierpoint at the White House

Above
Marvin Kalb and Bernard Kalb
working at Marvin's house

Left
Ben Bradlee in the
Washington Post newsroom

Opposite top
Connie Chung and her
parents at home

Opposite bottom
Bob Woodward and Carl Bernstein
in the *Washington Post*
newsroom

Above
Eric Sevareid telling his daughter
Cristina a bedtime story in
his study at home

Left
Eric Sevareid and his daughter
Cristina after her riding class

Opposite
Eric and Cristina

Stew Alsop at home, March 29, 1974

HOPE AND FEAR IN WASHINGTON (THE EARLY SEVENTIES)

HOPE AND FEAR IN WASHINGTON

(THE EARLY SEVENTIES) THE STORY OF THE WASHINGTON PRESS CORPS

BY BARNEY COLLIER WITH PHOTOGRAPHS BY MAGGI CASTELLOE

THE DIAL PRESS
NEW YORK 1975

Material on James Reston, Eric Severeid, Helen Thomas, and Art
Buchwald was previously published in abridged form in *The
Washingtonian* magazine.

Chapters 24 and 25 appeared in a slightly different form in *[MORE]*
magazine, February, 1975.

Manufactured in the United States of America
First printing

Library of Congress Cataloging in Publication Data

Collier, Barney, 1938–
    Hope and fear in Washington (the early seventies).

    1. Journalists—Washington, D. C.—Correspondence,
reminiscences, etc.   I. Title.
PN4899.W29C56   070'.92'2   75-23417
    ISBN 0-8037-5375-6

All of the characters portrayed in this book are as real as they cared to make themselves. Barney, Maggi, Kate, and Buckeye Dog are coincidental. The I is the author's imagination.

*This book is dedicated
to the memory of those
who lost their lifes during
The Voltairean War*

To hold a pen
is to be at war.

Voltaire

He loved life and she
loved death and they
loved each other madly.

Due de Balloon

HOPE AND FEAR IN WASHINGTON

One of the ideas behind this book is that in order to more nearly understand the news from Washington you must more nearly understand the life of the person who tells you what the news may be. News is a point of view. What's news to me may not be news to you.

Most of what is in this book about Washington news people was news to me. I had never looked at them or myself very closely before. I had been among them, and I knew how they worked, who filed their copy on time, who had respect among colleagues and who didn't, and a lot of professional opinion, but in most cases I simply absorbed and never bothered to digest.

So for this book I went back years later to look at the working news people who were the companions of my boyhood as a reporter, and to see different people I'd never met before who are in the business now. I looked very hard at from sixty to seventy people; harder than I'd ever looked at people in my life before. I looked so hard I nearly got a hernia of the mind. I left out only two honest friends and the people who were weak and boring. No matter who they are or what I saw, the people who appear in this book are in it because they ring true.

There are several ways these people might have been looked at. The easiest way for me would be to see them either the size of red ants or the size of the heroic David in front of Goliath. It was very difficult to look at them as mortal human creatures. So I decided to look at them as if time and memory, and truth and humor, and life's realities and phantoms and daydreams and nightmares are all part of a mind that is a flower with many petals and can change substance and form in a blink.

As far as facts are concerned, I stuck as close to the facts as the people would let me. I asked for only one document. I did double-check each birthday and place of birth. I was scrupulous about remembering and, whenever there was any doubt, checking what people said; and I observed only one technical rule: Nothing whatever was off the record. I told every person I talked to that I didn't want to hear anything so private that it was off the record, on the grounds that I might forget and write it.

I asked any question that came to my mind, no matter how private it might seem to be. I never asked a private sort of question out of leering curiousity. I want to know who loves who and why, and how much money people get paid, and if they panic like I do, and how their mind works and what games it will play and whether it's happy or lonesome. And other things.

To ask people such questions, you should be willing, up front, to explain a part of your own life and love at a particular time, too. Otherwise you are clothed in armor against the people you would pretend to respect, and can poke at them without respect from behind your blank-eyed bodyguard of personal secrecy, and report the answers in stiff summations. You are shielded in a pretentious suit that is the trademark for soberness and respectability.

This book was not written to be sober and respectable.

This book was written for wild and funny, wide and frightened, wicked and ferocious, wonderful and free eyes.

What it says briefly about Barney, Maggi, and Kate is much too sentimental and silly to be anything else but true.

HOPE AND FEAR IN WASHINGTON (THE EARLY SEVENTIES)

If the poor could hire the rich to die for them, Cowards would be a dime a dozen.

Marcus Atticus Septimus

I was at first preoccupied with the vision of dying in wartime. I had no physical courage to speak of. It had been an effort of will for me to jump from an eight-foot wall, in order to sneak into the Detroit Zoo as a ten-year-old; the thought of jumping out of an airplane in a parachute behind enemy lines reflexively tensed my jaw muscles and hardened my eyes with defiance. I cringed with shame inside at this lack of enthusiasm for risking my neck. Like most men I admired physical risk takers, with one qualification: they survived past fifty, and still lived. The saying among airplane pilots was, "There are old pilots and bold pilots, but there are no old, bold pilots." I repeated that often.

So among the first people I drove into Washington to see after lifting the pen and returning to The Voltairean War was Stewart Alsop.

I wanted to learn about courage in wartime. I had heard stories around Washington that Stewart was more courageous than his brother Joe, and I thought Joe had a lot of courage. I heard Stewart had joined the British army a year before the Americans entered World War II and later, with the American army, parachuted at night behind German lines in France to link up with the Resistance. I also heard that he now had an incurable case of leukemia, which he lived in spite of for two years.

Stewart chose one o'clock lunch at the Federal City Club, a private club mostly used for business by journalists, public relations men, and Washington lobbyists, located in the west lobby wing of the Sheraton-Carlton Hotel, whose elegance was dying of cheapness and function.

Stewart shuffled into the club barroom. He was slightly stooped but tall, in a baggy brown suit. Despite his worried appearance, Stewart was still able and alert. A smile of genuine relief loosened up my face, showing my strong, slightly yellowed teeth, which I rarely show in a smile. (Childhood orthodontic braces had turned my smile shy, and the pulling of eight teeth from my boyhood mouth had made me fearful of dentists.) Stewart's expression was puzzled, as if to say, "Why is that man smiling so boldly at me?" He dared a small, uncertain smile in return.

We ate in the club dining room, a place too large and uncheerfully peopled, mostly by older men dining in small groups and old men with the solitary companionship of a newspaper. The walls were painted a synthetic lime green, a color designed for fast, businesslike eating. The tall windows along one wall let in a cold, dirty light. I quickly came to the point.

"I want to talk to you because I admire physical courage."

Stewart's naturally ruddy complexion reddened additionally, and he cast down his eyes. He was flattered and slightly embarrassed.

It was thereafter easy to coax a war story from Stewart. At first, he talked at length about his continuous battle with leukemia. He explained the choices open to a leukemia sufferer. With medicines and blood platelet transfusions, a person fighting leukemia may see days, or perhaps years, of always threatening death, with only the faint hope of a remission. The other choice is a "treatment" whereby his or her bone marrow is sucked out, and this is followed by nine or ten months of lingering life followed by certain death.

Stewart explained that he was writing a book about it, including the mechanical details, down to the sizes of the needles and tubes that doctors hammered through his bones into his marrow to test, not to suck. This information was contained in the first part of his book.

"Are you interested in that kind of thing?" Stewart asked.

"I think it's gory as hell," I replied honestly.

"So do I," Stewart said. He smiled again, with more confidence. "When I got halfway through the book, I decided I wouldn't write any more about the 'gory' details and I'd finish with stories about other things. The odd thing is that the second part of the book comes out sounding funny. . . . But there's something not quite . . . right . . . about a funny book about leukemia."

"Are you going to finish it?" I asked.

I looked as hard as I could into Stewart's eyes to see the answer, and a fountain of greenish fear swelled up and out.

Stewart used no words to reply. He crossed the fore and middle fingers of his right hand and silently held them up for me to see.

We sat at the table too long after the coffee. At least it seemed so in the efficient atmosphere of the lime green room. Stewart wiggled restlessly when I ordered a second pot of coffee and then asked for details of his risking his neck in the European war.

Stewart told about a British recruiting sergeant who, in a British military accent Stewart enjoyed mimicking, said something like, "Bring your runabout, of caws; and don't forget your personal arms, and your dinner jacket."

He remembered asking if an old farm shotgun they used to shoot crows was suitable for "personal arms," and the sergeant said, "Of caws, of caws."

But by the time Stewart reached the climax of his tale, about how he had jumped behind German lines, it was ten past two o'clock and the dining room crowd had thinned to those few tables with a woman to hold the men's interest, and tables at which sat men with no office to go to and no particularly urgent work to do, passing time peering into the odorless air and waiting for an irresistible call of nature to urge them away from their lonely spot. Stewart did not want to be numbered among the last to leave, and he moved as if to stand and go.

"I do want to hear that parachute story," I said.

"Next time," Stewart said, rising commandingly. "I can't sit here all afternoon talking about *myself*. I must get back to the office. Got the column to write."

He was writing then a column each week for the last inside page of *Newsweek* Magazine, and writing his leukemia book, too, with a deadline of sometime that summer or his death, whichever arrived first. He recognized and nodded to men still seated at their tables, whose names are faintly remembered from another age.

"They were really something in this town once," Stewart commented. "I wrote about some of them in my book, *The Center*. That's what's become of them. I very seldom come here any more."

It was a sunny, clean-smelling afternoon outside. Without top-coats, we walked down Sixteenth Street to Lafayette Park, kitty-cornered through the pigeons, to Pennsylvania Avenue and Jackson Place, which is a narrow street that runs for one block beside the public park and one more block between the White House and the gray Executive Office Building. That block is shut off and guarded on both ends by iron gates and sentry houses.

A ghostly spirit chose that moment to leak out of an upstairs window of the White House which someone had left just a crack open, to drift over the lawn through the bare horse chestnut trees, over the black iron fence and across the wide avenue. It disappeared, like greasy smoke, directly into Stewart's left ear.

Suddenly, without other apparent cause, Stewart started doing what so many Washington journalists habitually do in the company of others, and sometimes alone with their typewriters. He babbled knowingly about politics.

"I've been thinking about a Watergate column, . . ." Stewart said, and he proceeded for fifty or so paces to explain an idea about the use of "black" dirty tricks and other wartime intelligence tactics by the President and his cynical men against fellow Americans in peacetime.

I had lost Stewart's attention, so when we reached Seventeenth Street, I made an excuse for walking the other way.

"Barney," Stewart said abruptly, interrupting a political sentence, "What kind of book is this going to be?"

"A funny one," I replied. "Hopefully."

"How the hell can there be a funny book about Washington journalists?"

"Well, . . ." I hesitated, being none too sure. "Probably the same way there can be a funny book about dying from leukemia."

Stewart appreciated that I had a problem.

II

Fiction has continuity;
Life, damn it, doesn't.

O. Porterhouse

Mel Elfin, who is the chief of the *Newsweek* bureau in Washington, believes in ghosts. He sees and feels and smells and wishes to communicate with ghosts, and he believes ghosts are almost all nostalgically wonderful, whether they are live ghosts or dead ghosts. He works in the office building at 1750 Pennsylvania Avenue, a block and a half from the White House, on the twelfth floor. There are thirteen floors in the building. The building sits on ground a few doors away from the funeral parlor to which they brought Abraham Lincoln's body after he died in a little house near Ford Theater, crosswise on a bed too short for his body. Mel can see the funeral parlor quivering in the air, even though an office building is sitting over it today.

Mel leans over the railing of his balcony and looks across the street. He sees down below in F Street the ghost of a man who was one of President Lyndon Johnson's closest friends. The ghost crosses the street late on a dark night and walks into the front door of the YMCA building. Mel follows the ghost, down to the men's bathroom where a few minutes later the man is arrested by the vice squad police. "He left our office-opening party to go there," Mel said. "It makes this office part of history for me." Out of decency, Mel looks the other way, at the Executive Office Building that was once the Department of State, and he sees ambassadors in swallowtail coats and striped trousers who work in Victorian castles. Hidden from his view on the other side of the castle is the White House, which everybody already knows is so haunted by presidents that at night you can hear them talking and drinking and smoking and making merry by themselves and with each other, now that they don't worry any more. Harry Truman plays poker with his pals, while the ghost of Teddy Roosevelt stomps around smacking his thigh with a riding crop and Calvin Coolidge tries to get some reading done, while President Johnson is playing with ships and planes and soldiers in the basement, and while President Nixon is playing cocktail hour piano and taking folding money in his beer glass in the East Room.

Mel cruises the streets of Washington in search of ghosts that practically nobody else can see. He looks at a house on Sixteenth Street and sees Harry Truman the night he found out President Roosevelt had died in Warm Springs, and he was now President of the United States. Mel can see a neighbor lady preparing supper for President Truman because his wife, Bess, was out of town.

Georgetown, near where Mel lives, is elbow-to-elbow with ghosts.

He knows what ghostly business has transpired all over Washington for centuries.

But the ghosts Mel loves best are the ones who lived in the 1940s, especially the singers and musicians. He was in high school then.

Mel works long and hard, and luckily he was assigned to Washington, where he could indulge his passion among more ghosts than live anywhere else in America. He said, "I'd be happy if I *never* left here."

There is a reverence about the way Mel sees ghosts. He is a priest in the Church of History. Hundreds of people all over Washington speak confidences in his ear.

Mel has two of the commandments of that church taped under the glass of his desk.

The first one says:

"It is required of a man that he should share the passion and action of his time, at peril of being judged not to have lived."

The other says:

"The poetry of history lies in the quasi-miraculous fact that once, on this earth, once, on this familiar spot of ground, walked other men and women, as actual as we are today, thinking their own thoughts, swayed by their own passions, but now all gone, one generation vanishing after another, gone as utterly as we ourselves shall shortly be gone, like ghosts at cockcrow."

III

What has four wheels and flies?
A Gypsy's house.

Old Rumanian joke

There are two major daily newspapers in Washington and four television stations. Only one well-circulated national magazine, *U. S. News and World Report,* is headquartered there. Nevertheless, there are hundreds and hundreds of writers, reporters, editors, cameramen, sound men, directors, stars, propmen, producers, field producers, film editors, and thousands of people with part-time or amateur status at these jobs who work on and off as accredited, bona fide members of what is sometimes called the Washington Press Corps. They cover the people and operations and machinery of government, most of the time in groups; and two or three times almost every weekday they appear in town in swarms.

Most of the Washington Press Corps is from somewhere else, like most people in Washington are from somewhere else, with their memories, way of talking, the way they grew up, their manners, their ideas, their loyalties, their mothers, fathers, sisters, and brothers living in some other part of the country or the world. These are a collection of transplantable people, who put down roots quickly wherever they land. The roots spread wide but not deep, and tomorrow they are pluckable, to be transplanted somewhere else.

Scotty Reston's mind is still on the River Clyde in Glasgow and his church is the Church of Scotland, even though he attends Church of England services in the National Cathedral. Doug Kiker's mind is in a treehouse and too scared to go back of the barn in Griffin, Georgia. Art Buchwald's is with the Seventh Day Adventists on Long Island, who taught him guilt and sin. Helen Thomas was born in Kentucky and grew up in Detroit, but her mind has roots that reach to the bazaars of Lebanon, when women wore veils and spoke fluently with their eyes. Joe and Stew Alsop are transplanted from a tobacco farm in Connecticut and their efforts to sink roots into the marble and granite of Washington were terrific. Dan Rather has a root that is a dark greenish brown and runs from his eyeballs down into the ground back to a mountainside in Kentucky territory, where a pioneer trader and an Indian woman met and fell in love. Roland Evans still thinks about Main Line, Philadelphia, and Bob Novak's heart is in his boyhood bedroom in Joliet, Illinois; but their common mind, "Evans and Novak," is deeply rooted on the thirteenth floor of 1750 Pennsylvania Avenue, which makes that mind rare in Washington. Lawrence Spivak's roots run back to a little, teeny crack in a New York sidewalk and then down through the earth to the land of the Hebrews, on the other side of the world. Harry Rosenfeld's mind was rooted in Berlin, Germany, until he was uprooted by a storm trooper and an SS sergeant with names and faces like Haldeman and Ehrlichman. Sally Quinn has no roots at all; she's a creature who lives on the road and travels by truck cara-van. But she dreams she has roots in the Old South, near Savannah, where girls wore pretty picture hats and hooped skirts to cover thick legs and ankles, where everybody cut everybody else with a man-nerly, deadly drawl, and where she would have been called "Miz Sally" by the Black Mammies.

Ben Bradlee's full, artistocratic name is Benjamin Crowninshield Bradlee, and his name goes back to Boston and New York for half a dozen generations of family ups and downs. But Ben is in truth a rootless one. Or as the Black Mammies rolled their eyes and said it down in Savannah, "I'se skeered a him, Miz Sally. I'se watched him and I'se heard tales about him, and, Miz Sally, dat man he *rootless!*"

IV

How often at night
When the heavens
Are bright
With the light
Of the glittering
Stars,
Have I stood there
Amazed
And asked as I gazed,
If their glory exceeds
That of ours.

From "Oh, Give Me a Home
Where the Buffalo Roam"

The most gossiped about young woman in Washington that winter was a *Washington Post* reporter named Sally Quinn.

Her job was to attend and write about "Washington parties," which meant cocktail receptions, government functions, embassy dinners, and other more intimate but well-staged gatherings, for which the party givers expected publicity for themselves and their guests. The way Washington parties work, their real purposes and their intricate mechanics, could fill several manuals bound in leather. They are not designed for fun. There is a determination to make Washington parties work.

To virtually every Washington party, a journalist of some sort is invited, either to entertain by babbling knowledgeably about politics, to have a "bug," as they say, placed in his or her ear, or to "write up" the party the next day, with a photograph or two of important guests with the host and hostess, when possible, for the magazines and local newspapers. Sally, among the write-up party reporters, had distinguished herself from the others by carefully building her own personal reputation in her articles, with planted words and phrases that called attention to herself as a desirable and alluring young female, a "liberated" woman in the predominately sexual sense of the day, and at the same time a person of refined experience, who spoke Swiss-school French, and lunched habitually at the fashionable Sans Souci restaurant. In one article she had also revealed that she commuted on weekends to Manhattan to live with her boyfriend of six years, whose name she exposed as Warren Hoge. She had attempted to create the image of a fast, easy thoroughbred.

When I read Sally Quinn's stories and the advertisements of her life, I had no sense for the reality of the girl.

By coincidence, I saw her in the flesh at the National Galleries at an opening party of paintings by American artists in prison in New York. I had an assignment from *Saturday Review* magazine to write about the show for $500, provided enough celebrities attended to sparkle up the unmerry subject of prison art. Most of the work consisted of cries of anger and pain and humiliation. Halfway through the show, none of the celebrities had arrived, and while I was asking a sad-faced museum worker what went wrong, the man's dull eyes lighted up as he glanced over my shoulder, and cried out:

"Look, there's Sally Quinn!"

I accept the words people speak as literally as a child to whom "I" means the same thing as "eye" and "see" means the same thing as "sea"; I turned around expecting to see a striking creature. And then I was stung by the bee of reality, right in the eye that I used to see.

Sally was of middling height with a slim torso and heavyset rump held up by thick, sturdy legs. She was built for work and not for speed, as she had insinuated in her stories. Her hair was a commercial blond and fell to her shoulders rather softly. She wore smoky colored aviator sunglasses over her eyes. Her expression was rushed, worried, and angry. Her nose was not large but rather nostrilly, and her mouth was drawn tight. Her face was flushed in splotches. Her arms were slim, and her hands were pretty remarkable. They were a creamy white and very soft looking, and the fingers were neither too long nor too short, but slim and tapered, and they were tipped by faithfully manicured and flawlessly polished pointed red nails.

I was disappointed in my own expectations and irritated at myself that I had allowed Sally Quinn to pull the wool over my eyes. I blurted out loud, "Overrated."

She was, in fact, a juiceless, hardworking, unhappy reporter, standing in the crowd very stiff and tensed, turning her head jerkily from side to side searching for a face she'd recognize, with her pretty, remarkable hands holding a notebook and pen.

Damn reality. I was looking for youth and beauty.

I introduced myself brusquely to her and she was instantly made uncomfortable by my seemingly unreasonable anger. Her voice was up in her nose, and she had no particular scent about her. She acted distantly businesslike. However, she agreed to see me, "because I don't refuse interviews to other newspaper people, since I ask for them myself."

People who think they know me tend to believe that I am unrealistic, so at times I go out of my way to listen to somebody's story, and note it all down, so that they get their impression of themselves precisely on the record and I add any other impressions I choose.

I was so annoyed by her flimflam that the desire to kick her in the behind almost overcame me each time she moved into my presence. Simulated sex is as disappointing a commodity as contaminated oysters; you may think upon first consuming them that they are one of the earth's delights, and when your eyeballs turn yellow and you throw up all night, you know they fooled you. A man who's eaten one contaminated oyster is for a long time leery of strange oysters.

A few weeks later, Sally sat in the *Post* lunchroom, her legs covered in white woolly slacks, with her shoe soles together in front of her crotch, opening and closing her legs like the wings of a moth on a cabbage plant.

I renamed her "Mothwings" in my mind.

I wanted to see her claws. I found them attractive.

But she was frantic to keep her sex image. She batted her moth wings back and forth in a manner both indelicate and unupsetting, and when I asked her, "Sally, do you have any friends?" she took me to mean only male friends and she reacted as if it were a very personal and prying question.

"I live with a man," is what she said.

I asked who.

She said *everybody* in Washington knew because it was no secret. It had been printed before. And she named Warren Hoge, without passion.

I thought a disgusted sound, "Eccch!"

"We've been together six years," she said. "I commute to New York on weekends. I've got a deal with the *Post,*" and she explained how the *Post* paid her way to and from New York if she wrote stories about New York parties. She lived in Warren's apartment, and that saved a lot of money on hotel bills, and she loved

New York and was bored at home in Washington where her daddy was retired from the army and in private business involved with army supplies.

"Do you love him?" I asked, meaning Warren.

"Yes, of course!"

"You do?"

"Yes!"

"Why, for heaven's sake?"

She said, "Because he takes all my shit!"

Sally found it a terrible interview and she told me so when we got up from the table, with dreggy plastic coffee cups fallen over on it, and an ashtray full of someone else's cigarette butts. She said, "I get terrible vibes from you, and I don't know why."

V

Heads I win, tails you lose.

A trick played on children

I'm drawn to natural ugliness, in the same way I'm drawn to natural beauty; I'm drawn to sunsets and cemeteries, flowers and toadfish, swans and bats, sun porches and dungeons, ballet dancers and severed heads, balloons and coffins. The madness, of course, is seeing one always tied to the other, like life is to death.

I was angry at myself after seeing Sally Quinn for seeing her so harshly, snooping under the phoniness she hid in the medicine chest and the dresser drawers and the old purses of her mind. I had asked her merciless questions, never letting up, although she finally closed up and stopped moving, poor moth, toward the end.

I thought my eyes were probably too unbearable for Sally a second time, and I was upset with myself for having ruined my chances to check impressions again.

I called Sally on the telephone a few days later and took the blame for making her feel so ''terrible'' inside. I said: ''Sally, I just wasn't up for you that day; I'm sorry. I have to get up to have a good interview, and some days I'm up to it and some days I'm not. I wasn't when we met in the *Post* lunchroom. I'd like to take you to lunch one day and see if we can't do better.''

She agreed.

We lunched at the Peking downtown on Thirteenth Street.

I got to the point.

''Do you really read palms, Sally?'' She had told me at the *Post* that she believed in astrology and palm readings, and had asked my sign, and I told her a Leo.

She said yes.

''Read mine.''

She obviously enjoyed palm reading. It was easy for her to do, and she could blame her own honest impressions on somebody else's hand and not on herself. Palm reading, tea leaf reading, coffee grounds reading, and the reading of cards of fortune are rarely dishonest acts because they carry no sense of guilt or responsibility in them.

I offered Sally my hand and after some coy reluctance, she took it (it was the left one) and held it uncomfortably because it was poked awkwardly across the table.

"I have to see the right one," she said. "And right-side up." She left her side of the table and sat beside me.

"Whatever happens," she said, "is going to go on for a long time. It's an endless lifeline."

I straightened up with pleasure.

"That is *not* necessarily synonymous with omnipotence," she smiled.

She bent and flexed my fingers and peered at the lines.

"A very confusing hand. Traits that contradict each other a lot. *Peasant* hands. . . ." She looked at me to see if I'd reacted to that with anger, and I smiled.

"*Very* peasant hands . . . but an *intelligent* peasant. Hands right from the earth. A lot of conflict. . . . First conflict in professional bent. You're torn between two directions—one authority and leadership, the other creativity. Maybe you should be a theatrical producer? The creativity prevents me from telling about leadership. You could make a great deal of money.

"There's a major conflict in your love life . . . I see three women in your hand. Those three people are all of equal strength and they will consistently come in conflict with each other—and tear you apart.

"When you make the final decision you could have the real marriage. There's a crisis. That crisis has to do with the women. It is in some way directly related to your decision about your career.

"Not a happy time. A major disaster. You're pulled in every direction. But really, it's a very healthy hand. It could have. . . .

"Conflict in every area. Religion or no religion . . . something unclear about moral stance. . . .

"Basically a very sensual hand. You probably find a major conflict because you don't know whether to be sensual or not. Socially in conflict. You do a lot of things you don't want to do. . . . A deep resentment you have for somebody you know and love very well . . . hostility . . . you feel put upon by and don't know how to get rid of it."

She bent and flexed my hand again.

"Very flexible in some ways. Very flexible but somehow it doesn't move some ways. Stubborn.

"A problem with women. A certain sense of your own worth

. . . either by women . . . may recognize for the wrong . . . makes you angry, hostile, resentful. You have to take it out on somebody—usually somebody you love.

"A traditional hand, a sense of tradition. You might come across as more iconoclastic than you really are. . . . You may give an impression——"

And then she sighed, put down my hand, and returned to her side of the table.

After that, I was somewhat kinder and gentler. I let her know a few facts about me, as little as possible because I felt nothing I told her was safe from some eventual abuse.

The things she told me about herself were that she thought she was a member of the "upper middle class," now, but not always. An early hero of hers was Scarlet O'Hara.

"My mother," Sally said, "always said you could tell a lady by her hands. I creamed my hands to death. I can't stand to go a day without Jergens Lotion. . . ."

She held her hands out for me to see. They were treacherous.

"I was fat and pimply as a child. The pimples went away after I started taking birth control pills."

Once, in Smith College, Sally recalled herself in a duel of wits with the girl she said was "the dumbest girl in school, Beatriz." Beatriz was graduating *summa cum laude;* Sally was on the "registrar's list" ready to be kicked out.

The battle was over the word "dilettante." Sally had what she called "a complex" about knowing what words meant, whether she did or not. But after the duel, Sally recalled being forced to the dictionary to look dilettante up and realizing, for the first time, it meant something she wanted to be.

She recalled the dictionary definition as "someone who dabbles, who knows a little bit about a lot of things."

She said: "I wanted to be a female dilettante.

"My knowledge of anything is very limited; I am an expert on carrying on five minutes of cocktail conversation. The definition of being a journalist—not at the *Washington Post* but for most people at most places—is to have more knowledge than most people about most things."

I asked her how she learned to be a dilettante.

"Learning how to be a dilettante . . . it's not hard for me. Being an army brat helps. . . . Never can stay in one place long enough to learn anything about it . . . I never lived in one place long enough . . . twenty-two schools and twenty-two jobs before I came to the *Washington Post* and I've been six years out of college.''

Then, in listing her jobs, she insisted on stressing the sex again.

''I was a go-go girl . . . it defined 'male chauvinist pig' for me.''

''Where?''

''In New York.''

''Where?'' I felt her implication, communicated with a bored, knowing, girl-of-the-streets-and-alleys attitude, was theatrical. Besides, I was realistic enough to look at her body closely, which embarrassed her, I supposed, because she blushed.

I said, ''It must not have paid well.''

She said, ''It didn't.''

''Where did you work?''

''At the New York Coliseum.''

''In front of a crowd of people?''

''Well——''

''A stage show?''

''Well, no.''

''Well, what was it then?''

''I was doing . . . a new products directory . . . for a car show.''

''What happened?''

She put her hands up behind her head, lifted up her hair in a come-hither way and wiggled her top and bottom, like a show-offy little girl, and said, ''Get your new——''

''Did you wear anything on top?''

''Yes. I was doing it in front of a bunch of cars. I was a sex machine . . . and people came around and stared at me.''

''People?''

''Men!''

I thought, on Broadway there are girls who wriggle topless in the bars, and the bartenders leave the doors open, or a venetian blind cracked, so that passersby can watch from the sidewalk. A crowd forms, and not only Sally's ''men!'' but fascinated women, teenagers, boys and girls, curious babies, and strange creatures of breeds you never knew existed, all want to see a sex machine gyrate.

She bravely carried on.

"I was a Girl Scout . . . wore a green ribbon. I was cheating my way through a swimming badge. Did three pieces on George Wallace and his family for the *Post* . . . they were such *great* characters . . . *great* material. They liked it. . . . Told Barry Goldwater. . . . Gave me a great deal of pleasure. I showed them as they really were . . . funny, interesting. Warren Hoge? . . . rich . . . father is the only person to have a smokehouse on Park Avenue."

She explained that Warren's father was from somewhere in the South, where people know about smokehouses.

"My father, he was always the commanding officer. . . . It's like being a princess. . . . He got his first star when I was ten years old."

"What's 'like being a princess' mean?"

"Always the biggest house and the biggest car and everybody salutes. There is no life like life on an army post.

"In Germany . . . I went to a school in Switzerland called Le Torrent, at the Chateau d'Oex."

She spelled the French.

"It was the only truly happy year of my life . . . like Heidi . . . a fairy tale . . . cowbells. I read Heidi about ten times."

"Was it fun?"

"Yes. The girls were all hell raisers. It was innocent hell raising, never anything evil or ugly. Money was a problem. Mother took me to shop in the government employees' merchandise store for my dresses."

Then she asked me: "Who else is in your book?"

I said Art Buchwald, Eric Sevareid, Evans and Novak, Helen Thomas, Doug Kiker—

"I can tell you a good story about Doug Kiker."

"Are you sure it's *good?*"

"Of course. He's a friend of Warren's. They were roommates together."

And she proceeded to tell a story about Warren and Doug, in their younger days, running up and down the backstairs of the apartment house they lived in, repeatedly "fucking" the same girl. Out of her mouth it was an altogether unattractive story. When it was over I said: "Sally, may I ask you something?" She said yes.

"Why would you tell such an ugly story, Sally?"

Tears came to her eyes. I can't swear any fell on her cheek, but they wet her eyes.

"Why is it ugly?" she asked. "It's a story *they* tell on themselves. I've heard Doug tell it over and over again."

"Why repeat it?"

"Because it's *good*. It's funny. Other people in Washington have liked it. I've told it a *dozen* times."

"Is it true?"

"*They* tell it—— Barney, why do you hate me so much?"

I said, truthfully, "I don't."

VI

The sky is falling! The sky is falling!

Chicken Little

Ralph Douglas Kiker was a little boy with a long red face, who lived on a farm near Griffin, Georgia. The farm grew mostly cotton. He wasn't very pretty, and children know before they can talk if they are pretty or not. He not only had a long red face, but Doug— that's what we'll call him—also had ears that stuck out like a ventriloquist's dummy and a mouth that fell open a little when he was thinking, and a funny bump in the middle of his forehead. The bump was like a third eye that was closed, and you can imagine what Doug would look like if somebody took a paint set and painted in an open eye, bulged out and staring.

Doug had a grandfather and two great-uncles. Their last names were Bunn, and as a joke people called the Bunns by as crazy names as they could think of, so Doug had uncles who were named "Sugar Bunn" and "Baby Bunn" and, don't laugh now because it isn't nice, there was "Hoss Bunn." Hoss Bunn was Doug's mother's daddy. Doug always called him "sir." But it made you laugh to think about "Sir Sugar Bunn" and "Sir Hoss Bunn," and when it wasn't funny it was very cruel, the way children are sometimes about things you can't help.

Doug was a boy who loved to read books. Some children read books only when they have to, when they are sent to their room for punishment or they must make a report in school. And some read to disappear from the world they're in into another world. Some children are better than others when it comes to traveling into other worlds, and almost all children are better at it than any adults. Children love fantastic worlds; they are shy of what is in the real one.

Doug Kiker's real world hurt him. His mother and father worked very hard and they didn't have time for a funny-looking boy who loved to read books. His father had drifted down from the mountains of northern Georgia. His mother's family, the Bunns, had a little land, somewhere. They also had a passion for alcohol. They were poor tenants. They never dreamed their boy would grow into a man whose face millions of people see on television, there was no television.

21

The way Doug survived was that he learned to tell stories that people would listen to. He knew how to use words from reading so many books, and as soon as he could he wrote a novel, a book about a Southern man called *The Southerner*. Then he wrote one about a sailor called *Stranger on the Shore*. If you read his books carefully, you will see that Doug was dreaming himself up and telling stories. Stories are little dreams, and books are postcards from other worlds.

Did you ever look at a grown-up person and see him or her turn into a monster with fangs, or into a little boy or girl right before your eyes? If you haven't, watch carefully the next time you see people remembering back to when *they* were children, or making angry threats about how one day they are going to hurt somebody if that somebody doesn't watch out! Watch how their eyes get very clear but far away, and how the little muscles under the skin of their cheeks start pulling and changing. Little blood vessels that haven't opened up in years and years fill with blood, and grown men, like Doug Kiker is now, blush. When Doug talks truthfully about Sweet Bunn and Hoss Bunn now, his face turns red as the inside of a sweet watermelon, his eyes start to laugh and crinkle up, his mouth, that looks like the top of a tied laundry bag, opens up, and his jaw-bone drops down so his face is long, long, long, and if you ever see him that way, you know Doug isn't going to tell you a lie. But then, sometimes, you might see him with his fists closed, and the blood gone from his face so that he is blotchy white as a haunted old house, and the strings in his neck are sticking out. He'll say something like, "Barney, if that bad-name Clark Mollenhoff starts up again, I'm going to climb all over his back. That's true! I will!" Don't believe him then, because when the blood goes out of Doug's face he's usually fibbing.

You can also tell when he's fibbing, or isn't really sure of what he's saying, when he talks like David Brinkley. If you listen to television news for the sound of it, you'll notice that a lot of the reporters talk like each other, and a lot of them sound like David Brinkley. What they do is what they call "punch" their words. That means that when they read a story on television, they *underline* certain words so that they say them harder . . . "punch" them, in order to keep their voices from droning along and putting people to sleep. David Brinkley, who grew up near Wilmington, North Carolina, trained the Wilmington accent out of his voice and made himself sound so original and interesting with his word-punching system that people going into television news reporting tried to copy his way of singing the news. Copycats are usually afraid of something, so when Doug Kiker sounds like he's copying David Brinkley, you can bet he's afraid of something, and reporters are usually afraid of themselves.

People in the news business are always worried about getting their head on straight; and what makes a job in television news so hard is that the bosses say you have to get your head on straight every day. Not a little bit cockeyed, not a little bit dreamy, not a little bit tilted or loose. On television when the red light over the camera goes on and you know that millions of people all over the country and sometimes all over the world are staring at your face and trying to decide if you know what you are talking about or if you are fibbing up a storm, you can't, if you are a grown-up, go banging the side of your head, or pounding your forehead, and say, "Ladies and Gentlemen, I don't have my head on straight this afternoon. One moment please while I adjust my head so I can read my lines right."

For reasons called "show business" this isn't done. News people who appear in front of the camera are trained to appear completely prepared, with their heads bolted down like one of those old-fashioned deep sea diving helmets. Only a few people, who are very sure of themselves, tell someone his head is on crooked. The rest fib their way through, and while most people are too polite to say so, children who know how it feels to tell little whoppers can feel it when somebody on television is telling some, too.

Can you?

Since most people on television are acting or fibbing most of the time, the best actors and the best fibbers all get together and have contests to see who can act the funniest or saddest or cleverest act, and who can make most people believe they know what they are talking about. For example, the Watergate television show.

Sen. Sam Ervin played the gray-haired, sorta funny country lawyer who flapped his dewlaps like an old rooster and said wise sayings like a very old Cocky Locky in Chicken Little. A senator from Tennessee played his young son, Little Cocky Locky. The other senators who sat at the long table were other barnyard animals. The senator from Florida was a white rabbit. The senator from New Mexico was an old turkey. The senator from Georgia was a smart hog. The senator from Connecticut was a bird dog. The senator from Hawaii was a strange, exotic bird of the Orient. They were all cared for by a lot of people who played ants. The people who came before them as witnesses played animals from a farm down the road. The lawyer who tattletaled on President Nixon played a brown rat, with round eyeglasses. His wife played a hot canary. The two men closest to the President played shockingly realistic roles as a cottonmouth snake and a black cobra. One old man who still worked in the White House played a dying old horse, and there were also a lot of weasels and pigeons and jackasses, and a man who was once the honorable attorney general of the United States played a bedraggled old rooster whose feathers had all been pecked out.

As you know, around every barnyard there are—except in China where they swatted almost all of them—flies. There are little gnats and houseflies and horseflies. If you were ever bitten by a horsefly you know how it hurts, and if you were ever in a swarm of flies you know how you think you're going to go crazy. There are also honeybees and yellow jackets and wasps, and they buzz around all the time. There were a lot of reporters at the Watergate show who played all the swarming, biting, stinging insects.

For about two months in the summer of 1973, "The Watergate" was the hit of Washington, and for those two months, when the brown rat with the round eyeglasses was on stage with his hot canary wife, it was almost as good as "As the World Turns," and "The Guiding Light," and "The Edge of Night."

Doug Kiker was one of the reporters playing a fly.

The part of the NBC fly who works for the NBC peacock calls for a man or woman to act very proper and serious about the great events taking place on the stage, especially on the Washington stage, which is the hugest in the world and seems so gigantic that human beings appear as little as dwarves against the big marble buildings crawling with ants. But Doug was having too much fun. He knew all the barnyard animals, and he enjoyed the good feeling of playing on the big stage so much that he'd get excited and stay up all night babbling on about it, and the next morning, he put his fly head on crooked. It wobbled and flopped around and Doug kept trying to adjust it back straight in front of the camera, while everybody was looking. He thought nobody could see.

One day, Doug let his fly head fall off altogether.

It was during the last act of the Watergate show that day. Doug's lines were supposed to be serious and deep, and in a tone of voice that would let everybody know that Doug saw how the players were men of great importance to the country, and that their play was supposed to make you angry and sad.

You were supposed to get angry with the President and sad about the way people live in America.

But Doug was so excited about all the drama that he ran in front of the camera, clutched a microphone in his hands, looked at the red light turn on, and opened up his mouth to say something very important, and his fly head fell off. You could see Doug's real long face underneath, with his funny hair, and if you saw his face in color you'd have seen it was the color it gets whenever he tells the truth.

Instead of saying his Sunday school lines, he looked up at the camera with his ears sticking out and a big smile from one ear to the other, and said a lot of words that all together sounded like, "Wow!"

Doug was too excited to notice that his head was lying on the floor. He said he had never seen a play with such spectacular action, and he told what marvelous entertainment it was and how much fun it was to watch such great actors play such interesting critters. He said the plot was wonderful, and he babbled on and on about what a wonderful time it was for a country boy like him to play on the same stage with "The Great Sam Ervin," who could read the Bible and make it sound like Shakespeare.

He was supposed to say something else, and to look like a four-teen-year-old boy *wasn't* the way he was supposed to look. But he was so excited he was bobbing up and down when he talked. People who saw him blushing and telling the truth knew that he'd be sternly warned to have his head back on the next time, or else.

The critics were upset with Doug. People called up and told the NBC peacock that one little boy in the cast was telling people how much fun the tragedy was, and people who wanted to be angry with the President and sad about living in the United States didn't want to hear anybody saying how much fun it is to be on the stage. If they wanted to feel good, they said, they would watch the Flip Wilson show, or Walt Disney.

Later, Doug felt ashamed about losing his head. He decided to screw it on tight next time. But heads that can be lost are like gloves and galoshes and umbrellas; they get lost no matter how hard you try.

Doug believed that if you dare tell the truth about what you think, other people will scoff and hoot at you. But something inside Doug made lies hurt and the truth feel good; still, it was considered evil to feel too good, like a sin. So when Doug told a truth that felt good, he blushed, because he was committing a sin, which was supposed to feel bad. All that mixed-up in a person's mind causes him problems in keeping his mind on one thing for very long; worse, blushing is very revealing if you can pin down exactly why a person blushes, and provided you can see the blush. There is a Black man who writes a newspaper column in Washington who is known as the best nonprofessional poker player in town. You can almost never see him blush. But Doug has thin white skin; when he gets good cards it shows all over his face.

What Doug enjoyed was daydreaming; nobody made him feel bad for telling the truth in a daydream and nobody said how "professional" he was when he had just told millions of people a bunch of whoppers.

When Doug was a little boy he read a book he never forgot. He has forgotten the name of the book and who wrote it. But he remembers what it looked like, and how the pictures were, and what it felt like to hold in his hands, and what it was about.

It was about a boy in the country who dreamed everything in the world was where he could see it, and touch it and play with it. The boy dreamed himself up more and more things to play with, and traveled to more and more places to see, and soon his empire was worldwide. No space was big enough to hold it all, so he decided to move his whole gigantic empire up away from the ground, so he could look down and see how funny people are when you are a giant and they look like children.

The little boy Doug read about gathered all of his toy empire together and moved it and himself into the biggest space in the real world he knew, in a tree outside the banging screen door. He called it "World Headquarters in the Treehouse."

VII

There are two kinds of people in the world.
Those who love bacon grease,
And those who love butter.
I love both.

Lord Renston

Dan Rather's opening words with me were: "Sure, Barney, of course I'll do it. I'm sure its a . . . worthwhile . . . project. I'll see you, sure. We'll have . . . lunch."

On our first lunch he brought a girl along as a distraction. We waited to be seated at a "good table" closest to the front door at a restaurant called Provençal, which CBS people nicknamed the "company cafeteria." Dan spoke in cabbage chewed many times. The only spark in his eyes flashed when I said, "Dan, I don't believe a lot of what you say. You say no when you mean yes and yes when you mean no."

"It's *possible* with me," is all he would admit. But he agreed that a man who walks into a poolroom sporting a long stick isn't necessarily a hustler. Dan paid for three lunches with a CBS credit card.

Next time he set a date for lunch, I waited until one thirty and called him at his office. A girl at the CBS news desk said he was at La Toque d'Argent. The maître d' who answered the phone said he was with a young lady.

When Dan came to the telephone, I said (in a shaking voice): "Dan, I'm waiting here at Provençal where we were supposed to have lunch at one o'clock." My anger nearly cracked his self-control. It was the first time I'd ever heard him sputter.

He said, "Oh, Christ, Barney, I'm sorry. I forgot. Christ, I'm not *that* kind of guy. Oh, it was some mistake, Barney. Let's see . . . ahhh . . . it wasn't . . . well, the secretary didn't put it . . . Barney, I'm really sorry, I'm not the kind of guy who doesn't keep appointments . . ." and so forth.

There were other Washington Press Corps people who had trouble keeping luncheon appointments or when they came to lunch they spoke chewed cabbage, too. At Washington restaurant prices, I couldn't afford chewed cabbage.

I was paying my own money and, for the most part, the people I wanted to see exercised expense accounts that allowed their company to be "The Big Man" standing behind them.

So I made myself a rule that obeyed no logic, only feeling. "He who names the place pays the bill or splits it." I wanted to name a good, inexpensive place. In some of the places I named my guests would try not to be found dead. Joe Kraft, for example, remembered for almost two years that once I had asked him to talk about Joe Alsop and not Joe Kraft. He was extremely upset by this, but he was almost mortified with shame when he prepared his mouth for the style of the Rive Gauche and I staked him to two hot empanadas and a Coca-Cola from a machine against the wall of Sam Weinberg's Argentine Bakery.

I made it a rule to pay when I named the place, and split whenever the other person wasn't acting "Big Man." I made, as best I can recall, three exceptions: John Chancellor, Meg Greenfield, and Johnny Apple.

I let John Chancellor pay the whole bill for several reasons. First, although I named the restaurant, the Peking, he insisted on a branch of it far up Connecticut Avenue, when I wanted the one downtown. His choice was a damp, dark place, with dirt on the floor like you see in a subway. We sat in a dark booth in the corner; John said he ate in the restaurant often. He talked loudly in the nervously friendly way of a man who hasn't any true friends.

He smoked Salems, or a similar brand of mentholated cigarettes, one after the other, because he had a cold, it seemed, from what was apparent in the hairs of his nose.

Finally, I started looking around and sniffing the air. Very unobtrusively at first because I could hardly believe that a dead rat could be decomposing under the table.

I tried to forget about it, but whiffs of it would blow at me, and just as I was about to say, "John, let's call the waiter and get them to move our table," I took a last analytical sniff and realized that the dead rat smell was mentholated.

I sat through it, but I made only the weak offer to pay when John reached for the check.

"That's okay, Barney," John said generously. "It's on NBC."

The other exception was Meg Greenfield.

She is an efficient girl. I say "girl" because it is truer, I think, than spinster. Anyway, she is a girl to me, with a man's whiskey nose, and the rest of her neat and trim and tailored as a little fiddle case.

She named Chez Camille, a French restaurant near the *Washington Post*.

Somewhere inside Meg is a tragedy, a something, the most interesting part of her life, that happened once that still hurts; but it's so deep I never got to it, and I knew very soon I wouldn't. Meg's hurts are too precious for her to reveal, except to a true lover, and I don't think she's ever had one.

So we chatted about her work, which is to write editorials for the *Post* that have a "woman's point of view" as well as what Meg called the "straight" editorial point of view.

I asked her, "What's straight?"

"Oh, gun control, for example. Got that one now. These subjects get into the rotation and one day something like 'gun control' comes up and I get it."

She admitted, with a shrug, she knew nothing about gun control except what she'd read, and certainly she was *for* it; she'd never bought a gun, anywhere, for any reason, and didn't want to. But she insisted that the laws are too lax about guns and she would argue it in an editorial.

"Go out and buy one and then write about how you tried to buy a gun," I suggested.

"Oh, Barney, I'm not going to buy a gun!"

"Why the hell not?"

"Because I'm *not*."

"I'll pay for it. You try to buy a gun, a little hand gun if you want, or a rifle or shotgun in Virginia, and I'll pay for it. . . . Better yet . . . let the *Washington Post* pay for it. See what happens."

"No." She was giggly irritated. "Don't be silly."

I dropped the matter after a while and ventured to women's salaries at the *Washington Post*.

"I'm satisfied with mine," she said.

"What do you make?"

She put her hand up to her throat.

"I'm not going to answer that."

"Why not?"

"It's not important to what we're talking about. Just say, 'I'm satisfied.' "

"Why not tell me how much?"

"Because no matter how much, I'm satisfied."

Then, she tried to play it both ways again, by letting me buy the entire lunch. She did all the purse-rattling, lipstick-applying, hair-primping things that a woman who dresses in a dark suit and wears her pumpernickel-colored hair in rolls on her head does when she wants to communicate: "You're the man. You invited *me* to lunch. *You* pick up the check. *I* have to go back to the office."

I said to myself, "Meg, if you're liberated, pick up the check yourself," and three pots of coffee later she finally reached for it, with her teeth clenched, and paid her half.

For me it was the principle of the thing, and when we parted outside the front door it was agreed silently between us that we would not soon meet again for lunch.

I may have missed an exception or two, but they weren't scientific samples.

VIII

The gourmet eats a pound of Beluga caviar and
 cares not about the cost.
The banker examines the gourmet's feces, and
 says,
"Only yesterday this was worth one hundred dollars."

Salmon Chase

Johnny Apple is an exceptional exception.

We met at Jean-Pierre's, another French restaurant two blocks
from the office of the *New York Times*. Johnny greeted me when he
arrived fifteen minutes late, with a big, meaty handshake and a chop
on the shoulder.

He was round and solid-fleshed as a cooking Winesap, and his
eyes were shiny, big, and innocent. His hair fell to his shoulders
and was greasy as a baby girl's after a meal with her hands. I
wanted him to put his napkin on like a bib.

He told me about his childhood in Ohio, where his father was a
German grocer. His name was Apfel. Now his father owns a string
of supermarkets.

Johnny would turn into 290 pounds of lard if ever he let himself
go; but his position with the *Times* holds him back.

Before Johnny was "on the *Times*," as they say, he was a writer
for the Huntley-Brinkley television news show. He was a winking,
girl-patting, pantingly direct wanter of anything he thought might
make him feel full. Big, voluptuous things made him feel that way.
Dinner was almost always done with wine; a hotel must have a
swimming pool; he drinks at world-famous hangouts; he pays with
the best of credit cards.

When he had to, he used his writing skills for the *Times*. The rest
of the time he wallowed like a hog. At our lunch, he wallowed in a
pound of butter, bread, calf liver, lettuce salad, and two bottles of
red and white wine.

It was so much fun eating lunch with a wallower for a change that
I paid for the pleasure by paying the check, nearly twenty dollars.
Johnny protested, but he let me pay.

However, I asked when we got outside the door, "Johnny, would
you please invite us home for dinner one night."

He thought I was joking, but he promised he would. I reminded him twice on the telephone before he set a date to invite us over.

Johnny had said he and Edie shared the cooking chores; she one day, he the next. "But I get the extra day," he'd said, "because I'm the best cook." Taking him at his word, I arrived at Johnny's as a food critic; I named his place "The Pink Apple."

Here is what the critic said:

"Cooking is a creative outlet for some men. But Johnny Apple's art is in the tasting.

"He greeted us at the door on a cold and windy night. His feet were bare. His feet were very dirty.

" 'What manner establishment is this?' I asked myself, but then I noticed the contemporary furnishings, the warm town-house living room with low-slung wood-and-leather decor, and a bar stocked with brandies, cordials, glass decanters, and goblets. The ceilings are low, the rooms well lighted, and we were asked immediately, 'What will you have to drink?' This question is common at Washington house parties, and almost always precedes any question such as, 'How are you?' If you say no to a drink, there is an embarrassed silence and the inevitable next question: 'Are you *sure?*' Non-drinkers in Washington are suspect.

"After a decent interval of small talk about the decor and the little nipping Apple dog—Edie Apple appears. She has substantial hams and drumsticks. She enjoyed putting her hands on food. She wears shoes. She is nervous but competent; she wants Johnny not to look like a fool. Problem is, Johnny *is* a fool; most endearing fool; unacceptable behavior most places, but he can write well enough to stay on the *Times* and be a fool on the side; *ergo,* The Pink Apple.

"Soon we were led downstairs to the dining room, with a spot-lighted glass table already set.

"The stemware is durable. Johnny apologized that the glasses were really too thick, but said they were packed and unpacked often and had to last. The tableware was bought overseas.

"Behind the table posed the evening's bottle of wine. A corkscrew lay tensely beside it.

"Beneath the stairs, only partially hidden from view, was their wine cellar. Johnny said he owned nearly 1,200 bottles of French wine stored in his house and other places in Washington. The collection was selected by Johnny and several wine brokers whose taste and advice he seeks. His investment is meant to grow in value each year. Johnny is involved with a company that imports wines; in the summer Johnny and Edie spend a month in France touring the vineyard country, to taste, he says, 'With an eye toward investment.'

"The financial details of Johnny's wine operations are not precisely clear; although he will not open a bottle of his $5 wine for the average visitor with an untutored palate. For them he reserves an excellent $2.50 wine (retail) with a French chateau label. He is both a restauranteur and businessman.

"We were then allowed a visit in the narrow Apple kitchen. Johnny and Edie stand back to back and bottom to bottom. Johnny stirs a bubbling, dark sauce in a shallow frying pan, and a pot of spaghetti is on the boil on a back eye of the stove. Both cooks enjoy bumping each other.

"A bit of tender rear-bussing aside, Edie expertly crumbled egg yolk in her fingers over a lettuce and everything-else-you-can-think-of-good-to-put-in-it salad.

"We were seated opposite one another; too far apart to touch. This too seems to be a Washington house party convention. Couples are split to opposite sides of the table, or as far apart as they can be arranged, apparently to mingle with the other guests in the belief that most Washington couples need as much time away from each other as possible. This critic, however, finds communication almost impossible beyond two interesting persons; to be forced by convention to mingle constantly with strangers is boring. Mix it up, I say. Seat couples together and more sparks will fly.

"Therefore, with nothing better to do, we watched Johnny and Edie eating the food they had cooked. It was a sight out of the American ordinary; they chewed the juice right out of every rich and heavy mouthful, and there were no delicate bones about it. The conventional way is to eat daintily and make remarks about the fresh, 'almost prancing,' quality of the pasta sauce; but in Johnny's case, one must think 'thick and hearty,' a taste that has gone out of fashion here.

"Coffee was not memorable or I would have remembered it. Desserts were huge, massive mousses. Halfway through they were painful to eat. Maggi suffered the pain. I didn't.

"We (as we used to say as children, me, myself, and I) rate The Pink Apple with two washcloths for cleanliness, which is next to godliness, one nose for wine, three bellies for food (almost three and one half, had the lettuce in the salad been a trifle less bruised by rough handling). Reservations are required in advance and can be made by calling Johnny at the *New York Times;* he is extremely finicky about his guest's clout in Washington and New York. So don't be disappointed if you have to call two or three times.''

So said the critic.

Soon after he stopped cooking and eating, Johnny plopped into a chair upstairs in the living room and almost immediately began to babble about politics. We had been joined for after-dinner cordials by two of Johnny's friends, one a former CIA station chief in a province of South Vietnam, the other a young scholarly man. They told Johnny, ''We came to watch you get interviewed.'' They were most interested, however, in babbling about politics. So we left.

The most genuine feeling Johnny mustered was to recall, as he had in Jean-Pierre's, when I paid, the single most happy year in his life: 1969, the year he spent in Africa for the *Times* before returning to New York. He recalled the African air, the giant moon, and the cries and grunts of the wild animals, and he could still see the stars. On the other hand, Edie remembered the strange house they lived in, the amusements and troubles with the native servants, and the upsetting ways of life in Nairobi. But you could see both sets of eyes light up when Africa was mentioned and Johnny explained that a lot of his time in Africa was spent with Edie by his side, in the days before she worked and he worked apart.

He longed for the times when they were together, and it was a genuine and bittersweet longing for better days.

''Now she works in a place where they have top secrets,'' Johnny said.

Her job was at the Voice of America.

''She makes a big *point* of not telling me any of her secrets because 'if a secret gets out' they'd suspect her,'' he explained, as gracefully as he could.

Anyway, I consider Johnny paid for dinner at his house, although I named the place.

I saw Johnny again several months later. In the meantime, a skinny-faced young man who watched Johnny work during the 1972 presidential campaign recorded in a book called *The Boys in the Bus* some of Johnny's bragging. One of the brags was, I was told, that while Johnny was reporting for the *Times* in Vietnam, he had shot two human beings dead. I did not bother Johnny with a confirmation or denial of his man-killing ability, or his true death score, because that would be like asking Santa Claus on Christmas Eve how much workmen's compensation he paid his elves, and does the North Pole have collective bargaining? Some things are better left unknown, and Johnny Apple's dreams of notches on his pistol butt are some of those things. Nonetheless, he took a hard, sharp, wicked rap from his own flapping tongue. When I saw him again at Jean-Pierre's he was embarked on a new sideline to his *Times* career. He was writing food criticism for the local *Washingtonian Magazine*.

He was thinner, firmer, and very much more nervous, like a man recently off the bottle who is miserable and at the same time proud of himself for doing what is socially acceptable for a change. The Apple was no longer pink. It was mature.

Johnny Apple had become a man, so much the worse for all who know him, because the shiny child's eyes were hurting with a stern self-control and only occasionally, as if through a crack in the nursery door, did the playful pink Apple peek out and smile for fun.

He was juicy flesh for critics before; now he knew better, and he was a critic himself.

IX

You cannot be
any better
than your breath.

P. Sodent, L. Avoris,
S. Cope and H. Kerchief

Dan kept our next appointment for lunch, unescorted. I chose the Jefferson Hotel. I told him:

"I once had a crush on Jean."

He blinked his eyes. That's all he did.

"I assume you knew it," I said.

"No," he lied.

His hands put down a knife and fork and reached for a napkin to wipe his mouth.

"You know what I thought of Beverly," I said. "And Jean was happy and fun and very smart. So I developed a crush on her."

"No, I didn't know," Dan said. His eyes said he didn't want to make an issue of it.

"Jean is a very smart girl," I said.

"She's country smart," Dan said, right then and there. "I'm street smart, but she's country smart."

I saw the Dan I had seen ten years ago, and he looked like the man I wanted to see.

He was a package from a swanky men's store. His wrapping was in the best tradition. His suits fit at the rump and shoulders. His fingernails were fanatically manicured.

His shirt cuffs were clean and unfrayed. His hands were the hands of a man doing pantomime. They were well shaped in a squarish, masculinely hairy way, and well treated, and they will lie calmly on the table in front of him without moving for a long time, under complete nervous control. They appear relaxed and calm, but there is a tension in them, and if Dan's hands were a sleeping animal, you wouldn't sneak up and touch it for fear it would whip over snarling and attack you.

The hands hold a glass of water like a glass of wine. The hands hold a knife and fork in imitation of royalty. When the mouth is talking the hands sometimes twitch in their sleep. They hardly ever move, but you know they are alert and under control. When the hands light a small, black cigar, they do it with the care of a man in a gambling casino on the Mississippi. When they shake hands they are businessmen from the East, cool, confident, a little bit aggressive, and under control.

The mouth has pouty lips, but it is under control, and before Dan goes on the air, you can watch this control take over in the few seconds they show him fixing papers and getting ready for his program. You can see him suck in his lips so they are thin and hard, and his jaw muscles tighten like a bunch of horse reins when you want to stop, and the mouth will be under control.

The hair is cut by a barber who cuts it with a kind of scissors the manicurist uses. Every hair is in its place. Not a single stray hair hangs over his ears. The hair ends are tapered and terraced so that all the hair stays quietly in place, and when the wind blows across the White House lawn, Doug Kiker may look like he's standing in a storm at sea but Dan Rather looks like he's on a stage with the White House a part of the scenery in the background and his hair is unruffled by the elements. It isn't easy at all to get your hair under control because hair is nerveless, and Dan's has a small wild sprout at the back end of his part, that sticks up sometimes no matter how hard he tries to slick it down.

Suddenly I was back in today.

Dan sucks in his belly.

Dan is getting fat. Not horsy fat, but fatter than the slim iron man I had remembered. Then I saw bags under his eyes. Then I saw him one day in the White House smoking a cigarette.

He held it between his right thumb and forefinger and sucked furtively on it through little pursed lips like a kiss.

I said, "Dan, I never saw you smoke before."

"Oh, yeah, I hardly ever smoke cigarettes. I usually smoke those cigars, but I forgot to get some and I ran out." He patted his pocket.

"It's so strange to see you puffing on one."

"I only smoked twice before," Dan said.

His face was pale. His eyes weren't sure. But his trousers were flared at the bottom in the style of youth.

He was getting gray.

Dan prowled the White House like an experienced old tomcat hunting among the garbage cans.

X

Some mother tossed a handful of magic beans out the window, and next morning, Jack was climbing up a giant beanstalk to fetch the goose that laid the golden eggs.

Fairy tale

Dan's voice is now under the weight of control, but years ago when Dan first came to Washington, Dan's voice was lighter.

One day I drove over to his house to pick him up on my way to work downtown. I knocked on the front door, but there was no answer. I tried it and it was unlocked. I walked in and heard the shower running. It was a long, long shower, the kind of shower a man takes when he is driven to soap and scrub, and wake up his numb skin. The sound of water stopped. Then I heard loud singing sounds, "Hoooooooooooooh" and "Haaaaaaaaah." No man makes those sounds in public, so I called up the stairs to warn him I was in his house so he wouldn't do it again.

"Come on up!" he called down.

He was standing in front of the sink in a steamy little bathroom shaving, very carefully so as not to make any nicks in his face. His mind was already at work. His body was hairy and muscular, and his feet were a little bit flat. He concentrated on his face in the mirror while I stood watching from the top of the stairs.

"Be ready in a minute," he said. "Sorry I'm late."

"Okay, but I thought you were wounded?"

"Voice lessons," he said.

"How come?"

"Good for my voice. Teaches you control and how to breathe from the diaphragm."

"Doesn't it hurt your throat?"

"The way I talk now hurts my throat. Too much strain. I have to learn to breathe right. Otherwise I breathe too much and that makes too many pauses. It hurts my throat trying to talk too deep."

"How long have you been taking singing?"

"Two weeks."

"Can you really talk deeper with practice like you're doing?"

"You can get down a full octave, if you work on it, my singing teacher says."

Dan took the blade out of the razor, then washed his face carefully. He examined his face in the mirror. He splashed a stinging shaving lotion on it. He carefully combed and brushed his damp hair, and flexed his shoulder muscles.

He turned and strode manfully out of the bathroom, a long white towel wrapped around his flat belly, and extended his hand for a handshake. I was surprised, but I shook it.

"How are you? Good to see you," Dan said, shaking my hand at the top of the stairs. "Be right with you. How things going?"

He strode into his bedroom to get dressed and I followed like a curious child.

The bedroom was a wonderful mess and a pang of jealousy struck me. Dan padded around getting dressed and finding an unwrinkled shirt, his cuff links, a dark suit, a carefully tied dark tie and polished dark shoes.

"Sorry about the mess," Dan said. "Jean's gone to take the kids to school. Otherwise, she'd have coffee ready."

"That's okay."

If Dan knew about my crush he didn't show it. He quickly dressed. We went downstairs to the kitchen. Dan mixed frozen orange juice, he made two cups of coffee, and we chatted about what was going on in the White House. He asked how Beverly was and I asked how Jean and the children were and we both answered, "Okay." We drove downtown together and my heart was full of sorrow and Dan was under control.

Anyway, many years later, Dan was explaining how Jean is "country smart."

He said that he and Jean were at a large dinner party in a Washington hotel and a well-dressed man from another table walked over and said hello. The man was someone who had seen Dan on television.

Dan was snappish with the man, and after the man went away, presumably ashamed for having bothered a television star at dinner, Jean said:

"That wasn't smart."

"What wasn't smart?" Dan asked.

"Being rude."

Jean told him that she'd been noticing whom among his fans Dan is rude to.

Jean noticed that Dan reserves his rudeness for people who apparently have money and people who dine in good restaurants and go to large parties like they go to. But when someone who looked young or poor comes around to ask him for something, he's always kind and sometimes takes too much time with them.

"I never noticed it before," Dan said. "But she was right."

That's what Dan meant by "country smart."

The city smarts was for Dan to have Nate Beanstalk as his business agent, negotiating his contracts with the network, promoting him among Nate's business friends and associates, and taking 10 percent of Dan's earnings over the ten years since Nate agreed to take Dan under his wing. Nate is almost fully retired now. He is in his late seventies.

Nate managed the business affairs of several CBS newsmen. For one, he managed the business of Eric Sevareid. That's a reason I can't believe that Eric is as poor as he poor mouths to be, no matter how much it cost him to pay for the mental care of his first wife. Nate was almost always careful and honest with the money of his clients. If they took his advice, and sometimes Nate made his advice forceful and fatherly in matters of money, they would never be rich, but they would feel a tiny bit more secure. The prima donnas listened. He told me once how he convinced Eric Sevareid to ride a bus from his home to the CBS office. The way Nate did it was to put Eric on a strict allowance and let Eric find out how much taxi rides cost when you had to spend within a strict budget. But it was demeaning to Eric to be recognized standing alone at a bus stop. Eric obeyed grudgingly and for a very short time. Dan was also kept on a strict allowance. Jean had to beg Nate for extra money. Jean complained about it to Beverly.

"The worst thing that can happen to them," Nate told me, "is when they find out they've got some money and then they think they've got to spend it."

I knew about Nate because Dan recommended I see him if I wanted to get into television news. I telephoned Nate in New York and made an appointment to see him. I didn't know it, but Nate was a legend in the business. He looked like a little old Jewish man to me. I always called him Mr. Beanstalk, but his real name is Beinstock.

Why I called him really is that I needed discipline.

My idea was that if Nate would be my business manager he would insist that I live within my income, less 10 percent for him and 50 percent for long-term investment, and I could say to Beverly, "We've got to live on a budget," and she could say to me, "Well, stop riding taxis downtown then." And I would stop taking taxis because my agent and business manager would have made a firm decision on the matter and my mind would be free to be undisciplined in other areas, like my work.

I flew to New York and saw Nate in his office. First Nate tried to sell me on how good an agent he was. He told me how much he'd helped Dan get his business straightened out, and make decent money. I didn't need selling.

"Jean told me about the allowance," I said.

"She did?"

"How you're a tough man to get money out of."

He laughed a puzzled sort of laugh.

"I like to keep my people on a very strict budget," he said.

"That's what I want."

"You do?"

"Yes."

"What is your financial situation?"

"Terrible," I said. "I'm making a pretty good salary at the *Trib,* but it's gone before I get it."

"Are you planning to stay with the *Trib?*"

"Sure," I said. "Unless there's a very good job in television."

"The *Trib* has real trouble," Nate said. "They can't be paying you much."

"It's quite a bit," I said proudly.

"How much?" Nate asked.

"About two hundred a week and overtime," I exaggerated. "Plus I get expenses from my trips to South America."

Nate was too polite a man to say a bad word, but 10 percent of $200 is $20, and here I was dealing with a legend.

Nate took a long, appraising look at me. It's the same kind of look you get if you take a ring into a pawnbroker.

"If you get into television, we can work that amount up," Nate said. "You're a presentable boy, you look a little like Dan. I can do some things to help you."

I didn't dare tell him at that point that I really didn't want to get into television, that I was happy at the *Trib* and hoped it would live forever, and that all I really wanted was some discipline.

I asked Nate, "What can you do?"

"I can get you appointments. I know these guys. I know all of them on business. I'm business manager for some of them. I can go up into their buildings and walk into their offices without an appointment, and I see them at lunch and they do me favors."

I was admiring, but I didn't quite believe him.

I had never known any shrewd Jewish businessmen; just poor ones, like my father. I didn't think Eric Sevareid would want to be seen at lunch with his pawnbroker.

Nate scribbled a note on his desk calendar.

"Okay," he said. "You go back to Washington and wait for me to call. I'll see that you get appointments."

"What about the budget?" I asked.

"What budget?" he asked.

"What kind of budget could I use in the meantime?"

Nate looked at me very puzzled. I stood there while he appraised me again to see if I wasn't cracked.

"What do you want to budget?" he asked.

"My money," I said.

"You told me you spent all your money before it came in. What's left to budget?"

"Well . . ." I thought to myself, "I could *not* pay the telephone bill, and *not* pay the rent for a while, and *not* bring anything back for Beverly from this trip, and cut out the taxis and *not* eat lunch out so much, and charge more on my expense accounts, and *then* I'll have something to budget."

Nate had figured it out by now and he swiveled around in his big leather chair and offered his good-bye hand.

"You've got to have something to budget," he said. "If you get in television, I'll show you how."

"Will I hear from you soon?" I asked.

"A week or so," he said.

I thought to myself that I could hardly wait to get into television so I would have some money to budget, and Nate Beanstalk, whom I considered a wizard, would help me.

Nate was as good as his word. Despite the fact that I called his office every other day for the next month, he saw his people and got them to agree to interview me. Nate called it "screen testing."

I had it set up so that I had two tests in one day in New York. One in the morning, the other in the afternoon.

"Are you sure you want to do two in one day?" Nate asked me on the telephone.

"I can do it," I said. "Get them over with."

"I want you to be *good*," Nate said.

"I will be." It was a Barnard Law Collier promise.

"Won't you be tired?"

"I'm used to being tired," I said.

"Well, remember, they'll try to *help* you. Listen to what they say. They want you to do a good job."

I didn't believe him. I thought they were there just to record. I thought that unless I brought it all with me, and did it with cold, hard-eyed professionalism, without slipping into any slovenly naturalness, like hair blowing out of place or my voice coming out sounding too high . . . if I didn't bring it all with me, then all of my weaknesses would show on the film.

I went to ABC first. It was a cold, rainy day in Manhattan and I was scared but calm. I figured that Nate Beanstalk must have seen something potentially worthwhile in me or he wouldn't have sent me to his friends. I'd also practiced. When nobody was in the house the week before the interview I sang "Hoooooooooh!" and "Haaaaaaaaah!" from deep down in the stomach to lower my voice. I didn't think I could possibly lower it an octave without going to Dan's teacher and spending $50 a week I didn't have. But I hoped I could lower it three or four notes.

I had also picked up a tape recorder. The man in the store knew me as a reporter for the *Herald Tribune,* and a card pal of Art Buchwald's. He agreed to send me a bill. I didn't have enough in my overdrawn checking account to pay with. I wrote a news story script and read it over and over into the microphone while I stood or sat in front of a mirror. I tried to sound as bass-voiced as Chet Huntley and the way I did it was by pulling in my chin, lowering the volume of my voice and trying to let the sounds rumble out of my chest. The strain slowed my words down and it took me three minutes to get through a two-minute script. So I tried to speed up my words, but the more words I spoke the higher pitched my voice got, and when I got down to two minutes in time I sounded too high-pitched again. I did it so many times my jaw muscles began to ache from the strain and my throat was sore.

I asked Dan about the problem.

"You don't really have to worry about that," Dan said. "You're a *great* writer. They don't really care how a guy sounds, as long as he gives the news, and that means great writing and reporting. You're a good reporter . . . a *great* reporter. You're a much better reporter than I am, so you shouldn't have any trouble at all. Don't worry about it. Concentrate on your writing and let the on-the-air part take care of itself."

I tried to be comforted by what Dan said, but I had a feeling, a feeling you get with strange dogs and wild horses, that Dan was only to be trusted so far.

So I kept on practicing and singing, and I put a sunlamp on my face and got a haircut and bought a blue shirt.

ABC had a big turnover of young talent. But they had respect for Nate and the man in charge of screen tests told me to sit down, take my time about writing a two-minute news script, and then he'd put me on film for the executives in charge of hiring to see. I was allowed to take the wire service copy from the day before to use as raw news for the script.

I sat down at a typewriter in a corner of the newsroom in New York and, recalling Dan's advice, tried to create the best-written news program on television. I wanted all of the previous day's news, and explanation of that news, insight, drama, oddity, and a wide range of national and international subject matter, all squeezed into two spoken minutes.

I used powerful, imaginative words. I thought up a clever, informative lead for the first story. By the time I'd done that, an hour had passed.

"Are you finished yet?" the producer asked politely.

"I'm getting there," I said. "I want to make it good."

He smiled and walked away.

Somebody on the other side of the room stopped the producer and asked, "Who's the new guy?"

"He's writing a book," the producer said.

Half an hour later a man from the news desk came over and stood behind me and looked over my shoulder. I rolled my typewriter roller around so he couldn't peek at my script. I did not like anyone reading my work over my shoulder, but I turned and nodded at him.

"How're ya doin'?" he asked.

"Fine," I said. "I'm doing a two-minute script for a tryout."

"You've been working a long time," he said. "I can't help but noticing. Are you having trouble?"

"No, no," I said, shaking my head.

"This is a different business from the newspaper business," he said. "A two-minute script can't take too long to get right. You've got to concentrate on making it easy to read on the air. You can't worry too much about how much you pack in it."

"Thanks," I said. I turned back to the keyboard.

"There are some other problems, too," the man said.

"How so?"

He explained patiently and simply.

"We have what we call a union. It's not like in the newspapers. This is a *real* union, or a bunch of unions. They all want more and more money, and every second they work they get paid for. So we in television can't waste any of their time. A cameraman has to get paid. A sound man has to get paid. The floor crew gets paid. Now it's getting lunch hour and if they wait around and make your test over the lunch hour, they cost the company so much money in over-time people around here get sick at the thought of it."

The man saw that I missed the point.

"Those guys aren't the Newspaper Guild," he said. "They're a bunch of *real* unions."

"That's too bad," I said. I felt that unions were a pain in the ass of creation.

"Yeah," the man said. "So you'd better get that script done before lunchtime."

I knew that was impossible. I got up and found the men's room. Then I went to his desk and told the man that the producer had told me to take as long as I needed to write the script.

"I've been talking to him on the telephone," the man said kindly. "He thinks you ought to be about finished by now. So wind it up if you can."

When I finally went into the studio to read what I had written in front of the camera, there was a feeling of tense, unhappy bickering in the room. Still, everyone tried to help me look good. The producer had me go through it once more than necessary.

When it was over, I asked him how it was.

"Not too bad," he said. "You've never done this before."

"How long does it take to get it developed?" I asked.

"Not long."

"Can I see it?"

"Don't worry. It's not too bad," he said. "I've seen worse."

I thought that was an optimistic remark.

"Thank you for coming in," he said. "You'll hear pretty soon."

"Contact Nate Beanstalk," I said.

The producer snorted.

I took a taxi to Sardi's and drank a Bloody Mary and ate bar cheese for lunch.

After a Bloody Mary and bar cheese at Sardi's, I felt very New Yorky and a little bit famous. I pretended I was a famous foreign correspondent for the *New York Herald Tribune,* who roamed the world in search of adventure. I turned up the collar of my London Fog raincoat with the alpaca lining and walked with my head bowed against the chilly rain, from Sardi's to Rockefeller Center. I wanted to be at NBC on time. I was seldom late for an appointment.

I filled my head on the way with thoughts of the revolution in Cuba. I thought of Fidel Castro and the week I spent with him on his island, and the front-page attention my articles received in the *Trib.* On the radio I could still hear them playing a commercial to promote my stories. The title of the series was "Seven Days with Castro," subtitled, "We Called Him Max, for Maximum Leader," and in the commercial the pitch was put to the tune of "The Twelve Days of Christmas."

The commercials had stopped running months before, but they still played in my head.

I thought of men kidnapped in the Bolivian mountains, and of playing draw poker with the "Purple Skullcap," whose hands had strangled a man to death the night before our card game. I thought of a sculptress in Mexico, and Charles de Gaulle, and a bloody body in Caracas. I thought about Carlos Lacerda in Brazil, and how he kept a machine gun on his desk in the governor's office, and Mike Rougier, the *Life* photographer, who passed out in the thin air of La Paz while I, a foreign correspondent of the *New York Herald Tribune,* quick-stepped around town and drank beer the first night. I thought of the long-haired sister of a Bolivian painter; the painter hated Americans and hated his sister for working for the money in the American embassy. I thought of watching Fidel Castro wipe his bootsoles, filthy with cow manure, on a white silk sofa, and how it wasn't a good idea for a foreign correspondent to take a Cuban girl to bed for risk of blackmail. By the time I thought all of these uplifting thoughts, and a few more, I was at NBC with the shoulders of my London Fog adventurously wet with chilly New York rain and my face as refreshed as if Manhattan skies rained bay rum.

I wrote the NBC script practically from memory, in less than thirty minutes in a little office with only a typewriter. I read it over a few times for timing, cut out some extra words, read it over again in my newly imagined voice, and told the producer I was ready. I was glad I tested at ABC first so that I had had a little practice.

The producer told me that the set I would use was used by David Brinkley when he was in New York. It was a tall desk with a green metal swivel chair behind it. The chair was locked in a swivel slightly to the right.

"That's the angle Brinkley wants it," the director said. "It makes him look best."

I thought it was pretty good luck to sit in Brinkley's chair. I could feel that the NBC people were behind me because I was a famous foreign correspondent.

The lighting man took a lot of time with the lights and I sat in David Brinkley's chair trying to be a famous foreign correspondent with a little bit of stage fright tickling me in the loins. I thought about having to go to the bathroom, but I rejected the idea as cowardly. I looked at myself in the monitor, I took out a comb and combed my rain-wet hair.

"Too much shine on his forehead," a light man said.

A voice from the control room said: "Makeup, get some powder on his forehead."

A man came over and rubbed my forehead with pancake makeup on a sponge.

"His nose shines, too," the voice from the control room said.

"Okay," the makeup man said, and he rubbed pancake on my nose.

I submitted manfully.

"Can we do anything about the hair?" the voice said.

"Move a light," somebody said.

I took out my comb and combed it neater.

"Okay, Barnard, we'll start in thirty seconds. Get ready," the voice said.

I thought about Fidel Castro, dynamite in Bolivia, the Mexican sculptress, and I pulled in my chin, straightened out my shoulders, and put a serious look on my face.

"Twenty seconds," said a man with flipcards with the seconds printed on them.

I looked over the script and silently tested my voice. It was the voice of a serious, adventurous foreign correspondent. I forgot fame altogether.

"Ten seconds."

The tickling in my loins started up again, but it was too late, and I was too cowardly to say, "Wait, I have to go to the bathroom first."

"You're on."

I read the script slowly and deliberately, making every word as clear as I could with my throat tightening up because of the strain and my mouth filling up with saliva. I looked up from the paper into the camera lens. But when I looked back, I'd lost my place. My eyes darted back and forth across the paper while my mind tried to remember what came next. Luckily my eyes fell on the next line. There was only a little pause. I talked on but I was afraid to look up at the camera, so I let my eyes run a little bit ahead on the script to memorize it while I read the words. It worked. I looked up for a second at the camera lens while my mouth kept reciting words and then I looked back down and found my place exactly. I did it three or four times more while the script lasted. Then, at the end, I signed off. I looked directly at the camera lens and said, in the deepest tones I could, "This is Barnard Law Collier, NBC News." I had practiced it dozens of times.

There was a silence in the studio after I finished. I was relieved that the silence was broken by the voice. It said, "That's a run-through, Barnard. Let's try it again to see if we can't do it a little better."

The producer walked over and put his hand on my shoulder.

"Loosen up," he said. "Breathe once in a while. And look at the camera occasionally. You've got your eyes glued to the paper."

"I thought I *was* looking up."

"You weren't."

"How was the voice?"

"Don't worry about your voice. Everybody isn't Chet Huntley."

"What do you mean?"

"I mean relax. And emphasize a few words so it doesn't all come out sounding flat. Where are you from?"

"Washington."

"I mean, where were you born?"

"Michigan."

"You don't have any accent, so punch some words. Pick out a word, like a strong verb, and come down hard on it. And don't trail off at the end of your sentences. It sounds like a Chinese when you trail off. Make it come *up*. Don't say, 'This is NBC news.' Say, 'This is NBC,' and pause for a split second, and then say *'News,'* strong."

I tried to drink in all his advice and make it a part of my blood so that it would come out perfect next time.

I went through it three more times. The last time everyone in the room was weary and I'd forgotten I was a foreign correspondent and my voice was tired from a day of strain.

The producer was very kind. "It was pretty good," he said. "You can do it if you try."

"Have you ever seen worse?" I asked him as we walked up some backstairs to the executive offices.

"Oh, sure," he said.

"Many?"

"Lots."

"Do you think there's a chance?"

"Aren't you a good reporter or something?"

"Yeah," I said. "I was just in Cuba with Fidel Castro for seven days."

"Then there's always a chance," he said.

He took me to his office where he had a big television set. It was connected with the studio. He made some telephone calls and the executives came in to see the test. There were two producers and Reuven Frank, who looked like Dr. Sam Bernstein, my pediatrician in Detroit. He was kind and gentle and tall and gray haired and smoked a pipe and dressed in tweeds. I trusted Reuven Frank's opinion as I trusted Sam Bernstein's.

The screen lighted up and my test started. I stood up in the doorway to watch. I was wearing my London Fog. I saw on the television screen that I was wearing a dark suit and a dark tie. My face was white and I had dark circles around my eyes. My eyes looked like the eyes of a man who has to go to the bathroom. My body was rigid with my shoulders thrown back, and my head was tilted down looking at the paper so that when I looked at the camera only my eyes moved in a mechanical doll way that I never saw again until I saw President Nixon do it on television. He was pretending to be President and I was pretending to be a famous foreign correspondent.

Then I heard the voice. It was the voice of a eunuch.

I looked over at Reuven Frank, who sat on a sofa puffing on his pipe in the dim light. He watched the whole series through. Once he commented on some item of news I'd put in the script.

The lights in the room were turned on, and Reuven Frank stretched and looked at me in the doorway.

"You want to know now or later?" he asked.

"Now," I said.

"You did everything wrong that ever was done wrong." He smiled. "I never saw anything like it."

I laughed.

"There must be something there," he said. He shook his head slowly.

I looked at him as if I thought he was kidding, just in case he was.

"I'm not kidding," he said. "You made every mistake there is. It's not that there isn't anything there. I know something's there because I've seen your stuff. But nobody ever covered it with so many mistakes before."

"I know the voice is bad," I said.

"It's not bad," Reuven said smiling. "It's terrible. Every word was the same in tone and stress and volume. It was a constant drone. I have a theory about that," he said.

He puffed his pipe like a professor and dared me not to ask what his theory was.

"What is it?"

"I think that Americans are afraid of their language. I think they're afraid to make it sing. You speak Spanish, don't you?"

"Yes."

"Well, I'll bet when you talk in Spanish you aren't afraid to make it go up and down and sing a little bit. But when you talk English in front of a television camera, you drone."

I tried out a few Spanish phrases to show him I spoke a few words of Spanish, and I naturally sang them a little.

"That's right," he said. "It has some life in Spanish."

"It's not too high?"

"You can get singing lessons to bring it down an octave."

"You can?"

"It won't do you any good," he said.

"Why not?"

"You've got too many other things to learn. Don't waste your time with singing lessons."

He stood up, shook my hand, asked when the *Trib* was going to fold, and left.

"Are you going someplace else?" the producer asked.

"CBS," I said.

"Can I give you a piece of advice?" he asked.

"Sure."

He put his hand on my shoulder and guided me out of the door and down the hallway.

"It would be a good idea to let your hair dry out and use a brush before they test you. It makes a nicer appearance."

"Thank you," I said.

"Good luck," he said.

CBS tested me later in Washington, and Bill Small was the man who gave me the bad news.

XI

Time is relative. Is a minute longer eating
ice cream or sitting on a red hot stove?

Chauncey dePew

Sander Vanocur is dickering with Ben Bradlee about writing a column for the *Post*. Ben is playing with him, not giving him a yes and
not giving him a no. Sander wants to think that Ben is tantalizing
him over to the *Post* against Sander's will. But Sander's legs are not
crossed anymore, and Sander is on his way into Ben's arms. I
talked to Sander on the telephone and he said:

"Barney, Ben Bradlee is the most seductive man in Washington."

"I don't think so," I said.

"You don't?"

"I like long love affairs. Ben Bradlee is a ten-minute man."

"Oh, *no!*" Sander said, "He'll take you out to lunch."

"Yeah. But as soon as he's seduced you, Sander, you'll be lucky
if it's ten minutes before he'll be gone."

Sander laughed.

"You know," he said, "you're right. Ben's a sprinter."

"He's built like a sprinter."

"That's right," Sander said.

XII

If the lunatics get out,
The politicians will go to jail.

Dix Hill

There is an almost imperceptible crack in Art Buchwald's iron eyes, and out of the great darkness comes art . . . and a twinkle.

I had a very hard time finding a way to look into the crack, and then, after thoughts of Mark Twain and the Marquis de Sade and Toulouse-Lautrec passed through my head, I stumbled on the word *depravity*.

I said, "Art, I think you're depraved."

The crack did not open.

I said, "Art, the part about you I enjoy most is your depravity."

The crack opened . . . and a twinkle of anger twinkled out.

"Whaddaya mean, 'depravity?' " Art said.

I never did explain. I spent my time looking into the crack.

He said, "I'm not depraved."

I said, "You are, too!"

He said, "Whadda hell do you mean?"

I said, "I think you are the most depraved man who has the guts to work openly in Washington."

He said, "Whaddaya mean, 'depraved'?" I'm not depraved. I'm . . . I'm . . . I'm . . . Moral!"

"Shit," I said.

"I am!" Art said, and a twinkle of fun shone out.

"I don't think so," I said.

"Well, you don't know what depraved is, then!" he said.

"I do, you don't."

"What is it?" Art demanded.

"A man who sees the truth and can still make it sound funny. That's depraved," I said.

"What does the dictionary say depraved is?" Art asked.

"Let's look it up," I said.

The dictionary gave the common meaning. It was a common, college-level dictionary.

Art was willing to go by that dictionary, which stressed the immoral and "perverted" sense of the word.

I chose the *Oxford Universal Dictionary* to define a certain aspect of the word—as follows:

"Theol. the innate corruption of human nature due to original sin (often *total* depravity) 1757."

Art said he would agree to the word "praved" to describe him. I suggested he might better choose "unpraved." Maggi suggested "repraved."

However, I clung to depraved, and pried and pried and pried at the crack with it.

XIV *

If your spine ever tingles for some unknown reason, it means someone is walking on your grave.

Harry Proshan

---

* There is no thirteenth chapter in this book. Here is why.

Barney Collier has Gypsy blood. His mother's mother was terrified of Gypsies. Gypsies stole babies, which was very bad, but Gypsies also made babies, which was worse. Somewhere back in his mother's mother's family, probably back in Russia in the 1800s, a Gypsy had turned up to add his blood to the line. His mother would go far out of her way to listen to a violinist whose bow trembled when he played, "When a Gypsy Makes His Violin Cry." She believed that dreams on Friday nights were prophetic, and also in good- and bad-luck words, and the *fige,* which the Brazilians call a *figa*—the thumb sticking between the first and second fingers of either hand. When a baby is born with its fingers making a fige or a figa, it is a sign that the child has the power to ward off evil spirits. It is a very lucky charm if Gypsy blood runs in your veins. Kate was born with the fige in at least one hand and, Barney thinks, in both, but he doesn't want to overdo her credit.

It's Gypsy blood that makes him want to move around the world. The Gypsy is why he enjoys wild eyes. He is sentimental and believes in omens. The dead bird outside the windows, which is better than outside the door, and infinitely better than inside the house, which means death within. The whippoorwill singing "Let me go" for ten minutes without taking a breath is an unburied soul begging to be laid to rest.

True, an ominous cloud hung inside his skull. In the sunniest joy he saw the roots of blackest sorrow. To him, the world was full of portents, of events sending their signals ahead of them. He prayed to gods unknown to spare him the sorrow of losing those lives he loved, for many, many, many years.

In the morning, he shook his shaving lather can exactly twenty-five times. It had something to do with how many more years of life he wanted. In his right pants pocket he carried a horsechestnut called a buckeye, for luck, and a .22 caliber bullet for sexual prowess, which he liked to think of as a symbol for a symbol, because he couldn't easily carry a mortar shell in his right pants pocket. He also carried his own version of mad money: coins enough for at least two telephone calls in case he was stranded.

He made superstitious gestures. If salt spilled, he tossed a spilled grain or two over his left shoulder; he tapped wood; he avoided speaking of good dreams out loud for fear a spiteful Fate would replace the dream with a nightmare. To himself and half aloud he would say, *"Kin ahora,"* which is what his father and mother said to take the curse of the mouth off too openly admired lives, especially pretty children.

Therefore he spoke as little as possible about Kate's round, happy face or the possibility of her keeping her exotic bloom for as many years as he and Maggi lived. He avoided for the same reason telling Maggi of her natural beauty, although he was drawn as nothing else had ever drawn him to the unfathomed blue oceans of her wide-set eyes and pleased beyond description by the rest.

Barney's black hair and olive skin and dark brown eyes that can talk are Gypsy traits communicated from some unknown dead ancestor, and if Barney ever walks on that ancestor's grave, Barney thinks he'll know it. He knows that ancestor's taste for food and lights and strange languages and romance in perfumed places.

Barney also knows the quizzical nature of his father's people. He stands sometimes, and looks through his father's witch hazel eyes, and the world seems very puzzling, and some order must be made of it. There must be laws to tame the jungle passions of nature, and man's life must bend to man's laws. Rather than fortune-tellers, his father's people were the sages; men who interpreted the law as handed down by Moses, men who believed in the book.

Barney knew his father's nervousness at being confronted in a world without the rules of law and the belief in logic.

But Barney loves growling and sentiment, and stories that bring lumps to your throat and tears to your eyes, and the deepest and most complete connection between a man and a woman, with all accompanying animal sounds and feelings, with a chorus of laughter to toast the fact that we are human and only humans can laugh and make love at the same time.

In the case of thirteen, the Gypsy wins out over the sage.

XV

For ambitious lovers,
Work always comes first.

The Headless Horseman

I told Art I was writing about Washington journalists. His eyes sized me up and he leaned across his desk and pointed his finger toward the door.

"You're going to do *them,* aren't you?" he asked through his nose.

He was pointing toward the office of Evans and Novak, which was across the hall.

"Sure," I said.

"You'll *do* them, right?"

"Right."

"Okay," he said, "if you *do* them, I'll help you. I always like to help someone from the old *Herald Tribune.* We'll have lunch and talk about it."

You must be admitted to Art's company at Sans Souci, and my admission had been paid ten years before when I gave him $600 in a series of gin rummy games in his office. One day I lost $120 after being triple blitzed in two games and double blitzed in the third. Two days later, Art opened the *Trib* office door and cried out, in the voice of a triumphant fishwife, "Hey, fellas, look what I got!"

He was holding it out for everyone to admire. It was a gold wristwatch.

"It's beautiful, isn't it?" he said to the reporters who came around to see. I went over to look, too.

"I've wanted a gold watch for a long time," Art said. "And now I've finally got one."

To be polite, someone asked where he'd gotten it. "Oh, it was a gift," he said. "From *Barney.*"

There was a pause.

Someone said, "Barney, who?"

"Barney *Collier,*" Art said.

Everyone was flabbergasted, including me.

Art turned to waddle out. He poked his head back in and said:

"Oh, thanks, Barney. You're the greatest gin rummy player in the world."

Do you think I learned a lesson? Not a chance. The Greatest Gin Rummy Player in the World went on playing great gin rummy for years before it dawned on him.

Occasionally Doug Kiker lunches with Art. While my $600 admission was prepaid in cash, Doug pays his admission in a different way at the table.

Doug told me another adult story he tells around Washington:

"Sit down," says Art.

The way Doug tells the story, you know Doug sits down proudly. In Doug's circle of Washington friends, it is fashionable to sit at Art Buchwald's table in the Sans Souci.

There's a little chitchat, a drink is ordered, and then Art leans over to collect his admission.

Doug hesitates shyly, but Art is not subtle or elegant about it.

"Well?" he says.

Doug grins bashfully.

"C'mmmaahn," Art says loudly. "What was she like?"

And according to Doug, "I tell him about this gorgeous girl I had the night before."

Art sits enthralled. When Doug pauses in his story, Art is afraid it's over too soon and goes: "Yeah? Yeah?"

And Doug, who wrote two long novels, prolongs the climax.

"Art loves it," Doug said. "Especially when I get to the fucking part. He keeps saying, 'Yeah; Yeah; Yeah.' "

Once I had lunch with Art at Sans Souci.

Sans Souci is designed as a small, intimate theater. Anyone who enters must play.

A player makes his entrance through a proscenium archway, with a curtain at the side. Then there is a narrow runway from the archway across the stage platform and down two steps into the pit.

Art was seated at his preferred table, down in the pit with his back to the wall.

I was led to the table by Paul, the maître d'hôtel, who has one warm eye and one glassy eye that looks off wild in his head.

Art reached out to shake my hand. His handshake was soft and puffy.

He said, "Hi. How can I help, Barney?"

I said, "I don't know. Let's just talk."

We talked about Washington, while I watched him.

His attention was over my right shoulder, on the archway.

He watched the entrance and act of each star player.

In between scenes, Art turned his attention to me. He was businesslike. He gave me some ideas for the book, and he suggested a title.

He said, "I name lots of guys' books."

I said, "Okay, what's your name?"

He said, " 'Clout in Washington.' "

I said, "Who's 'Clout'?"

"Clout, clout, like somebody with a big fist."

"Who's got clout? Among the journalists?"

"Oh . . . Scotty Reston's got clout . . . Lippmann had clout."

"Do you have clout?"

"Nah . . . nah. I don't have clout. Everybody in Washington loves me."

"Does Ben Bradlee have clout?"

He hesitated. He hesitated. He hesitated. He hesitated.

"You're not going to *do* him, are ya?"

"Isn't he your friend?" I asked.

Art nodded his head, yes.

"I'm going to do him," I said.

Then Art saw something coming that caused him to hunch up his shoulders, suck in the left side of his mouth, close his left eye, cock his head to the right and up, and shake.

Behind me I heard the footsteps, in a prancing trot. Then, as a lady in a pink pantsuit, with her neck skin hanging, leaned her belted belly over my shoulder, I smelled the aroma of Joy.

She put a kiss on the part of Art that he offered her—the upper rim of his left ear.

Almost every weekday lunchtime when Art is in town, he takes in the show at Sans Souci. He watches with screwy eyes.

In his eyes, it's the most wonderful living theater in this part of the world, and if it ever closes before Art moves away or dies, he will miss it to the bottom of his heart.

When the meal was over, Art asked the waiter to bring him a cigar. I was astonished with myself. I had watched him very closely the entire time and I hadn't realized he hadn't been smoking a cigar.

Art said, "Ya got whatcha need?"

I said, "I don't know."

He said, "Ya don't?"

I offered to pay the bill. Art said, "Nah, I got it, Barney."

I said, "No, I'll pay half."

Art said, "I sign the tab at my table. And I'm gonna sit here a little while and talk to some friends."

He looked over at the table to his left. A former Cabinet officer was lunching with his pantsuited wife. He turned to his right and Mel Elfin was sitting there with a tiny Italian ghost with the faded name of Jack Valenti. It was almost two o'clock. I said, "Thanks, Art, I'll get back to you."

He said, "Awright, Barney. See ya."

I walked directly from Sans Souci to the office of Evans and Novak in order to start doing them.

XVI

A promise is a promise is a promise.

From "What You Always Say"

The story about how Art has tried for years to bust up Evans and Novak came from a bald-headed man of thirty who works down the hall in the *Boston Globe* bureau.

He said that Art tried to make Rolly mad at Bob for making too many long distance telephone calls. Art would say things like, "Rolly, if something happened to Bob, you could have the whole column to yourself and make twice what you're makin' now. And he wouldn't be around to run the telephone bill up all the time."

Art knows that Rolly couldn't do the job by himself, so if Rolly got rid of Bob, Rolly would be done for and they'd be broken as a brick after a karate chop.

I went into the Evans and Novak office and saw Novak standing in their inner office doorway. I asked Novak if the story had any truth to it, and he smiled a toothy smile, and said, "No. It's just for fun. It's nothing serious. We've been together twelve years now."

XVII

Wisdom often comes from disillusionment.

Recalled from Little Orphan Annie

Rolly is pale-skinned, blue-eyed, liver-spotted, and slim. His fine pale hair is thin. He has trained himself in the social graces, and he plays the game of a girl—a little bit coy, a little smile of come-hither teasing, and sometimes, an almost shy way of bending his body, almost to the point of bringing his hand limply in front of his mouth and giggling behind it. He's also playful with his words; they don't always mean what they say.

His teeth are very long. Yet, Bob Novak sells him as "almost as active a squash player now as he was when he was young—a fierce competitor."

Stewart Alsop had called Rolly "my best friend." Stewart enjoyed a man on trips who would be fun to play with and who paid his own way, and Rolly will play games day and night, and almost always pays his own way. Stewart told me about a travel game he and Rolly played on an around-the-world trip together. One point of the game was who registered first at the next hotel. The first to register would approach the desk clerk, and in the tone of voice and accent both men can imagine Joe Alsop using, he would give his own name, as if he were military or royalty, and then say condescendingly, "I also need a room for my boy. He's outside, you see, carrying in the baggage. A very *small* room, down the hall, will do."

The one who won the point paid the big cost for the big room, and the one who lost paid for the small room.

There are few professions in which men travel as intimately together away from home as in the higher ranks of the Washington Press Corps. There are still very few traveling women journalists, so there is an armylike comradeship about men at an Indian reservation in South Dakota, journalists bumping into each other at a house party in Saigon, at an airport in Atlanta, at a hangout in New York, in a bar in Montevideo, and on the corner of Seventeenth Street and Pennsylvania Avenue, NW, in Washington.

If you bump into any, they will tell you war stories that are real to them but sound like fish stories.

They sound made up because the man lives a fiction when he is out and abroad and without a woman to share his reality. Men-without-women is a world of risking life and limb in the pursuit of danger at night during the Black riots on Fourteenth Street, or in a mountain village 20,000, well, maybe 18,500, feet up in the Bolivian Andes, or in a canoe on the Au Sable River in Michigan.

The fiction is that a woman's flesh and mind could not withstand the rigors of that sort of life, so they can't come along. The truth is, very few women ever pay their own way.

If you walk into a bar or a restaurant or hotel lobby and introduce a woman to a pack of men journalists as "my wife," the pack's reflex is to snap shut its mouth. It bites its tongue for whatever time a wife is around; the pack makes it clear by the way it fidgets that a wife is more welcome someplace else.

On the other hand, if a woman is a mistress, you can introduce her with some respect. She is certainly more beautiful than a wife, on the grounds that an ugly mistress is an insult to a man's intelligence and an unforgivable slur on his wife's honor. She is also more sensuous by definition.

But, if you have the great good fortune to introduce a woman who is clearly your lover, and you are clearly hers, then you have unanimous respect, no doubt about it. Lovers are introduced with their own names, with no "my wife" or "my friend" implied or attached.

Few men have the lucky good fortune to be married to their lovers, and in the eyes of most men I've known in the Washington Press Corps, and among foreign correspondents who love to travel in pairs and packs, it's completely unrealistic for a wife and lover to be the same person. They'd rather you brought along Rolly Evans any day than any woman.

Rolly Evans has a wife. She is a reddish-haired woman whose eyes in old photographs from her days at Vassar were like a dark-eyed serious kitten. Her eyes, the single time I ever saw them, in the Evans house in Georgetown, were now lost and resigned.

She spoke to Rolly the morning I saw them together with an edge of bitterness. It was a quarter to nine in the morning on a cloudy fall day.

Rolly and I had breakfasted together twice before at his Metropolitan Club, but I wanted to see his house and family.

The house was quiet when I was let in by Rolly, except for a radio playing back in the kitchen. The front of the house had the polished old wood odor of heritage and refinement, and an old piano that implied music.

Rolly led me to the back of the house where a small breakfast table was set in a room with a glass ceiling and glass walls like a greenhouse but as tall as a two-story birdhouse, with the birds flown away. He said the glass was tinted and extra strong to withstand hail. He said it had required thousands of dollars of architecture and engineering to build. Rolly was extremely proud of it; it was what he seemed most proud of about his house.

I asked him how he managed to pay for such a project, and he said, "Oh, I've got plenty of money. Actually, it was from the money Bob and I made on one of our books."

Outside the windows of the structure, in a space that used up the entire small backyard, was a swimming pool in the style of a Grecian bath. The water was mirrory still and dark and the terrace was of a blackish stone. Ten-foot-high columns supported the low sky on each side. Fall leaves and apples floated in the water. It was impressive and strange.

Rolly said:

"It's a terrific pain in the ass, Barney, but I like it."

Rolly and I ate fried bacon, tea, white bread toast, and honey. Rolly was very careful about the honey. And he was possessive of the honeypot. When I reached for it, he said, "Careful of that."

He took his knife and showed me how he buttered his bread a little first, and then put honey on it, never touching his knife to the bread so as not to transfer crumbs to the honeypot.

It was a lesson in manners. I did my toast the same way he did.

I wondered why he attached such special significance to honey.

He told me that his father, who still lived near Philadelphia, was a spry, healthy man still active after eighty-two years.

Each time I talked to Rolly at breakfast, he had mentioned his father, and he said, almost in the same breath, "He still plays tennis. We played together not long ago."

He told me again about his father as we ate bread and butter and honey, and then he said:

"You know what my father says? He says honey is an antidote to death."

"Wonderful," I said. "I'll eat some every day I can from now on."

I was very pleased to get some useful advice from him.

Then Mrs. Evans appeared. She scuffed into the porch and told Rolly about a telephone call she'd answered for him. Rolly said, "Barney, this is my wife," and he said her name. She said, "Hello," and disappeared into the kitchen. Then she scuffed back out to a telephone nook at the foot of the stairs.

We ate quickly, and as I left the house with Rolly I saw that Mrs. Evans worked in that nook. Her work for the day was to organize a dinner party. I noticed a list of food to be bought at the "French Market," names for invitations, a recipe, and telephone numbers to call.

From the sound of their matter-of-fact conversation, I gathered the party was for Washington business more than for pleasure. There was no spark of spontaneousness in it. Almost everything was organized to the last detail, and guests' social calendars checked, and the possible arrival of "a special guest" planned and hoped for.

From time to time before he died, President Kennedy visited Rolly's house for a party, and by Rolly's account, he enjoyed himself.

XVIII

"Those are liar's proofs," they said behind his back.

"A Piece of String"

"Barney? How you doin', baby?"

"Hi, Rolly, how are you?"

"When's your book comin' out?"

"As soon . . . . as I—as they put it in print."

"What do you think?"

"I think . . . February, March, April, May, June——"

"Are you nice to us?"

"I don't know. I called to ask you a question."

"You've finished the book."

"Well, I've finished except for checking."

"Uh-huh." Then what I didn't say about being nice dawned on him, and he turned on the tone of a schoolmaster bawling out the classroom dunce.

"You don't know . . . ?!"

I let it pass.

"Well, I've finished except for checking, and that's a very important part of the book."

"Well, what do you want to check?"

"Two things. Number one, you told me one day when we were at the Metropolitan Club that you'd be fine and dandy to have your income tax return looked at, so I want to look at it."

"Oh, *shit,* not a chance. Why should I let you look at my income tax returns?"

"I don't know, you made the offer."

"Well . . . chhchhk . . . I——"

"Were you kidding?"

"No, I mean, if a . . . a legal or, ah, ah, an IRS question raised about my income statements, ah——"

"Right."

"Ah, obviously they'd be looked at."

"Well, you told me you had nothing, you said something about having absolutely nothing to hide——"

"Absolutely nothing——"

"——And that if I wanted——"

"I don't let any, I don't let any——"

"And that if I wanted to look at your tax returns, come up to the office and you'd let me. That was your words."

"Yeah, well, I wouldn't let any stranger, or any member of *my* family look at my income tax just because *they* want to."

"Right, so while you said it, it's not true."

"Well, I don't remember saying it, Barney. Have you got a note on that?" It was a nasty, sneering I gotcha' tone. "Let's see your notes. . . . I'd like to see them. . . . I don't think you *took* notes."

"Well, I didn't take notes, but I do remember what you said."

"Well, I don't think . . . if I said in a colloquial way, a guy could say, 'Jesus, I don't care who comes up and looks at my house and every, every closet in my house is open for inspection.' I don't have any skeletons——"

"Right."

"Including my income tax statements . . . but if you think I'm going to—some guy calls me up, you or somebody else says, 'I want to see your income tax,' not a chance."

"I understand that. I wondered why you said it. I thought maybe you were putting me on."

"If I said it . . . I mean, I agree I said either that or something like it. What was the context of the conversation?"

"The fact that we were discussing finances, how much you made, and you said, in the course of the moment, you said, 'I'll show you my income tax returns,' and I said, 'When?' and you said, 'I could show 'em to ya, I've got some at the office——' "

Rolly interrupted sternly.

"Well I *couldn't* have said *that,* Barney, 'cause there's never been an income tax file of any kind except on the newsletters, or newsletters——"

"We were also discussing the newsletter——"

"I have never had a *single* shred of paper in this office on my income tax. . . . Nothing!"

"Well, you must have meant the newsletter then."

"And I frankly am not in a position to let you look at the newsletter file 'cause I've got two partners."

"Right."

"Novak and Gutwillig, and I—I guarantee you that they'd be against it."

"Okay."

"And——"

"So then you just take it back. Period."

"Well——"

"We'll just leave it that that was not correct."

"I just can't imagine ever saying it, Barney."

"I would never have invented it out of thin air, you know that. It had to come up somewhere——"

"I'm sure something like that came up in a context of a politician or a government . . . hiding his income tax . . . saying, 'I've got nothing to hide, I don't know why anybody else would.' But to draw from that ahhh . . . an understanding that I would let somebody come up and look at all my income tax statements is nonsense."

"Okay. . . . So that it isn't right."

"If you say—You can say anything you want, Barney. I mean, I'm being perfectly honest with you. I would never let anybody come up and look at my income tax statements. They'd find information in there that would involve my *children*——"

"Right."

"I . . . I wouldn't *dream* of it, and I, I can't imagine ever making such a statement."

"You did. Maybe you were kidding."

"What?"

"Maybe you were just kidding."

"It was maybe a colloquialism——"

"We were talking about Nixon and other people doing it——"

"Yeah, but I'm not President of the United States. . . . I mean if, if it were . . . I may have said it as a colloquialism that *I* have nothing to hide in terms of, ah, illegal transactions or deductions. In fact, I, ah, have very, very fe . . . low deductions, for . . . ah, ah . . . considering that I could have. I may have said that."

"Okay." I laughed.

"I'm serious," Rolly said.

"So you want. . . . Let's drop that issue then," I said.

"Yeah. If I, if I said that, ah, absolutely . . . you say—you say anything you want, I mean I'm just trusting you. . . . I was surprised that you never took any notes at all during three hours of conversations . . . and unless you have total recall——"

"Well, I have pretty good recall and then I go back and make my own notes."

"I hope that. . . . That really shocks me because if there's gonna be . . . if there is a similar situation to that that you're going to put in your book that I . . . I . . . ah . . . ah——"

"Well——"

"That would take me as much aback as this, I'll be very god-damned unhappy."

"Well, any quotes that are quotes of yours, I'm going to check with you anyway."

"I don't even mean *quotes,* but I mean to say that Evans says anybody could come up and look at his income tax returns 'cause he has nothing to hide. I mean, I mean, that makes a man a *fool*."

"Maybe you were trying to take me for a fool?"

"What?"

"Maybe you were trying to take me for a fool."

"Oh, *bullshit,* Barney."

"Well, you did say it and I wouldn't possibly have dreamed it up, Rolly, you know that."

"Well, pal, I'll tell ya, I've been in situations in reporting many times when I, in retrospect, I, I put a connotation or a word in something that I think I heard a politician and I *know* I was wrong. That's why I take notes. Verr-rry careful notes."

"Did you ever get your notes wrong?"

Rolly paused for a second.

"I thought I have," he said very softly, "I don't know."

"I find," I said, "people have been very upset about me not taking notes, but I find that notes—I've seen people take notes of things that I've seen and then come back and do something totally wrong because they got their notes wrong. So I find that notes and other things of that nature don't . . . I mean, I know it makes people nervous, but I really do have quite good recall . . . and I've done several pieces, just to put your mind at ease, and nobody ever came back to me and said I misquoted 'em."

"I am not saying that. I'm saying that I wish I could recall the construction, I wish I could reconstruct that conversation. I could see if we were talking about . . . I just can't see where we would get into that."

"We were sitting up at the Metropolitan Club and you were discussing people and income tax, and we were discussing your financial affairs, and how you and Bob split them up. And how your income was split, divided down the middle, and how your expenses were divided down the middle."

"Yeah."

"And several other things, and I said, 'How about your income taxes? Do you file joint returns?' And you said you filed separate returns."

"Of course," Rolly said.

"Well, but I didn't know that when you said it," I said.

"I don't know *anybody* who files a joint income tax return, except with his wife."

"But I didn't know whether or not you might file them as a partnership. I mean I didn't at the time know how your business works."

"Um-hmmm."

"I had no conception at the time how your business works——"

"Well, we do file one partnership return on the newsletter."

"Right, and you said that would be fine, you can look at my returns, we don't make that much money and our returns are *open* and we don't have anything to hide, and I said, 'Well, I don't know, one day I'll take you up on it.' "

"Well, I think the key word there is 'open.' Anyway, if I said that, it was a colloquialism, and I was not saying, 'Barney, come on over now.' I mean I might have said right then, 'Come on up to the office, I want to show you my income tax returns.' "

"Well that was the impression you gave me."

"Well——" Rolly said.

"Maybe this is just your general openness when you talk to people," I suggested.

"Well, I would not show *anybody* my . . . I mean . . . let me tell you what's *involved* in a person's income tax returns."

The words sounded as if they were spoken down a schoolmaster's nose, with Ben Franklin spectacles perched on it.

"I got a few," I said.

"Yeah, well, you know what it. . . . ."

He sounded embarrassed at his arrogance.

"There are certain things that have *nothing* to do with me."

"Right."

"That I would not—that—that I wouldn't for one minute let anybody look at."

"Right."

"That have nothing to do with *money* . . . but there are all kinds of——"

"How about the President?"

"Well, he's . . . I think a public officer is an entirely different situation."

"Right. That seems to be the case."

"I mean, I don't think reporters run the. . . . Reporters have no responsibility to . . . ah, make political decisions that effect the future of the country. They aren't elected to high, ah, *noble* office. I don't even feel I'm obligated to come up with a program to solve poverty or Vietnam."

I laughed again.

"I *mean* that. You know. A lot of guys say, 'Well, you're criticizing all the time, what's your program?' Well, shit, I don't have a program. I'm a reporter. I'm not a programmer."

We chatted for a while about the second thing, which was making an appointment to check facts for the book, and Rolly asked about the photographs.

"She really worked hard that day," Rolly said.

"She did work hard. I mean you're hard. You're hard guys to work on."

"No, we gave her every possible courtesy, I thought."

"Well, you did give courtesy, but . . . you——"

"In fact, we wanted her to stick around."

"I don't blame you," I laughed. "I don't blame you."

Rolly said he wanted to buy one of the photographs for the *New York Post*. "They use a picture of us that was taken about twenty years ago, and it's so terrible, and we wanted to buy it."

"Twenty years" was another colloquialism, I realized.

"I know she knows," I said.

"Ask her. Give her a little plug on that."

"She doesn't forget things about business. She'll get back to it when we get this. . . . She's got a big job now to finish up and by the middle of February she'll probably get back to you."

"Okay, fine," Rolly said. He sounded dissatisfied.

"And on the *other* thing, Barney," he said, "Just have to use your judgment. I would not——"

"I'll believe what you say," I said.

"I would not under any circumstances let *anybody* look at my tax returns, except the IRS, and I, of course, they've, ah, they've done several audits on me."

"Have they?"

"Ye-ee-ah-ah!" It was an unemphatic sound.

"Have they *really* done several?"

"Yeah. I told you about that. I told you all about that."

"No you didn't. You never told me about audits."

"Oh, hell," he said.

"You must have told other people. I didn't know they did audits on you."

"Oh, sure. I've been audited at least three times."

"In the last several years?"

"I think the last one was this year; last year's."

"Did they catch you with anything?"

"No. No. No, in fact I got a two thousand dollar refund."

"Did they?"

"Aww, about seven or eight years ago——"

"How about recently?"

"——Which I refused to take, 'cause I didn't think I deserved it. But legally——"

"What was it about?"

"It was an expense account thing. I can't possibly give you the details. It was something about, ah, they treated some expenditures as, ah, business connected which I did not think were."

"Um-huhh. And you said, 'I want the government to have the two thousand dollars better than me'?"

"I never applied for it," he explained.

"You *never* applied for it?"

"No," he said softly.

"Do you have an accountant? Or do you do your own?"

"Oh, hell, no, I have an accountant."

"Yeah."

"Out in Minneapolis."

"Oh, in Minneapolis."

"Yes."

"Uh-huh."

"Okay?"
"Okay."
"I got two calls hanging."
"Ciao."

XIX

Be kind to losers and they'll
always be kind to you.

Albert the Knife of Soho

Bob Novak is the dark one.

His eyes are brown and aggressive.

He wasn't afraid of me, he never asked me to be nice, or to be kind, either to him, or to the Evans-Novak "us."

He was not ashamed of himself, including his belly that bubbled over his belt.

I found that out by asking him, "Bob, aren't you a little overweight, out of shape?"

He patted his shirt over his belly and said, "My wife sometimes is bothered about it, but I *like* it."

I was also impressed that he stopped a forty-cigarette-a-day habit. He gave up Luckies and Kools because of asthma attacks. He said:

"My wife stopped smoking with me, but she cheated by smoking a few here and there when I wasn't around."

"Did you ever cheat?" I asked.

He gave me a penetrating look, to see if I knew if he'd ever cheated—and whom. He said, "No!"

I started to think of him as "Eyes."

"How observant are you?" Bob asked.

"Not observant enough to suit me," I said.

"Did you notice that I've got glasses?"

"Yes."

"They're something new. Last six months."

"Why?"

"Old age, Barney. They're wearing out."

"Were your eyes really that good to begin with?" I asked.

"Yeah."

"Twenty–twenty?"

"They were good."

"But were they *keen* eyes? Was it your eyes that got you the stories at the *Wall Street Journal* when you wrote for them? Or the state capitol stories in Illinois before you got to Washington?"

"Well. . . ." He twisted and shook his wiry, salt-and-pepper

right sideburn, put his chin up in the air and started thinking, his
eyes cast upward.

"Well . . . I'm not a great eye-witness," he said. "In covering
a prison riot other guys could take in a lot more in a scene of ruins
than I can. But I'm fast, well organized, and I have an incredibly
good memory, better than normal analytical ability—the ability to
see a scene and analyze it."

He said it as straightforward as that.

"You depend mostly on sight or some other sense?"

"It's not that much based on sight really. It's by facts. I guess
it's mostly by reading, looking for the telling word."

"So it's not really sight for you, even with such good eyes?"

"No. I've got closer to what some people call a phonographic
memory——"

"How perfect? Truman Capote says his is ninety-nine percent
perfect or something enormous. Over seventy-five percent."

"It's *almost* perfect, but not perfect." Bob was careful not to get
into a betting contest on numbers.

"How are you different from Rolly?" I asked.

"He takes a lot more notes than I ever do."

Then I started to think of him as "Ears," too.

Another important thing about "Eyes and Ears" is, as they say,
he puts his money where his mouth is. He makes bets on everything
from basketball games to politics. He bet early on whether or not
President Nixon would resign; he bet no, and hedged only a little
for insurance. He prides himself on paying off promptly when he
loses, and he wants to collect promptly when he wins. He mostly
makes bets with people he knows in the back rooms of politics and
in the Congress, and he keeps a book in his head about who is a
slow payer, who is a fast payer, and who doesn't pay off at all. He
refused to tell who doesn't pay off, so I asked him, "What *kind* of
people don't pay off?"

He sneered.

"They're children who can't live in this world."

If anyone has *ever* welshed on a bet with Bob Novak, he or she
has a lifelong dedicated enemy.

On the other hand, Bob was pleased to recall a man named Bob
McCandless, who worked for Hubert Humphrey's election campaign. He bet $1,000 against Bob's $1,000 on the results of the
1972 election.

The payoff was based on a complicated formula. Bob said it took into consideration the popular vote and the electoral college vote and a lot of tricky percentages. The bet required a business mind to figure out the winning odds.

Bob said, "It was a very bad bet for him."

Sure enough, McCandless lost. Within a week he paid off.

Bob said, "*That* impressed me. He made a bad bet and he accepted the consequences. Neither one of us are millionaires, and that was a big bet."

But Novak bet $20 on Bobby Riggs. And when I asked him why, he said, "I knew he'd lose but I hoped he'd win."

XX

If you call a canine nomenclature, he will lacerate your epidermis.

Tickle

For many years I shared with Art Buchwald the urge to peep into the Evans and Novak inner office, but only when the door was closed.

Their inner office has been in the same spot since a year after they joined together on May 15, 1963, when their first column appeared. They each have a desk and typewriter; there are bookshelves against the wall. Piles of newspapers, magazines, and press releases make a warm, papery nest around them. There is a curling poster-sized, after-the-wedding picture of the couple, on the job with the *Herald Tribune*. He is smiling dark and he is smiling light. Bob was slimmer then, Rolly has kept his figure.

At eleven o'clock, or close to it, Evans and Novak close their inner office door to the world. The door is decorated with gaudy decals and political bumper stickers. Once the door is closed, telephones are answered by one of two secretaries who will interrupt only with urgent messages.

How Evans and Novak think and work together is private. A peep through the door, left slightly ajar, shows that Novak broods and paces and Evans is most often talking on the telephone. Novak talks about money, and Evans talks politics, and sometimes a little bit of baby talk.

There is confidence and trust in the little office. There are no locked drawers to hide secrets. Roland's desk is in front of the only window which mildly gives the impression that he is a senior partner. He is also ten years older than Novak. But there is very little friction.

I wanted to know if money was as useless a way of trying to bust them up as it seemed to be. So I asked Novak about it.

"We've had very few disputes about money of any kind," he said.

I said, "You're doing all right *now*. How about when you weren't doing so well, in the beginning?"

"You're *wrong*," he said. "People who are money oriented are the same way about money no matter whether we're talking about

ten thousand dollars or one hundred thousand dollars a year. It's
what's important to you. Not only how you live your life, but what
you spend your time doing. We have no money problems. It depends on what you're oriented toward, and we'll never 'fall out over
money.' We're oriented toward success. Can we put out a good
product? We very much enjoy it when we get something good.''

That is exactly what he said, and just that directly.

"And there's no senior partner?" I asked.

"No senior partner. We do things *absolutely* even."

"That will be hard for a lot of couples to understand."

"Why hard?" he asked.

"In most cases, I think . . . I don't know . . . it will be hard to
understand."

XXI

Attack them first where
They love.

Albert the Knife of Soho

Carl Rowan has a deck of cards in his hands.

Carl plays card games for money, but he will also play for pride. Pride and twenty-five cents will buy a cup of coffee in the drugstore. Pride and too much money will get you cheated anywhere. Pride and $120 will buy a gold watch for Art Buchwald.

Art tried to teach me a lesson with the watch, but I never thought he cheated me. I was too proud to require cheating. I'd rather think I gave the games away because I was very stupid than to think I was cheated. I was sure Art Buchwald played fair. I never knew when *anybody* cheated.

I cheated every time I could get away with it. But I assumed other people never cheated me. Therefore, I assumed that Art Buchwald never cheated at cards, or with women, or in business, and I sat down across from him day after day and gave him my money the same way I was giving it to Beverly, with a good-sport look on my face. But to Art Buchwald, whose friendship I respected, I gave checks that didn't bounce. To many other players I gave rubber ones.

Another thing. They say cheaters never prosper. Art Buchwald prospered, so how could he be a cheater? A man can't be very proud if he *knows* he's being cheated and keeps going back again and again and paying for it. On the other hand, a man who doesn't think about being cheated never knows it. He plays some more, and he goes on playing, until the cheater's conscience starts to hurt at the terrible beating the victim is getting, with blood spurting out everywhere; but the victim stays on his feet, flailing like an imbecile child with his eyes rolling up and his tongue hanging out. At that point, the cheater feels so sorry that he steps back and watches the cheated stagger around saying, "Come on, one more game. I'm just learning something."

And finally the cheater quits playing and leaves the title of the Greatest Player in the World to the one who doesn't know he's being cheated. And the cheater goes off to cheat someone else. And the one who doesn't know he's being cheated looks for happiness with somebody who plays the best game in the world without cheating.

As I said, Carl Rowan has a deck of cards in his hand, and he is the Second Greatest Poker Player in Washington.

I played with him. I know some of his best poker advice:

The first thing is, I don't play cards, I don't gamble, with strangers.

A stranger is a guy you've never *seen* before, or a group of guys. For example, let's say I get on the train . . . and I'm going to the Rose Bowl game, and six Redskin fans, none of them I know, say, 'We're going to have a poker game. Come join us.' *No way!*

I tell you another reason for not playing with strangers. The card sharks don't have to have a marked deck. If you watch me deal the cards, I'm what you call a plain, old-fashioned plodder. I never wasted much time doing fancy deals. In fact there may be three, four times during the game when the guys will say, "Get him a basket." Because cards may fall everywhere. I just shuffle 'em and cut 'em, and so forth. But, you can sit down at one table and you see guys who can riffle the cards in the fanciest sort of way. . . . But all you need to do is sit down at a table once with a real card shark, and see what he can do with a deck of cards, to *know* how you can get your drawers taken off of ya by playing cards with a guy who looks like just . . . another . . . passenger . . . on the train . . . but who is a *real* card slick.

There are guys who make money going to parties showing what they can do with a deck of cards. If he comes here to show what he can do . . . God, he makes accordion deals, he does fancy things. But he gets on the train, he's a plodder. He looks like a stumble bum. But he's got cards up his sleeve and in his palm and coming out of his toenails, and he winds up in the crucial pots having ju-u-ust enough to win.

What do you want to know about a guy before you sit down at the table to play with him? I want to know what kind of game he plays. Whether he bluffs a lot. Basically I look to see if he plays an aggressive game or a conservative game.

If you want to know the truth, let me tell ya. You will learn at the poker table more about people's character than *maybe* anyplace else you know. There are guys I see at the poker table and I would not hire on a bet. There are also guys I wouldn't trust as far as I can throw this house. Because I have seen them *cheat* for fifteen cents . . . And I'm talking about guys making a hundred thousand a year. . . . If I see a guy who makes a hundred thousand a year cheat over ten dollars, then you can *bet* that this is no guy that *I'm* ever going to trust.

When you start a poker game, *even with close friends,* nobody breaks the seal on the deck until the game is under way, and everybody's there. We're talking about a *friendly* poker game. The *friendliest* poker game you can imagine.

I brought this deck out. The seal was broken. You'd be the craziest guy in the world to play poker with me. Absolutely crazy!

I look at everything I can see.

What I'll do, especially if my cards are just so-so cards, the first few hands, is I'll kind of fade out and lie back and watch what they do. I wait to find out whether he leaps out to bet without seeming to give it much thought—by way of trying to give the appearance of confidence. Or whether he fumbles nervously a little bit with his chips before he throws them out. Or whether he tends just to call or raise just a little bit, to keep the pot down. Or whether he throws the maximum raise possible out every chance he gets, if he's trying to establish his daring. Then I wait to see whether he's winning or losing on those hands. Because if he's in to the end, he's gonna have to turn 'em over—and I see what he's got, and I see what he's been bettin' on.

My only strategy is to try to pay attention to what's going on. To play an alert game. I suppose that's a rule that can apply to diplomacy or anything else. Because if you're running your mouth over to your left while the action is taking place on your right, you're gonna get screwed.

I see an awful lot of guys sit down at a poker table, who come in and wouldn't take a glass of Scotch and soda for the world because they're so *determined* to win they say you should never have a drink at a poker game. Yet, throughout the game, I will find that while the cards are being dealt and two or three bets are being made around the table to their right, two guys want to talk about what Richard Nixon paid for his house in San Clemente, or some girl they saw at the Democratic convention. In my view they'd be a damned sight better off to have *two* glasses of Scotch in their hands and watch the deal and the betting.

If there's no money, if nobody gets hurt, the pride is never that big. But if one guy gets hurt, you know it's almost like two boys out wrestling for fun, and one gets the other one down, and they go on off and maybe one didn't like losing, but it's no big deal. But let's say instead of a friendly wrestle, they have angry words, and they fight. And one guy blacks the other one's eye and he's got to go around knowing that he got beat in a fight. Well, that's a far different kind of pride, because one guy hurt. That's a different kind of pride from the lower degree of pride that was involved in a friendly wrestle.

You've got four or five guys who *can't afford to lose* . . . and you get a guy who's really desperate to win, and you add two bottles of beer or a shot of bootleg whiskey, and . . . maybe an *error*. He thinks maybe when you've played a split-the-pot deal the other guy counted faster than he did and got two dollars more out of the pot than he did. And so the argument starts. The next thing you know you've got guys calling each other nasty names and talking 'bout cuttin' each other, and whatever. Now *that* is an unfriendly poker game.

You survive by gettin' the hell out. That's the only way you survive.

An unlimited amount of money makes a tremendous difference.

You don't have to have anything in your pocket if you put five hundred dollars out on the table.

If people could make a rule, it would be an unfair rule, but the rule probably oughta be that only people who can afford to lose oughta gamble. But it would be an asinine rule, because it would go against human nature. It's the people who are most in need who are always the biggest suckers trying to get somethin' for nothing.

Interestingly, in all of the poker games I've played in here, sandbagging has been outlawed. You cannot check and raise. I think it's so because I think sandbagging is one of the places where you draw the line between a poker game where people are playing for the sport and the comradeship and the fun of it—eager to win some money, of course—and where people play for blood, or to make a living. We regard it as *unethical* to say to everybody else around the table, "I'm in such a shape that I cannot afford to bet." And then as soon as somebody bets, you try to take his drawers away from him.

I show my hand only when I have to.

There are some nights when the luck goes in such incredible ways you have to laugh at it, it's just so good or so bad.

If I'm say fifteen hundred dollars to the good, and a guy says, "Hey, gimme a break. I'll bet you fifty dollars that my up card on the next hand is higher than yours," or "I'll bet you fifty dollars that my next spade is higher than yours," I'll bet the fifty dollars, and for some strange reason, the guy who's winning tends to win that bet, too. The luck seems to run that way.

I might go out and win five straight times, an average of six hundred bucks . . . that's three thousand dollars. But if I went out the next time and lost a thousand dollars, losing the thousand hurt ten times as much as winning the three thousand felt good.

I'll tell you the truth, if I were playing poker for a living, children and women I wouldn't play. First of all, you tend to get a sense of over-confidence. You tend to play women and children cheap. And you can get killed. . . . Not just in poker, but in most of the games of life, people get in trouble by playing other people cheap.

You've got to act as if you're bluffing sometimes when you're loaded.

If you make a guy upset, the assumption is that the next four or five hands he'll play badly.

There's some guys we play with, God, you hear them groan . . . you *know* they've got a pat hand.

The columnists. Hell, he least of all is playing for his life.

You hate to lose some things more than you hate to lose others.

My wife objects strenuously to my playing poker with women. Because she believes, and I think she's right, that psychologically men take women for granted, for being a little bit softer intellectually or weaker nerve-wise. Next thing you know they've got your billfold . . . and *gone*.

If my wife loses fifteen cents she cries a week.

Let's say that I gambled everything I've got now. If I won, I'd only have twice what I've got now. But what I've got now is enough. That's true. So I'd only have twice what I've got now, which wouldn't change my life so much. If somebody gave it to me, I'd take it. But I don't need to gamble. I don't know that at any moment since I got married would I gamble for twice what I had. But I'll tell you. When you're gambling everything you've got, you're doing it only because what you've got is so trifling that losing it is only a momentary calamity.

XXII

Holding out is almost
impossible not to do.

Duc de la Roche de Balloon

Early on the day before Easter, Barney unexpectedly came home from his war. He was thrilled to be home. He spent the entire morning in deep concentration with Maggi, building a rabbit cage. Barney said, "I'm not worried so much about the rabbit getting out, as something bad getting in." There were wild-eyed dogs in the woods.

On Sunday, the bunny was brought for Kate in an egg basket on a bed of shredded green paper. Kate's friends and babysitters, Judy and Carol, had bought it for her. Judy said, "We wanted to save its life. They were going to sell it to somebody who was going to eat it." It was brown with a white tail. Maggi named the bunny Happy.

On Easter afternoon, Barney walked into a store in Vienna named Peter Pan to buy an iron rake for the garden, and he walked out with a cardboard box and no rake. He put the box on the back seat of the car and scratching and cheeping sounds came out. Maggi looked inside and saw two yellow baby ducks.

Happy spent Easter night alone in his cage at the edge of the woods near Barney's office. Next day, Maggi found a rock to put on the ground in front of Happy's cage, so she could sit and watch him inside, as he chewed up dandelion leaves or a carrot. Kate shared with Happy the carrot she ate. Kate called Happy "Happum" and, in a few days, carrots in Maggi's and Barney's and Kate's house were known as happums.

It always hurt Barney's heart to see a vine of poison ivy growing out from under the watching rock and around the legs of Happy's cage. It refused to die. Hoeing and pulling and poisoning did not kill the poison ivy.

The two baby ducks spent their first night together in their box inside the house. The next morning, they walked in the yard and nibbled the seeds off the long grass. They were almost indistinguishable, except that one almost always waddled at least two baby duck waddles in front and slightly to the side of the other. Maggi named one Quick and Barney named the other Quack.

Quick and Quack lived in the house for a week. Then, Kate reached enthusiastically into their box to play with them, and she grabbed one's leg. It was hurt and it walked with a limp. Barney and Maggi never could be sure whether Quack was hurt and walking behind as usual, or whether it was Quick who was forced to drag along injured behind.

After that, Quick and Quack were put outdoors to roam free, and they patrolled a circle around the house day and night, never more than a few waddles and a few quacks apart. It was a beautiful sight as they grew big and white to see them from an upstairs window making their rounds, and one of the first sounds in the quiet at dawn was their slow, sleepy, good-morning "braaak" to the world. And on rainy days they made the overjoyed noise of drumming their beaks against the flooding metal drain spouts outside the front porch and the red door. They loved the rain.

"One day," Barney said, "I'm going to build them a duck pond."

XXIII

Be good to life.

Duc de la Roche de Balloon

I saw Stew Alsop again, this time in the warmer, less hurried atmosphere of the Sheraton-Carlton's lounge and main dining room. He appeared ten minutes late, but when he shuffled into the lounge, he was still strong and I smiled as boldly and happily as the last time. This time, he gave a good smile back.

Stewart ordered a drink. He seemed to enjoy the numbing effect on him of alcohol. But in the dining room, he put three tiny mounds of food on his plate from the big, festive buffet and he picked at it unhungrily.

Stew kept his promise and told me the story of how he jumped behind the lines, and I believed him.

"There were three of us. We parachuted from an airplane in the night over France and we were supposed to land close enough to be able to call to each other . . . rendezvous . . . and then find the Maquis base of operations. The Resistance was always on the move so the Germans couldn't locate it.

"There was no moon. I landed in a tree. I unhooked myself, climbed down, and buried my parachute. Then I tried to locate my companions. But I heard nothing in the dark. I was afraid to signal with a match or flashlight.

"I was very scared. I sat down under a tree and my imagination started to work. I imagined Germans behind every bush. I said to myself, 'Alsop, you're in trouble.'

"I remembered what I had in my pack. Two packs of Chesterfield cigarettes and a hip flask of brandy. I pulled out a Chesterfield and lighted it behind my hands so that no flame showed, and I took a sip of brandy. That gave me enough courage to start walking down the road to what seemed to be a little town. But when I approached the town, all the dogs started barking and they made such a noise that I abandoned my plan to sneak into town and ask to be hidden in somebody's house. So I went back to the tree.

"I lighted another cigarette and took another sip of brandy. Now Alsop began walking east toward where I thought the Maquis might be. I wanted to walk as far as I could before dawn. I walked about fifteen miles when I came over a hill and heard a grinding, roaring sound, and there below were dozens of trucks with fires burning on the back of them rolling down the roads and maneuvering in big circles. The trucks that had fires on them were burning wood to run their engines, because the Maquis didn't have enough gasoline for their operations. Those trucks were ingenious machines called *ga-zugens*. And then I heard a voice calling, 'Schtu! Schtu!' and at first I was scared shitless. I thought, 'The Nazis must be tremendously good to know my name,' and then I realized they were my companions, and I was saved."

It felt like a true story, and I said, "Stew, why don't you do it for your column."

"I'm thinking of giving up the column," he said.

"Why?"

"Well, for six weeks I've been having these night sweats. I get a fever that goes up to a hundred three, and I sweat like a horse. I have to sleep in two beds, one in our bedroom and one in the guest room. One gets so soaked."

"You look okay in the daytime."

"I'm feeling good in the daytime. It's at night."

"So why quit the column?"

"It's a matter of how much I can do. I can't really report like I used to. I can't get out so much; three times a week to the hospital . . . and I have the leukemia book to finish."

"How are you going to end it?" I asked.

"I don't know," Stew said. He grinned honestly. "I don't know what to say."

"I always thought that books about incurable diseases could only finish one way," I said. "That's the interesting thing about them. To see what a man thinks who is certain he's going to die."

"I quit for a while once before," Stew said.

"You did?"

"I was out of energy. I felt useless. It was a dismal period. I was dragging around. Then one day Rolly Evans called me on the telephone and said something like, 'Stew, you son-of-a-bitch, listen here. You just can't fuck around doing nothing. You're going to get out every day and have lunch and see people. Like a working reporter. I'm going to see that you do.' And he picked me up and we had lunch with such-and-such and I got back into it slowly."

"So why are you thinking of quitting again?"

"I'm feeling weak. These sweats. You know I've got to go to the hospital three times a week for platelets."

"Write about the *gazugens*. That'll make a good column."

"You think so?"

"Yes. I think fear of death is interesting."

"Well, maybe I could do it another way. Maybe I could put it in the context of the energy shortage. 'Here's the way the French Resistance solved the energy shortage.' That kind of thing."

"Any way at all, as long as you tell it," I said.

"It was pretty scary," Stew said, smiling to himself. "You know," he said, "I wrote some letters home to my mother during the war, and I ran across a packet of them not long ago. I read them. I was pleased to see I hadn't bullshit the war."

He thought back to himself as an adventurous twenty-nine-year-old in the darkness, with German soldiers lurking in the shadows, and he said to me, "Barney, it's your imagination that kills you."

A few days later Stew was in the hospital with fever and pneumonia. I made inquiries about him, and his condition was described as very grave. His fever was high. Then one of his sons called to cancel an appointment we had to visit his weekend house in the country, and the young man's voice was strained when he said Stew was "not too good."

The next time I went to Vienna, I bought two packs of Chesterfield cigarettes and prepared to buy some brandy in a flask to deliver to him. But I never could bring myself to deliver such a symbolic gift, because it might have been thought a cheap and sentimental takeoff on his war story, or a gift too personal from a man who was not known as his friend. But if thought is truly the father of the deed, I thought about it and bought the Chesterfields.

XXIV

Lily Belle, oh, Lily Belle,
I've taken lots of tumbles,
But here's why I never fell . . .
'Cause I got spurs
That jingle-jangle-jingle,
As I'm rollin' merrily along.

A song

I called information for Sander Vanocur's home telephone number and I said to the operator:

"I'd like Sander Vanocur in Washington, D.C."

And she said: "Oh, *thank you!* That's a celebrity, isn't it?"

"Yes. Why?"

"I like him," she said.

I asked when she last saw Sander, and she said, "Not in a long time." I asked how she knew him, and she said, "From television." I asked her what she liked about him.

She said, "When he *used* to be—when he used to be, and when he was associated with the Kennedys . . . I thought he was fabulous."

"I'll tell him that," I said.

She said, *"Thank you."*

So I mentioned it to Sander when I reached him at his number.

Sander responded downheartedly, "That's it, isn't it? The Kennedy thing."

We made an appointment for lunch at Jean-Pierre's.

XXV

In a democracy,
The majority defines sanity.
In a dictatorship,
The dictator defines sanity.
In a nation dictated to by lawyers,
Sanity is defined as
Knowing right from wrong.

Fortuesque Biles

Sander entered Jean-Pierre's in an obvious hustle, waving a newspaper in one hand, while the other hand patted the maître d's shoulder.

In a voice loud enough for anyone who cared to hear, the maître d' announced, "Oh, hello, Mister *Vanocur*. How are you today?"

Sander looked around for faces in the dimly lighted room.

He was shown to the booth where I was sitting drinking a Bitter Lemon. We shook hands.

His eyes said, "I know your voice, but I've never seen you before in my life."

My eyes said, "But I've seen you before. Sit down and we'll talk about it."

Sander squeezed into the booth beside me. He was tight-skinned as a big sausage, with punky cheeks, a bad-boy's nose, and eyes that not even he could trust not to exaggerate.

I remembered Sander and his wife Edith in 1965. They walked late into the house of an NBC news producer one night for a party. Sander and Edith entered as stars.

Sander had worn a dark blue suit and smoked a cigar. He gave off the important air of just having come from a private party in Georgetown, or perhaps from one of the Kennedys. Edith was round and short and wore black stockings under white fishnet stockings, and black leather shoes with spiked heels. They looked like stars to me. I was proud to be at the same party with them. I was surprised only when I heard Edith speak. Edith spoke with an accent that sounded like Yiddish to me. Sander talked English with an educated Englishman's quality that he had picked up when he attended a college in England and later worked for the *Manchester Guardian*. He oozed success.

Now, ten years later, more of his forehead showed, and a bitterness replaced his old playful sparkle. Edith had since gone to work as a cooking writer for the *Washington Post*. She was writing a book about one hundred ways to cook chicken. Sander said, "I've eaten chicken for dinner for almost a hundred straight days and I'm sick of the taste and the smell of it."

Sander ordered soft-shell crabs. I asked for baked clams.

Sander looked over at my glass. He said, "You'll have some wine. *Not* that Bitter Lemon."

"All right."

I knew Sander was preparing to pick up the check.

Sander stuffed his bread and salad into his mouth.

Sander spoke loud enough for people to hear in the next alcove and at the table across the aisle. The alcove table people did not appear to listen, but a long-haired boy and a finishing school girl, and their nervous mother did listen. Sander looked at their table until the boy noticed him, and I watched the boy's face as he worked to put Sander's voice and face together with some old television images. After a moment I saw in the boy's face the signs Doug Kiker once described to me as the "pop-eyed" recognition of a celebrity. Doug had said, "Once you see it, you'll always want it."

The boy whispered Sander's name. Sander relaxed, and looked vaguely satisfied. He lowered his voice and gave me his attention.

"Tell me something," Sander said. "You know Dick Wald from the *Trib*. Off the record, what do you think of him?"

"He's cold as ice and as mean as a weasel when it comes to money."

Sander smiled.

"I'm glad you think so," he said. "I think so, too."

"Is he the one who fired you?" I asked.

"I wasn't fired. It was a mutual understanding."

Sander explained that he and Dick Wald, who was then a vice-president of NBC News, had met in New York not long before his contract was ready to expire.

Sander said, "I told him I wanted a freer hand in doing news, including political news. Dick said, 'We'll see if we can work it out,' and told me to hold on a few weeks. I held on and nothing happened. So I called Dick 'cause it was getting pretty close to the end and I wanted to know something. Dick said, 'Hold on a little longer.' So I did, and then nothing happened again. So then with just a few days left, I called him and he said, 'I'm going to Fisher's Island . . . with Jock Whitney and his family . . . over the weekend. We'll discuss it when I get back, and settle it once and for all.' ''

"What happened?" I asked.

"Dick just said he was letting me go," Sander said. "He said they were having a budget squeeze. They figured I had a damned big contract and they might as well just chop it off."

"The Kennedy-Shirley MacLaine business didn't have anything to do with it?"

"Oh, hell. I don't think so. Not *that* much. They had a chance to save themselves a lot of money and they took it. I had a big contract then."

"Did you have an agent?" I asked.

"No. I never used agents. I acted on my own."

"Too bad. One might have kept you out of so much trouble."

The food came. Sander's soft-shell crabs were drowned in melted butter. My six clams were buried under a gray crumb putty.

The story in Washington about "the Kennedy thing" was that Sander too openly associated himself with the lives of the Kennedy family, instead of discreetly enjoying them on the side. Gossip said Sander had lost his journalist's mind. Sander was accused of openly praising the Kennedys, and making insulting statements about Kennedy rivals.

There was also the story about Shirley MacLaine. Maxine Cheshire was apparently the first to hear, and she reached Sander by telephone in California to ask him if it were true. Sander says to this day that he was outraged by the call and told Maxine that his personal life was none of her or the *Washington Post*'s business.

He said, "I called up Ben Bradlee—my friend Ben—and I told him, politely, that I didn't think that kind of story belonged in his newspaper. Ben said, 'Yeah, yeah, Sander, I understand.' But the story was published anyway."

I said, "How long did it last?"

"Three months," Sander said.

"Were you in love?"

"I want to skip the details. . . . It's hurt Edith and me enough, and I make it a policy never to talk about that . . . period."

93

After his contract with NBC expired, Sander went to work for National Public Television for $85,000 a year. It was said at the time that public television required newscasting celebrities to attract larger audiences. It was hoped that large audiences would in turn generate enough political power to persuade the Congress to give public television enough money each year to grow. Sander's salary was printed in the public record, and at first no particularly critical notice was taken of it. But Sander was an easy target for politicians who wanted to remove "Kennedy men" from government jobs. Sander said both the *Washington Post* and the *Star* printed stories about his salary. It was pointed out that Sander was making more money than a congressman. And so, in 1972, when his two-year contract expired, Sander was cut from the payroll of public television.

"Did people stop inviting you places?" I asked.

"They dropped off," Sander said.

"Do you still see the Kennedys?"

"Oh, Christ, I haven't been out there—we haven't been to Ethel's in months . . . months."

"Are you looking for work?"

"I call people."

"Do they call you back?"

A thought so bitter passed across his mind that his face was distorted into a snarl without his being able to help it.

"I'm keeping a list!" Sander said. "I'm keeping a long list of people who haven't returned my telephone calls. And one day. . . ." His hands were working at each other. "One day I'll *chop* them off. Sander Vanocur isn't finished yet. . . . I'll be back."

"Are you getting any offers?" I asked.

"They're not exactly tearing down my telephone to make me offers."

"Does anyone call?"

"People for Edith."

"What about Ben Bradlee?"

"Not yet," he said.

"Do you expect to hear from him?"

"We're still in the talking stage."

"It must be hard to live on less than eighty-five thousand dollars a year?"

"It's not that. It's—It's—It's that it's *killing* me not to be out reporting the Watergate every day. I can't stand just sitting back and not being out there reporting . . . doing my job.''

"Why don't you report for a newspaper somewhere?''

He bit his lower lip.

"Not yet.''

"Well, if it's *killing* you not to be on television, why not find some television station to report for? You don't want to kill yourself, do you?''

"I didn't say not being on television was killing me,'' he corrected. "I said not being able to report the Watergate.''

"So why not report it for a newspaper or magazine? Why work for some foundation that just 'thinks' about newspaper and television, instead of working in television? If it's killing you, why let it?''

"You don't understand,'' Sander said.

"You can't stand *not* working for television. It's *not* killing you *not* to be writing for a small town paper in Illinois, and it's *not* killing you *not* to be working for *Harper's* or *Atlantic*. It's killing you *not* to be on the television so people can see you again.''

I thought there might be a long chance Sander was going to tell me I'd gone too far, but Sander acted like a gentleman. He thought over what I said and nodded his head up and down.

"I guess so,'' is what he said.

Twice more Sander corrected me for saying it was killing him *not* to be on television.

"I didn't say that. That's what *you* say. It's not my quote,'' Sander said.

"It's what you mean,'' I said.

"Yeah, but it's not my quote.''

"I won't quote you on it.''

I ate all of my clams under putty, but Sander ate only half of his soft-shell crabs. When the waiter took Sander's dish away, I said, "Sander, you haven't finished.''

Sander had ordered the crabs at $5.50, and I had ordered the clams at $2.25. Sander had tried to entice me into crabs by saying, "Edith tells me the crabs are in season right now. They're delicious.''

When his dish was taken away with $2.75 worth of crab on it, Sander looked at me out of the corner of his eye and said, "Barney, I'm on a diet. Too damned rich for me.''

He grabbed the check. He gave the waiter a credit card. I said, "No, I'll take care of this. I invited you." I didn't say anything about him choosing the place.

"I'll take it. I'll take it," he said.

He blocked my arm with his shoulder to prevent me from reaching over to examine the check.

"Art Buchwald wanted to pay for my lunch the other day, too," he muttered to himself.

I was thinking how the tongue that once talked to millions of people on television was now left to talk too loud in Jean-Pierre's. Down the road may be dreary oblivion. Sander broke directly into my thoughts.

"You're not going to put me in that down-the-road-to-destruction character, are you?"

"I don't know," I said. "I hope not, but I don't know."

"Well, I'm *not*."

"I hope not."

On the way out, Sander said to the maître d', "Save me a salami."

"You have salami?" I asked the maître d'.

"Oui, monsieur," he said. "Maybe you want one, monsieur?"

"I don't know," I said.

"Monsieur Vanocur gets one here all the time."

I imagined how Jean-Pierre's would be a funnier place with salamis hanging from the ceiling. So I asked, "Are you in the salami brokerage business?"

The maître d' stood back at attention.

"Of course *not*, sir. Only occasionally for special people, like Mister Vanocur."

"Well, save one for me," I said. "For next time I come in."

XXVI

A driver is only a driver,
But a good chauffeur is a friend.

Fernando Federico

Ben Bradlee seems smaller and more frail than he truly is. He is the executive editor of the *Washington Post,* and it is not a Washington exaggeration to say that the *Post* was the ship that torpedoed President Nixon.

Ben moves with a tenseness in his body of a man under constant pressure over a long period of time. He is in full command of the *Post* torpedo room.

Ben is not the captain of the ship. Katherine Graham is the captain of the *Post,* and Ben knows how to be her first torpedo room officer better than any man Mrs. Graham knows, or Ben would be gone.

In the Washington world it is rare to find a woman captain, and Mrs. Graham does not flaunt her power in public. But her submarine, the *Post,* fixed the nuclear battleship ''President Nixon'' in its sights and, without apparent fear, it fired one salvo after another, day after day, week after week; it dodged, weaved, and its crew sweated while depth charges exploded. The entire time the big ships in the fleet stood over the horizon and trembled, firing only an occasional shot. They shied away from following her into action. They said, as gentlemen sometimes do, ''Ladies first.''

The fact of the matter is that she might have been sunk so many times that good luck is the only explanation of why the *Post* escaped undestroyed. The government attacked the *Post*'s radio stations and television communications, especially in Jacksonville, Florida, where President Nixon had a stronghold. Day after day, the White House delivered broadsides attacking the *Post*'s trustworthiness. To destroy the *Post*'s trustworthiness would be, put in terms of warfare, a direct hit in the powder magazine, and it would have been deadly. Trustworthiness, the ability to convince people that what you think you see has truth in it, was what was at stake in the battle between the *Post* and the President.

After the President Nixon damage was done, the timid fleet of the *Post*'s gentlemen friends appeared and bombarded the hulk of the President and ran over members of its crew while they flapped in the water. The *Post* won the Pulitzer Prize for journalism for her daring; if she had joined the battle as bravely on the side of the President, she would have won a medal of honor.

Feverish, romantic daydreams and nightmares occur in wartime, and Washington lived in wartime while the *Post* and the President first dueled, and then while war operations dragged tediously on.

Imaginations burned gaudy and hot with images of treachery and suicide and the lives of the soldiers vibrated at a more excited rate.

Sleep was either exhausted or troubled. Talk and gossip rose to peaks like a church chorus turned hysterical. An orchestration of Middle Eastern and South East Asian guns boomed in the background; there was the drone of traffic at rush hour, and on windless summer days a yellowish brown cloud of smoke hung over the earth up to the middle of the Washington Monument. Laughter was tense and telephones rang in the middle of the night many times a week.

The White House was more heavily guarded than ever. Secret Service agents made double and triple checks on identity cards of press members and screened almost all packages going in and out of the White House gates. A threat of President Nixon's assassination lurked in the back of minds all over Washington.

At night, the White House was lighted in the glare of white arc lights, and the drapes were drawn in the upstairs rooms. The building had a sanitary hospital look behind black, well-patrolled iron gates.

It was joyless in the White House, and while there was much hurried activity, there was also a sense of mourning, the kind of mourning I felt when my father looked at me one day and said, "Barney, it's black. It's all black."

I asked him what he meant and he said, "It's black. You'll see. I'm looking into it and it's black."

I was watching one of my father's favorite daytime television programs on the set in the library where he and I had often sat to talk. He was staring at "As the World Turns." I asked him why he liked it, and he said, "I don't know."

I looked into his eyes—his eyes were grayish green—and they spoke of so much terror that I was embarrassed and ashamed. I'd never seen a man before who was looking into the pit. It seemed unmanly to me for a father to show terror to his child. I was his child and I wanted him to survive, and when I saw the terror, I judged him a coward. It was a moment when my father wanted comfort, an escape from what was never true, nor false, but real, and I had no words to reach him.

I never broke through to his runaway imagination to say, "Here, Dad, here's a big dose of courage, just like a sulpha pill, and your reality will be gone and life will be bright, fresh and sweet."

He was wearing a tieless white shirt and baggy brown trousers and some old moccasins. His belt buckle was fastened loosely on the last hole. He was wasted.

It was the time in the Michigan winter afternoon when you must turn on a lamp or exist in a gloom; I didn't light the lamp. The only light was from the cold, white glare of the television set with its droning, meaningless sounds.

With my fingernail, I scraped a track of frost off the window so I wouldn't have to look at him. I wondered if the shock treatments would ever restore him.

I made talk, but I wouldn't look in his eyes.

"It's a matter of time," I said. The words didn't register. "It'll get brighter. You'll see."

He was so feeble of will by then that he didn't have the strength to move quickly any longer, but what I said about brightness shocked him into a rage. He pulled the arm of my chair so that it swiveled around, away from the television set, and forced me to face him. He was using some reserve power I hadn't seen since I was a baby, and he drew me into his mind with a force I thought had completely burned out.

"It's all black," he said. He was furious when he saw that I didn't believe him.

"It's not," I said.

"It is!"

"It's not!" I said. "You'll see, it's not."

"I do see," he gurgled. "It's all black!"

He slumped back exhausted. I started hard at him defiantly. That was the moment I went into mourning for him and the next time I saw him, about a year later, he was in his coffin. I knew he was telling the truth that gloomy afternoon about what he saw, and in the White House I had the feeling that the President was also a truthful man, like my father.

XXVII

I am going to be
The author of a book.
Hmm!
I will tell about my life.
I know myself better than anyone.
Hmm!
I can't think of anything
I want to say.

From "A Short Novel"

Here is an excerpt taken from a question-and-answer interview that appeared in the *Raleigh News and Observer* on Sunday, July 1, 1973. The headline was: "Uncommon Conversation: The Most Hated White House Correspondent." It is with Dan Rather.

Q. Correspondents sometimes seem to me cardboard cutouts. I wonder how much of what you really think is on the air.

A. As little as I can put there.

Q. You mean there's the public Rather and the private Rather?

A. I'd like to believe it. That's the goal.

The next question was:

"But aren't you a recorded announcement, too?"

"I try not to be," Dan answered.

In his photograph next to the article Dan's mouth is a tight straight line, his eyes glare into the middle distance, his hair is neat, his tie and suit are dark and his shirt is pale. He is soberly handsome, and if you look very closely, and you happen to know about it, you can see the redskin Indian in him—in the cheekbones, the steady blackness of the eyes, and the square jaw with a cleft in it.

Dan continued:

"When I go through the White House gates, insofar as is humanly possible, I leave my own ideological opinions behind me. I'm not paid to tell people what I really think. I'm paid to tell them what I hear, feel, and smell."

There are few odors to smell in the White House. The air is cleaned and recleaned and heated and refrigerated by the White House air-conditioning system. The air is kept very dry and cool.

The air is constantly in motion, and cigarette and cigar smoke is sucked away into ducts and never hangs in clouds as it did around politicians of old. Neither is there the fragrance of a lady's perfume because the air is guarded by special instruments that kill odors with electricity. The White House press room is often crowded with journalists standing shoulder to shoulder and hip to hip, and in that room there is the most potential for odors.

The press room is where Dan works at the White House. He has worked there since three weeks after President Kennedy was assassinated. On the day President Kennedy was shot in Dallas, Dan was a reporter for a CBS television station in Houston and occasionally covered stories for the network. It was a regional job and small notice was taken of it in New York. In the news business, people are usually promoted from local jobs in smaller cities to regional jobs in larger cities to national jobs in New York or Washington. A promotion to Dallas or Atlanta or Los Angeles or Chicago is often the best most reporters can hope for.

Dan had been assigned to the parade story. After the shooting, Dan recalls making only one serious mistake in the days and nights of solid work without sleep, while he covered for the network one of the most emotional weeks in the memory of people then alive. The mistake was that Dan said, on the air, that Mrs. Kennedy had "panicked."

"That's what I thought it was," Dan said.

He used "panicked" to describe the way Mrs. Kennedy climbed out of the back seat and onto the rear deck of the open limousine, in the seconds after her husband's brain and blood had been spattered over her by the force of the bullet.

"It looked like panic to me," Dan said, "so that's what I called it. But people called up CBS, and some of them were in a rage because they said Mrs. Kennedy would never panic, that she was just trying to help a Secret Service agent into the car, or something. The switchboards lighted up, but I was so damned busy I didn't even care, except to ask myself if I'd made a bad choice of words, and I didn't know for sure."

"How did you know it was panic?" I asked.

"I could feel it," Dan said. "It was the word that came out."

"I'm interested in panic," I said.

"So am I," Dan said. "I always wanted to read a book about

panic. Once in an airport I bought a book with panic in the title, and I read it on the plane. But I was disappointed because it was a cheap mystery and it didn't really talk about panic at all.''

"What is panic to you?" I asked.

Dan stopped to ponder.

"Panic is when you can't control your fear. When you just give it up and start to run or scream.''

"Have you ever panicked?"

"No-o-oo-o, I can't remember ever panicking,'' he said. "I am under pretty good control.''

"I've panicked,'' I said.

"You have?''

"Yeah, I can remember once standing in line for lunch in the first grade, and feeling I had to go to the bathroom, and the line slowed down, and just before my turn came, I couldn't hold it any longer, and I wet my pants, in front of the whole room. That's panic and humiliation at the same time.''

"Yeah,'' Dan said. "Now that I think of it, I do remember now—a feeling of panic. I can swim, but I never could swim very good, and when I was a kid we went swimming in the bay . . . and nobody'd taught me how to swim . . . so I just had to jump in and keep my arms and legs moving and try to keep the water out of my mouth—and pray to be able to get out or touch my toe on the ground.''

"How come you never learned to swim?"

"My dad never had enough time, he worked too hard. . . . Well, one day he did try to teach me. . . . I don't think, maybe . . . he didn't know how to swim himself.''

As the story Dan remembers goes, Dan is one-eighth Indian. His family legend says his great-grandmother on his mother's side, named Carr, was an Indian woman from the mountains above the Ohio Valley.

In 1875 the Carr family farmed near Bloomington, Indiana. They heard cheap land was available, and along with other farmers from the area they packed wagons and traveled south, across the Mississippi River, and down to the Gulf coast of Texas. They called the place they settled Bloomington.

Dan's father's was Daniel Rather. His middle name was Irwin. A tradition in Dan's father's family was to name the first son Dan or Daniel. Dan is the son of a Daniel, and Dan's son is a Daniel. Dan sees in himself his father's dark hair and his chin. He sees in himself his mother's greenish brown eyes, her sculpted mouth, with a clear dent on the upper lip, and her broad nose.

Dan's father's mother came from Mississippi, according to family legend. Dan says he can't remember her name. He called her Grandmother. He recalls Grandmother telling him stories about how, in her father's family, there was a kindly Civil War doctor, near the Tennessee-Georgia border, who doctored both sides. His name, Dan recalls, was Rather, too.

Dan's father was born near Houston in a two-room frame house. In 1973, the house was inside the city limits, but in 1932 it was four miles from the city line on the edge of a swamp. The people who lived there called it The Heights.

The Rather family owned no land in Texas. When Rathers farmed, they sharecropped; and when they worked, they worked with their hands.

Dan's father's nickname was Rags. He called Dan's mother Mutt. Dan Irwin Rather was Rags's and Mutt's first child.

Mutt, whose real name was Berl, had a brother whom Dan remembers as the only one in his mother's family who would talk to him honestly about the Carr family tree. Dan remembers him saying that Dan's grandmother's father "took an Indian woman" sometime before he arrived in Bloomington, Indiana. Dan remembers it was said exactly like that, "He took an Indian woman." It is the same way Dan says it.

Rags was twenty-one years old and he was in a crew of strong young men who were digging an oil pipeline ditch from the Gulf of Mexico to Houston. Mutt was a waitress in a small restaurant in Wharton, Texas. They courted and married in the weeks that Rags was digging the pipeline into, through, and down the road away from Wharton. Whatever ceremony there was came before Rags had to move out of his pipeliner's shack and leapfrog ahead toward Houston, to live for a few months in another pipeliner's shack.

Dan now remembers himself as a skinny boy. The kind of work Rags expected out of his first son was not the kind of work Mutt wanted Dan to do. Dan was forever anxious to please her.

Mutt had dreams for Dan.

Not on either side of Dan's family, for as far back as anybody could remember, had any child ever gone to college. Mutt saw that Dan was destined to be educated in college. As soon as a boy became able-bodied in a pipeliner's family, he was needed to work with the old man. But when Dan was fourteen years old he could not make Rags proud of his muscles. Dan's ankles and knees swelled after a day of shoveling in the ditches. Rags grumbled and shouted that Dan was acting like a puny sissy. Mutt took Dan to doctors, and the doctors found nothing seriously wrong with him physically. Then one doctor diagnosed Dan's problem as rheumatic fever. Mutt refused to hear talk that Dan was really only playacting about it. Dan remembers how angry Rags would get, and how he would describe a man's life, "You gotta keep your nose down and your ass up." He used those words to tell Mutt that her's was a foolish way to see the world from a frame house on cement blocks in The Heights of Houston. Mutt and the doctor insisted that Dan stay home and rest for nine months. He kept up his schoolwork.

Then, the next summer, Dan was forced to go back to work cutting underbrush. He fell sick again, and the doctor insisted again on absolute bed rest and recuperation. While he was still recovering, Dan put up with schoolmates who taunted him because he had a note from his doctor that insisted that all Dan's classes must be on one floor, and forbade him to walk stairs.

When Dan's sister was thirteen years old, Mutt decided it was time to move to a better neighborhood of The Heights in order to expose her daughter to a better class of young men.

Rags refused to move. He said in harsh words that still ring in Dan's head that he could not afford the money to move. But the Rathers moved to a new neighborhood, and Rags complained about the new style and the big mortgage and how they strapped him.

When Dan was in the eleventh grade, there was a Rather family discussion. Rags said it was about time Dan learned to work like a man. He wanted Dan to quit high school. Dan remembers him saying, "Mutt, he's got to learn to keep his ass up and his nose down!" Mutt replied that Dan was the one Rather who was going to college.

Dan was allowed to finish high school.

He received what he calls half a scholarship to San Antonio Teachers' College. It was a bus ticket to San Antonio, to try out for football. But Dan was slow from the waist down, and while his hands could hold onto a football, his legs were not fast enough. The second half of the scholarship was a bus ticket back home.

While Dan struggled to stay on the team, and was losing, a teacher whom Dan grew to love took him under his wing. He was the journalism teacher, and Dan wants his name memorialized. His name was Hugh Cunningham.

Hugh Cunningham rescued Dan from the football field, loaned him money, found places for Dan to work and sleep, and taught Dan how to see and to hear, feel, and smell—as a "reporter."

These are Hugh Cunningham's rules for reporting as Dan remembers them:

"You have to have the ability to take yourself out of a situation— like someone who has just strolled in on the situation—but someone across the street.

"When you see an electrocution you want to see it not as a prisoner in the prison would see it—or his family—but walk in as a detached observer. You begin to see things that way. I liked that feeling. I still like it."

"You do?"

"Yes. It's one of the things that drive Zeigler and Ehrlichman up the wall. They don't believe you can do it."

"Can you do it?"

"Not all the time. But when you do it, you can learn things about them. You can learn secrets they have among themselves and don't tell their wives. They are very good, but you can learn because somebody detached can do it."

"What do you mean?"

"I call it tropism. It's like having all your antennae out. You pick up all kinds of signals. When you walk into a reporting situation you leave all your psychological baggage in the lobby."

"Is that your definition of a professional?"

"Yes. The first thing you're taught as a boxer is when you're hurt, try not to show it. A boxer . . . you can knock the hell out of him, and if he's a good pro—the ultimate pro—he tries not to show it when it hurts."

After the Kennedy assassination, Dan remembers Hughes Rudd, a CBS correspondent, said to him: "The reason you're good, Dan, is that you don't feel anything."

Dan told the story with pride, but he added, "I was shaken by what Hughes said."

"Did you feel anything?"

"Yeah. A week later, when I was alone and had a chance to think, I cried all night one night."

"Where did you get the word tropism?"

"It's a novelist's word. I'm not sure where I learned it."

"Do you read much?"

"Well, I've not read too much. I am not well educated. But I'm taking care of that. I've read thirty-three of the books in the Chicago Great Book Series. There are fifty-five books, but I couldn't get through them all . . . yet. I stopped around . . . Montaigne . . . Montaigne. Eric Sevareid told me once that a man isn't educated until he reads Montaigne, and that you can read Montaigne the rest of your life and nothing else and still not get enough of him."

Dan's college was interrupted by the war in Korea. So many young men Dan's age were volunteering that Dan felt ashamed to stay on in school, and he enlisted in the marines. He recalls saying no when he was asked if he had ever had rheumatic fever.

In boot camp, the instructors threw Dan into the water to teach him how to swim. They used a long pole to prod him and keep him from dog paddling. Marines recognize that dog paddling is a symptom of panic. Dan swallowed his panic.

"Did you learn to swim?" I asked.

"Passably," Dan said, "but then, the next time there was a routine physical and the doctor asked me if I had rheumatic fever, I said yes."

"You didn't mark it on your forms," Dan remembers the doctor saying.

"It's true," Dan said. "My doctor at home will prove it."

The Marines sent him home and he was back in college three months after he had left. . . .

Twenty years later, Dan and Tom Jarriel, the regular White House correspondent for ABC News, were swimming with flippers and face masks off a beach in the Virgin Islands during a presidential trip. The ocean was rough with a strong undertow and without realizing it, Dan had ventured with Tom too far from shore. The color of the water was a dark, oily blue, and waves rolled into Dan's mouth.

Dan remembered looking back to the beach and knowing he hadn't the strength to swim back. He heard himself say, "Tom, I'm so tired I don't think I can make it."

And that, Dan remembered, was the instant when he knew a grown man's panic.

Tom, an excellent swimmer, said, "God damn, Dan, I'm tired, too."

Then Tom went on to hold Dan up all the way in.

XXVIII

We are warts on the pickle
of time.

Virginia Park

Sally Quinn left Washington in midsummer for New York. The *Washington Post* article that had announced her new career said:

SHOWDOWN AT SUNRISE

The article began:

Watch out NBC's Barbara Walters, here comes CBS's Sally Quinn.

From the beginning the two women were matched against each other, like Gypsies. Sally was sold as being ten years younger, and she was supposed to be fresher and more provocative.

The day before Sally left town I called her at the *Post* to ask how she felt.

"Scared," she said.

"Why?"

"I don't know why, Barney. You're supposed to be scared, and I'm scared."

"Well, good luck."

"Thank you. I'm getting ready to leave. . . . I've got to go."

"Have people been wishing you luck, Sally?"

"*Of course!* Lots of people. What do you think?"

"Do they mean it?"

"Of course——"

"Well, I mean it."

"Thank you," Sally said.

I am happy by my bellybutton.

Buba Lena

In the fall of 1973 the United States had a weakened President.

In Washington there was conversation that Richard Nixon was insane. The word "insanity" was mentioned more than once in testimony before the Senate committee on Watergate.

Washington's journalists took note of the talk, and questions about the President's sanity filtered into the newspapers.

There were signs of great stress on President Nixon. The President was being questioned at an unscheduled press conference in the White House press room. The hot lights were switched on, and the television film cameras were running. The air conditioning was extra cold.

The President stood behind the lectern answering politely asked questions, when he appeared startled by the high, demanding voice of a woman reporter on his right. Then a woman on President Nixon's left began to speak in a calm, strong friendly voice. She was asking the start of a new question. It was Helen Thomas. The President gave his attention to Helen because he knew and recognized her; but the other woman continued to speak. The President looked at Helen, but the other woman's voice rose. Helen continued to ask her question in a firm voice.

The President's body began to shake and his jowls began to shiver. Then his head began to snap back and forth between the women. President Nixon's eyes rattled with uncertainty.

His press advisers stood helplessly to the side. Finally, he found his way and pointed at Helen. He called her name. There was a release of embarrassed tension in the room as the other woman quieted down. Helen then asked her question again, from the beginning.

And then, in New Orleans, President Nixon pushed his press secretary with angry, uncontrolled hands. The action was recorded on film and widely shown on television and in periodicals.

President Nixon was heard to have said something like, "The press can't come this way," and "Get them out of here." Instead of a cool and controlled President, President Nixon acted like a man exasperated with his "native boy" because the boy had fallen asleep while his job was to fan away the gnats.

The gnats were getting to him. They were flying in his eyes and buzzing in his ears, and nowhere could he go without being bothered by them. The press was a plague of gnats, biting and biting and flying into his face and eyes, and if he tried to get away from them, in some hidden office, he would look at the fruit bowl, and there, flying above a peach, would be a gnat.

Gnats swarmed like reporters, and after a while it was hard to tell gnats and reporters apart. Only reporters were worse. They did not die with the first frost. They flitted day and night, every day, everywhere.

There were eyes everywhere. Mel Elfin sat in his *Newsweek* bureau, a block away from the White House, and he watched. His eyes were sharp. Dan Rather's watched. Helen Thomas's eyes were dark and very strange, they saw everything, and they talked, but never where the President might hear. Helen was almost always on duty. She hated sleep because sleep meant to her that her eyes had to close. "I'm going to be dead a long time," she would say.

The gnats were driving President Nixon to distraction. The gnats were more fierce than ever that summer because they were well fed by the mess of Watergate. They swarmed around Watergate in clouds, and the worse Watergate smelled, the more gnats came, it seemed from everywhere.

The gnats flew on the presidential press plane, with the best care and feeding. Two wire service reporters and a reporter to report to other reporters flew in President Nixon's official plane with him. They flew secluded in a press compartment, as if they were trapped in a bottle.

Within twenty-four hours of the pushing incident in New Orleans, reporters asked the assistant press secretary whether or not the President was *not* taking any medication, and he answered the next question, which was, "Why not?" by saying the President was taking no drugs because the President did not need any.

The gnats seemed more vicious than living politicians could easily remember, but stories about how thick the gnats were when Teddy Roosevelt rode up San Juan Hill, and after Harry Truman dropped the first atomic bomb—those stories were faded somewhat with age. People preferred to forget about gnats and to remember gnatless stories about how they killed the elephant with a single shot between the eyes.

No modern man ever made a great name for himself fighting gnats. President Nixon may be the first exception. His career developed fighting gnats. When he was elected to Congress, the gnats swarmed on him, and he swore that he would fight the gnats. He was elected. The common people do not love gnats. They invade everyone's privacy and they run picnickers inside and cause you to pull down your windows and cover the crock where the wine is fermenting, and they swarm over trash, and if you tried to make love in the grass in the summertime, the gnats would interrupt you.

Stew Alsop and a handful of other writers and reporters dined one night with Henry Kissinger. Kissinger was not driven into hiding by the gnatlike qualities of reporters. He smartly gave them honey in a bowl to keep them away from his head. It may be an old German saying that you can catch more gnats with honey than vinegar, but President Nixon never understood it. He hated gnats so much that he wanted only to destroy them. If there was a gigantic can of Black Flag gnat spray, the President would order it up, mount it on a flatbed railroad car, and choo-choo down the tracks spraying from Washington to Los Angeles. Henry Kissinger's visions were perhaps more diabolic. He would arrange to have almost all the gnats in the world trapped in a jar of honey of the variety the honey-dippers dip. Then, when the right moment came, he would dump the gigantic honey jar out of Air Force One on the heads of the enemy. They would die a sweet and ticklish death in a great yellow muck.

A pair of eyes
You never see
Is watching you.

Father John in the Park

I knocked on Helen's UPI office door in the White House press room. I saw through the glass that she was talking on the telephone.

I admire the wire service reporters who are expert at their work. The work demands an excellent memory, an accurate eye, a fine sense of orderliness, an ability to think in tight, short phrases, speed, and stamina. I counted Helen among the best in the business.

Helen motioned me inside with a nod of her head and a look in her eye that said, "Open the door."

I opened the door and stood in the doorway for a moment listening.

Helen held a notebook in her hand and she was tracing a line with a pen point on the paper. She spoke into the telephone in a steady, carefully paced voice, and I could tell from the phrasing that she was dictating to a good typist on the other end of the line.

Helen was somewhat in the middle of a story about a party President and Mrs. Nixon had arranged for the White House secretaries. Helen said, "It'll take about ten more minutes to finish."

I sat down and watched her. Then, for the fun of it, I decided to see if I could start a conversation with my eyes.

I said: "It's a pretty interesting story you're doing for this late in the day."

The story was about how the President had told the White House secretaries how pleased he was with their work. At the time, certain of the secretaries' "bosses" were secretly telling the FBI and a few reporters all they knew about the Watergate scandals. Yet it had never even been rumored that a woman, certainly not a White House secretary, had ever squealed.

"I know it's a good story," Helen's eyes said back. "It'll take me a little while longer. Please wait. I don't mind if you listen."

"I'm surprised your eyes can talk," I said.

"I'm surprised yours can," she said. "We must be on the same wavelength."

"It's a lot easier to trust somebody if they're on your wavelength. You can get a good idea what they're thinking without talking about it."

"You have Middle East blood," she said.

"What's yours," I asked.

"Guess," she said.

"Middle East somewhere. It's all the same to me," I said.

She told the typist at the UPI office about how the secretaries were . . . and she paused.

"Loyal," I said, out loud.

". . . loyal, . . ." she told the typist.

"I used your word," she said, out loud.

"Thank you. I'm glad you thought enough of it to use it."

"You've got good sense," her eyes said.

"I know."

"That's a pretty bold answer," she said.

"You like bold answers. If you got a bold answer all the time, you'd be in heaven."

"You're right," she said, and she blushed.

She interrupted her dictation and said into the telephone:

"Hey, Agnes." I think it was Agnes. "Come over here right away. I've got a handsome man in the office."

But she never took her eyes away from mine.

Eye talking is an art that requires a great deal of practice, like magic does, unless you are born a magician.

Helen was born in a small town in Kentucky and was moved when she was five years old to Detroit. Her father and mother were from Lebanon, and they were poor. Helen was one of nine children.

Helen remembered her father, George, as a strong, proud man. When Helen said, "My father," she straightened her shoulders, and lifted her chin and, sometimes, she balled up her fists. She remembered her father selling goods in a store, a cluttered hole-in-the-wall store such as many immigrant Arabs, Jews, and Turks operated on the east side of Detroit.

The most painful memories of her father did not easily pass her lips.

Helen's eyes may talk, but her mouth knows how to be discreet. Helen will either like you or not, because of a private inner feeling, and if she writes about you and she likes you, you will be treated with great care. What you said to her will come out in her stories sounding like what you said to her. If Helen doesn't like you, you will be treated exactly the same way as if she liked you.

But underneath in Helen's soul she has deep harbors.

You may enter a few of her harbors when Helen drinks alcohol, and her tongue is slightly loosened. She will remember out loud then the arrogant eyes of the Germans on Heidelberg Street where she grew up.

She will babble on about politics, and the sound of her voice, from a coo to a retch of disgust, will help describe the presidents she has watched during fourteen years at the White House.

Helen worked closely almost every day for fourteen years with Doug Cornell, who was the regular AP reporter at the White House.

They worked in honest competition—yet almost always together—and on presidential trips they would talk together in the special compartment of the President's plane, and during the other long times of waiting. They grew to be friends, yet remained rivals for every story. When they were not together on a story, they missed one another.

After thirty years with the AP, Doug retired in 1971. The retirement party was at the White House and Mrs. Nixon announced Doug and Helen would be married soon. She was fifty-one years old and it was her surprising first marriage. Doug had been married for many years, and his wife had died four years earlier.

Now Doug misses her more than ever. She still travels with the President and works the same long, hard hours at the White House; she drinks and dances late into the night, and listens with her heart to the sad stories of her friends. Doug tries his best to be with Helen as much as her time allows him. He chauffeurs Helen to and from work every day he can.

He misses her quietly and with dignity, and when they are together he treats her with gentle respect.

They agree on the facts of their wire service life together; they agree Helen was sometimes faster in getting to a telephone, but Doug more often found just the right word or phrase to make a situation come alive. Doug is a man who believes in facts.

When Helen said, discreetly, "My father had a store in Detroit," Doug interrupted her by touching her arm.

Helen went on with her story. Then Doug touched her arm again. She gave him her attention.

"You told me," he said, "that your father started out in Detroit by pushing a pushcart."

Helen's heartache ached in her eyes.

She said, "I didn't . . . I didn't want to say that——

"It's true," Doug said.

"I know," Helen said.

"You want to get the facts straight——"

"Yes," Helen said.

And her eyes talked about seeing her strong beloved daddy grunting like a field ox behind a heavy wooden cart in Heidelberg Street.

XXXI

I want no guards
on my borders.

Madame de la Roche de Balloon

Stew was in the hospital in May and out in June and he finished his book in July.

I did not know its title.

In his ordinary office at the *Newsweek* bureau I asked Stew what the name of the book was, and he said, *"Stay of Execution."*

Stew's face was red and dry. His eyes were somewhere else. We carried on an emotionless business conversation about Stew's arrangements with *Newsweek* and Stew said he had a contract that specified his work was to be printed as he wrote it, or not to be printed at all. He felt that over the years with his brother Joe, and then at the *Saturday Evening Post,* he had earned that independence.

Stew's mind was already far away from the cares of who would or would not be happy to read what he thought. He was worried about ideas, the kind of ideas a reporter who is good at his trade must pick up at lunches and interviews and in telephone calls. Stew was very tired. When I saw his face, I tried to smile and then stopped short so as not to cheat.

I said, "Stew, it's very difficult now to reach you through the veil of death."

He said, "I know."

We walked together to the elevators and down across the street.

"Where are you heading?" I asked.

"I've got a business lunch at the Metropolitan Club," he said.

XXXII

As luck would have it, the eyes
and ears of our mongrel beast, The
Press, are always open, and its
many noses sniff day and night.
When dangerous, furtive men
threaten us, The Press is the
first to know. Then our singular
beast sounds the alarm by
drumming on thousands of
teakettles until the sleeping
are aroused.

From "Run with the Rabbits,
Bark with the Dogs"

Happy was so unhappy in his cage down the hill behind Barney's office that one day Barney came out of his office, looked at Happy, and said, "Happy, we're going to move you into the sunlight where we can see you."

Maggi and Barney lifted Happy's cage, whose frame was a heavy wooden work table, and carried it near the black walnut tree, where the afternoon sun could shine in through the chicken wire front. Happy sprawled luxuriously in the sunlight, and now he was visible from the house. Maggi and Kate said hello to Happy every morning from the upstairs bathroom window, or the window over the sink in the kitchen, or from the window in the sunny dining porch. Almost every day they brought him a carrot.

Happy grew fatter and happy, but when Kate or Maggi did not play with him, he was lonesome. One day, with only small warning, Barney bought a big white rabbit with red eyes from a pet store, to be Happy's companion. They put the white rabbit in the cage with Happy, and after two days of chasing each other noisily, they settled down. The white rabbit's habit was to thump his back foot on the cage wire, and make a bang, bang, bang sound. Barney said, "Let's name him Banger." Maggi thought that was lewd. She suggested Lucky B. Rabbit. "And we will know what the B stands for."

One afternoon a strange car pulled into the driveway and a young man with a moustache got out.

"Is this kitten yours?" he asked of Maggi. "We found it wandering down the side of the road."

"No," Maggi said.

Barney saw the kitten in the back seat of the car, mewing, eyes blue-green and wildly alert. Its coat was honey colored and it was the size of three big cupcakes put together. Barney picked it out through the back car window and held it. He said, "If you don't want it, we'll take it."

The young man delightedly agreed.

Barney and Maggi brought the kitten into the house. It ran berserkly around the downstairs rooms, its fur and claws poking out everywhere. Then, after ten or so minutes, it began to rub against Barney and Maggi's legs, almost insane to be held and touched.

When it was set free outside, the kitten and Calico Cat decided within minutes to not fight openly, but the kitten was not sure about Buckeye's intentions and his loud, funny bark. The kitten climbed the vine-like limbs of a trumpet tree to the second story bathroom window. Its only footing so high up was on a branch no larger than a lady's forefinger. The branch bent shakily under its small weight, but the kitten somehow clung on, and cried and cried and cried to be taken in and held. Several times the kitten missed its footing and saved itself from a fall by catching its claws on the bathroom screen, then crazily regaining its perch on the branch. If Barney and Maggi were away from the house, the kitten waited for them, and sometimes, growing anxious, it would climb to the bathroom window and cry, just in case they were miraculously inside.

Barney wanted to name the kitten Kiss-Kiss for what it wanted. Maggi wanted to name it Fearless for what it was.

The kitten was most often called Kiss-Kiss, and sometimes, Fearless Kiss-Kiss.

XXXIII

I am no man's slave; I am a woman's.

Adam

Scotty Reston is fascinating. He appeared to me alone in the rugged foothills, walking in the brown stubble fields under a drizzling Scotch sky. He had leaned back in his swivel chair, in his office, his short, muscular legs open, his eyes dreamy looking. He puffed smoke from a curved pipe. He called me, "My boy," as if I were a son.

Scotty's voice was mellow and brooding.

"Where are all the great men?" he asked. "Where are the poets? *Where* are the philosophers?"

Scotty said, "The last great man . . . puff . . . to die . . . puff . . . was Mike Pearson . . . who was once Prime Minister of Canada."

He went on, almost without blinking. "The world's poets are now second rate and the living philosophers . . . puff . . . except for . . . Mao Tse Tung . . . are mostly *faddist.*"

In a puff, Scotty was transformed from a voice of prophesy and doom into a feisty little son of a knotty-kneed, left-handed shipyard worker on the filthy banks of the Clyde River in Glasgow. Scotty was suddenly angry and indignant that a furtive pretender like President Nixon had frozen Scotty Reston out of the White House, a house he had visited as an honored guest for twenty years. Scotty refused to believe that Americans would elect a man to the White House who didn't see the wisdom of simple, old-fashioned beliefs.

"Every day it's like a new drop of poison," Scotty spit.

Puff . . . Puff . . . Scotty was an oracle again.

"In Emerson's concept of the law of compensation," Scotty said, "it all tends to even up in the end . . . and the SOBs get caught . . . and the good are redeemed. It's a concept of religion and not logic. It's—It's Old Testament."

He went puff, puff, puff on his pipe.

"A lot of people think they see Old Testament vengeance in my columns. Religious themes are so out of general favor with the world of journalism. For anybody to invoke an occasional biblical phrase is rather odd . . . startling."

Then Scotty puffed. He suddenly looked up to heaven and invoked a biblical phrase.

"God will not be mocked!" he growled.

I was so fascinated I had to ask him about illusions. Scotty quoted Eugene O'Neill.

" 'Don't take away our illusions,' " he said.

I was about to ask him why not, but Scotty was working out an idea.

Puff. Scotty became a journalist.

"I don't think I would see it the same way they do," he muttered. "Ehrlichman and Haldeman are guilty of the *greatest* of *all* illusions—'that a small group of people in the White House, loyal to the person of the President, could run the country *better* than other men who believed' . . . who are presumed to believe . . . 'they are no better than other men.' "

"Ed Lahey," Scotty said. He was invoking the name of an old Washington journalist. "He told me once that most of the people who fell in Washington—the President, senators, reporters—they began to think they were what they merely represented. It reminds me of Maugham's essays. He kept a roll of toilet paper on his workbench to remind himself that he was mortal like other people."

He puffed, but Scotty remained a journalist for a while.

"I've never been as proud of my craft. . . . It's closer to doing now what the Founders had in mind. Vietnam. Television in the South to carry on civil rights. It has jumped into the visual. . . . It's probing away. Without cameras on the battlefield we couldn't have seen what the war was like. They are excellent at what they can do. . . .

"And then," Scotty said, with a puff on his pipe that turned him back into a feisty little Scotty, "We know from the Pentagon Papers the *lies* they were telling. . . . Puff . . . Puff . . . Puff . . . Puff-Puff . . . *difference* between the reality of society and the junk spoken out of the White House. There was the reality of Vietnam and how they can *really* fight. . . . Christ, you can see it's not like they say it is in the United States of America. . . . People never like to believe in illusions."

He puffed quietly for a silent moment.

"I grew up," he said, "in this business. I grew up during the rise of the dictators of the late twenties and thirties. I saw the rise of fascism endangering not only France and Britain, but the civilization of the West. The country living with illusion could do business with Hitler. . . . They said it was a fight among Europeans who were always fighting.''

He drew in a mouthful of smoke. Now he was a very young journalist.

"It ended . . ." he intoned to himself . . . "in 1941.''

And then he said to me:

"I . . . didn't have any illusions.''

He rocked slowly back . . . and . . . forth in his chair. His pipe ran out. He rocked forward to fill it . . . lighted it in puffs of smoke and flame . . . and rocked back.

"I don't think," Scotty continued, "the good life is something apart from . . . honorable . . . conduct. Nor do I believe that illusion is essential to man's well-being. I know some agnostics, and I respect their agnosticism. But it's not logical. There must be ethical standards . . . something in any society . . . higher standards of conduct. . . .''

He drifted off into silence, puffing.

After a decent time I interrupted him.

"What are your own personal illusions?" I asked.

He gave my inquiry respectful thought.

"I have the illusion that—" he smiled a charitable smile, "—that in my own life, the struggle to live up to the ethical standards of religious training have been good for me. I have the illusion that living up to ethical standards is a force for good in the life of the nation. This is a country in which good prevails over evil.''

He smiled again.

When I saw his smile I mentioned the name of President Nixon.

A rush of blood welled up in his face, and he made a quick, nervous rock forward. He jabbed the air with his pipe.

He said, "At the moment it seems to be an illusion . . . although it's *not* an illusion to believe in an ideal.''

The blood was dammed in his face, and he planted both heavy-shoed feet solidly on the floor.

"We are pretty realistic people . . . but we've never suffered . . . except the Civil War. This . . .'' he rocked back more relaxed, "has shaken our self-confidence.''

"How,'' I asked, "does it make you feel?''

"I don't for a *minute* confuse Richard Nixon with the President of the United States,'' he insisted. "Not for a minute! I don't think this is anything but a tight, narrow band in the White House.''

I didn't understand. I asked him again.

With a certain pleasure in the clean, unmistakable descriptiveness of his choice of words, Scotty said, ''It gives me the *scunners!*''

''The what?'' I asked.

''The scunners,'' Scotty smiled. ''It means disgust . . . puff . . . puff. . . . The *foulest* kind of disgust.''

XXXIV

Girls who wear long ball gowns
and evening gloves are sometimes
covered all over with hickies.

Mlle. de la Roche de Balloon

Scotty Reston sometimes lets his sad, sad, sad, sad eyes come out. They are covered with an old-dog membrane. He lets stubble grow on his chin. He ties his necktie carelessly. He lights his pipe and he draws in air with madly rapid sucks. The stems of his pipes are jaggedly chewed off. Only a proud control that he learned as a golfer in his youth keeps his hands from shaking.

I asked him one day, "Scotty, what was wrong the day we came to take your picture?"

He said, "Barney, I don't like psychology. I don't like psychological questions. I don't like talking in front of a stranger. I don't like it, and I don't trust it."

Scotty was especially upset when Maggi turned out to be a woman. He tried not to notice her. He tried not to take notice that she was clear-eyed and that she was graceful and lively. He looked at me. He refused to so much as acknowledge her presence in the world.

To Scotty, she was as fearsome a stranger as passengers on a train who want to lure Carl Rowan into an unfriendly poker game.

I asked him, "Scotty, who have been your clerks? Haven't they all gone on to rather good positions?"

"Yes, they have done pretty well." He named them with the help of counting on his fingers. They were all boys.

"Didn't you ever have a girl?" I asked.

"Well . . . oh . . . hmmmm . . . ah. . . ." He blushed at having forgotten. Her name struggled to stay in his mouth.

"Linda Greenhouse," I reminded him.

"Oh, yes, yes, there was . . . Linda." He grinned an unreasonable grin.

Then he caught himself and a look of absolute fright filled his eyes at the thought of anyone poking into his mind.

In every corner Scotty saw something that he was afraid was lewd, or, as he put it, "not uplifting of the spirit."

Movies with a sexual theme, they were never uplifting. Movies of the struggle-against-great-odds-allowing-the-poor-to-suffer-with-dignity; they were uplifting.

He told me the difference he believed there is between the Church of Scotland, in which he grew up, and the Church of England, in which he then worshipped.

In the questions of catechism that train little children into the forms of the church, the Church of Scotland's first question is, "What is man's chief end?" The answer to the question is, "Man's chief end is to glorify God and to enjoy Him forever."

The Church of England's opening question is, "What is your name?"

Scotty had published in one of his books the view he believed about women and country.

"We should behave toward our country," he wrote, "as women behave toward the men they love. A loving wife would do anything for her husband except to stop criticizing and trying to improve him. We should cast the same affectionate but sharp glance at our country. We should love it, but also insist on telling it all its faults."

The quotation was signed, "J. B. Priestly."

Scotty's world was suddenly gray and low to the ground. He and Sally, who is precisely a priestly wife, are sitting in a fishing lodge during a vacation in Scotland. An old man in a kilt enters the room. Scotty thinks the old man has a wonderful appearance, and he approaches the old man to "share a whiskey with him."

Scotty is shy with elders and betters, and he could not get to the point with the craggy old man. He talked about the terrible weather and other common subjects.

In Scotty's mind, the old man fixed Scotty with his flinty eye. In his rolling-tongued burr-r-r-r he said: "You are an American, are ye?"

"Yes," Scotty said.

"Are ye a Christian country?"

"Yes," Scotty answered.

"Then why duh ye tr-r-reat that Black man like ye do?"

Scotty could not answer. He was only trying to have some fun and the old man poked him in the eye with a sharp church stick. The gloom settled back again over the grizzled landscape of Scotty Reston's mind.

"Scotty," I asked, "What do you think of when you think for fun?"

He said, "I think on things amiable. Amiable. I think on things true . . . and beautiful."

"No! I mean *fun*. Do you ever go to the movies for fun?"

"Well, I've *never* seen, for example, a pornographic movie. I don't want to see *Last Whateveritis in Paris* and come away at the end of the evening having concentrated on lust and basic instincts."

"I don't blame you," I said. "I wouldn't either."

"It demeans love and life."

I asked him what movie he had seen. One was a struggle-de-spite-human-suffering-indignity movie called *Sounder*.

His eyes were momentarily bright with uplifted spirit.

"It was like two hours in church," he nearly whispered. "I seek that out."

"But you see a lot of other things besides uplifting people, don't you?" I asked. "Don't you ever see a little bit of foolishness in the world? Frivolity? Gaiety?"

He became guarded and shy. He took time to stuff his pipe.

"I know something about fucking and what goes on in the world," he said softly.

I hadn't expected that turn of events. I decided that if he was going to travel that road, I'd follow.

"Do you know about jerking off?" I asked.

His eyes stiffened up like setting glass.

"Yes," he said.

"What do you think?" I asked.

"What do you mean?" he asked. He was hearing unuplifting words.

"I mean I've found that Washington is full of jerk-offs. Have you noticed that."

"Yes, yes," he said. "But I never gave a lot of thought to it."

"I haven't either, but it's pretty clear," I said. "Lots of 'em in the press corps, too. But Christ, you see 'em jerking off all over."

Scotty squirmed. He couldn't open his mouth.

"I mean *mental* jerk-offs," I said.

He smiled a relieved, tobacco-toothed smile.

Scotty said, "Yes, I'll agree with that, Barney. I'll agree with *that*."

Scotty lighted his pipe. He proclaimed a great respect for the American Institutions, and a profound respect for women who mothered and married men of good character. Yet, Ben Bradlee was breaking up a marriage of nineteen years, and had invited Sally Quinn to share his new apartment. Joe Alsop and Mary Catherine were separated; Tom Wicker of the *Times* and his wife were getting divorced.

Scotty said, "I can't understand it. Wicker and his wife were so well matched. They had the same background in Carolina; they were together so long and seemed to be so happy. I was fooled. I was taken in. It must have been her. She was one of those plantation girls who want men to worship at her shrine of beauty . . . puff . . . I misjudged."

He complained about the wife of his elderly friend, Walter Lippmann. She was seventy-six years old and lived in Maine, while Walter, at eighty-nine, was living out his years in a New York rest home. Scotty visited Walter at least once a month. Scotty said, "Walter only makes sense in the mornings. He seems to make no sense at all in the afternoons.

"She could have at least stayed with him to make him his meals," Scotty said.

Puff . . . and he was at home in his small upstairs study . . . a fire burning very small in the little fireplace . . . and Scotty was dressed in a sweater and white shirt, with his hair combed.

I asked him: "Scotty, why does it make you so unhappy to answer 'psychological' questions?"

"Because happiness is being *outside* yourself!"

He puffed emphatically.

"Well what's inside?" I asked.

His eyes were the eyes of a man looking into his own grave.

"Demons and worms," Scotty said.

XXXV

If you squander only love,
you'll be a rich man.

Madame de la Roche de Balloon

News people, male or female, are highly regarded among their fellows if they are unemotional about death. "It comes with the territory," as Dan Rather and Bill Small will say.

My first brush with death as a newspaperman is inked indelibly on my vivid memory. I was riding down a road and a motorcycle driver ahead of me had swerved past a slow truck onto the shoulder. His head had been sliced off by a sharp-edged traffic sign. I arrived upon the scene minutes later. I did my best not to turn pale with horror, which you don't do if you are a newspaperman. I walked over and stared down at the red plastic helmet that contained the open-eyed head, its face caked with sweat and road dust and a little bit of blood trickling from a bruised lip. I watched its blue eyes, with a look of open surprise and wild panic in them. And I wanted to push the helmet with my toe to see if the eyes closed and if, as I thought must be true, the eyes could still see but nothing alive could understand. It is a beautiful and strange look into the future.

Stewart Alsop never trusted death to be as beautiful as it looked, and Roland Evans knew it. Stew told me that they were together one afternoon in a part of South Vietnam where the government held the main highway in the daytime and the Viet Cong held it at night. Rolly and Stew and a third man were visiting a village along the highway, and Stew was always on the lookout. Rolly had a noisy good time.

He mingled his paleness among the dark yellowish people. He talked in a loud voice, and made many notes. Rolly smiled as if he were having a good time. But it was getting late in the afternoon, and soon the sun was going down. Stew's imagination started to work.

Stew thought about the jeep ride back to Saigon in the long shadows. Thick clumps of bamboo overhung the road. They made perfect ambush sites.

Stew thought to himself about the way the Americans treated German prisoners during the war, and he didn't want to be treated the same by a Viet Cong patrol.

Stew kept calling, "Come on, Rolly."

Rolly loved to play games with Stew, so Rolly would yell back, "I got a few more questions." And then take his time.

Stew said he started to sweat.

"Come on, Rolly, it's getting late," Stew called.

"Wait a second."

"It's getting *dark,*" Stew said.

"The sun is shining," Rolly answered.

Rolly waits until Stew is pacing nervously around the jeep and wringing his hands. Then he saunters up to the jeep. Stew described a tiny smirk on Rolly's lips. But all the way back to Saigon, Stew was watching the shadows for the telltale sign of a gun barrel glistening. Rolly would pretend to snooze.

Stew's imagination could almost run away with him and kill him, but he always seemed to hang on to the shred of control. But imagination killed my father.

He was indicted by a grand jury for embezzlement of funds from a housing project he had an interest in. He was both the contractor and the lawyer, and he managed it all poorly. One of the people he annoyed went to the federal prosecutor and made charges. The story appeared in headlines. Not just little headlines, but the main, eight-column headline across the top of the front page of the *Detroit News* street edition. It said something like, *Local Lawyer Indicted.* The story gave his name, his address, and a photograph of him was included. My father reacted like a beetle shot with an insecticide spray. There is a moment or two of stunned, erratic flailing of legs, and some movement to try to get away . . . and then the paralysis sets in. There are a few tremors and the beetle tries once or twice to open its wings, like my father tried to reopen his law office after he was acquitted of the charges by a jury. But the wings fold closed again and only the head moves jerkily, and then there is a long moment while the beetle clings to the wall, and then the feet relax with a spasm and it falls dead to the floor.

My mother remembered the afternoon he died in the hospital. He had a very bad pain in his chest and the nurses came in and put him on a stretcher and wheeled him toward the intensive care room. He couldn't talk because they had clamped an oxygen mask over his face, but he could see, and they were wheeling him away from my mother, and he tried desperately to get the nurses to understand that he wanted her with him because he was afraid, but they wheeled him on. And as he was wheeled down the hall, my mother saw his fingers in a panic opening and closing in the please-come-closer, please-come-to-me gesture, and that's the last she saw of him while he was alive.

Those black headlines were a shot of insecticide for my father. The poison attacked his courage, and inhibited it, and his imagination ran away with him. The psychiatrists tried drugs, but his imagination continued to run wild, and it was a relief to know he was dead. I wish he had died of natural causes.

If it's true that men hate and rival their father, I can hardly have done a more deadly piece of business than to scoff at becoming a lawyer, ignore classes in college working on the college newspaper instead of studying, and then move away from home when he was weak and asking for courage . . . to make my living in the newspaper business that had destroyed him. Children can be cruel when they do what they want to do. It pays not to forget that. Only after I dreamed that my father was pieces of chicken in a milky chicken soup did I think that he was not worth fighting any more. He was dead four years by that time. That's about the same time I left the newspaper business.

There were a lot of stories floating around about why I left the *Times*. Embezzlement was one of them. My mother used to say, "The apple never falls far from the tree," and "As the twig is bent, so grows the tree." My expense accounts to the *Times* were bloated out of all normal relationship to reality. When I turned in an expense account, it was like the fat man in the circus. People in the *Times* office would have paid to take a peek at that grotesque, inflated, absurd creature.

Manny Friedman, may he rest in peace, was an assistant managing editor for the *Times* in New York, and he had a mind that was not at all amused by freaks. But some of my expense accounts were so colossally outrageous that he couldn't help himself from showing them around. I had never dickered for more salary at either the *Trib* or the *Times,* but I never hesitated to write down a fictional man's name for a $12.50 lunch, and I had lunch with fictional men at least three days a week, and if I were working on a story I thought was important enough to make the front page, I took fictional men and a few fictional women out to extravagant fictional dinners, and my fictions were all big drinkers. Manny Friedman, may he rest in peace, would look at one of my expense accounts and, as he'd read it, he would pinch his eyes with his thumb and forefinger and shake his head to make certain they were working correctly. I would sit at my desk or stand near the drinking fountain in the *Times* newsroom and watch my pieces of paper with so little writing on them make an old editor see something new.

Had I been the kind who salts away money, I could have lived on my salary and retired at thirty-one with money in the bank . . . instead of broke, in debt, and owing the *Times* for old bills I had never properly accounted for. It cost me $2,000, which the *Times* took out of my salary, plus what I borrowed, to pay back what I owed in unaccounted-for bills from Argentina. Manny Friedman, may he rest in peace, received calls for months from car rental companies whose bills I hadn't accounted for. I spent nearly $1,000 on rooms at the Concord Hotel, having no idea they were so expensive, while I slept outdoors at Woodstock. It was awesomely bad management, but it wasn't why I left the *Times*. The *Times* was *extremely* benevolent towards me.

In Buenos Aires, money leaked out of my office accounts in every direction. I set off on a trip to Lima or Santiago in order to postpone the harsh demands of fiction writing for Manny. The office account in a New York bank was overdrawn month after month; its bookkeepers called the *Times* and reached Manny. They asked him to deposit money to the bureau account. He did and sent finger-wagging warnings that my bureau accounts were absurd and ridiculous and must—he underlined words like *must*—be straightened out and explained. And in one letter he added: "If you can."

Then Scotty Reston paid a visit to Buenos Aires on his way to Uruguay to help write and report a meeting between President Johnson and most South American heads of state.

He and Sally were guests at a dinner party I conceived.

There were eight or ten for dinner. I did not attend to those kind of details. I was never sure in my mind who the guest of honor was. Scotty Reston was down from New York, and in his world he was considered a very powerful journalist. The other guests who made an impression on me were Stanley Grand, a man with the face of a white baboon, and his girl friend, whose name was Mabelle, and sturdy as an Amazon queen. He worked for the American government. I recall Stan's manners. They were almost human.

There were one or two Argentine couples; the wife of each was small, slim, and dark, and the daughters of old wealthy families.

The husbands were dashing young men who worked in the Argentine Foreign Ministry. Their manners were full of tight smiles and correct silverware.

Nicanor Costa Mendez was a small man with very fair skin and blue eyes. He walked with a cane and a limp. He was the Argentine foreign minister. He dressed immaculately in a dark blue, double-breasted suit.

The scene was an apartment that I compared in my mind to the Versailles Palace. The dining room was decorated, by a previous tenant, in the glass-and-mirrors style of Al Capone. When I walked into it, I would say out loud, "Where are the machine guns?"

That night the long, glass-topped table was glisteningly elegant under gold-rimmed, emerald-edged Wedgewood plates, the next finest Argentine silverware, with the forks placed tines-down in the French manner. There were Argentine crystal wine glasses, a clear one for the red wine and a pale green one for the white. The napkins were linen. The silver candlesticks each weighed four pounds.

Since I did not attend to those details, I can only recall part of the seating arrangement. Scotty was on my left about halfway down the table; Costa Mendez was across from him on my right. Sally was close by because I can recall her motherly conversation. Beverly was at the far end of the table.

Dinner was served by the Chilean cook and the Chilean maid, while the English governess was in the closed wing watching the children. Beatriz, the cook, passed the first course herself. It was a golden pastry shell containing the most delicate fish in the River Plate poached in a light, creamy wine sauce with shrimp and baby mushrooms. The pastry flaked mouth-wateringly when it was cut. She passed the dish ceremoniously. Beatriz, who had worked for the Chilean diplomat who had rented the apartment before I did, asked pointedly to know who ranked who before the dinner began. I said, "Beatriz, you decide." I was her *patron* and sat at the head of the table, but I was twenty-eight years old and young enough to be her grandson. She knew I had no desire at all to deal with servants. She understood that I never thought of her as a servant.

The main course was a rack of lamb, with fresh vegetables. There was silence in between courses. Costa Mendez tried once or twice, unsuccessfully, to compete with the overwhelming attention I gave to the food. He was defeated by the self-conscious chewing on everyone's part but mine. I thought the food tasted wonderful. Scotty struggled, bless him, to ask a few good journalistic questions to bring the orgy of eating back to grim reality. But after the delicious lamb was passed once, it was passed again. I took a big second helping, most of which I wanted and the rest in tribute to Beatriz, who was so proud of her cooking that it was an insult to her if second helpings were refused. I encouraged her that my guests would be expected to take more. Man or woman, there wasn't a stronger mind in the room than Beatriz's when she was proud of her work.

Dessert was a luscious fruit torte, and there was coffee and tea, and Argentine brandy in the small snifters. There was a traditional toast from Scotty to the foreign minister, and from the foreign minister to Scotty. Then came into the room a feeling of uncomfortable overstuffedness that everyone shared, it seemed, except me. I was still hungry. So I sneaked back into the pantry and with my fingers I ate a few more shrimp from the cream sauce.

The evening ended. Scotty continued on his way.

On a cold morning a few months later, Seymour Topping, the foreign editor, arrived in Buenos Aires, was taken to his hotel by the bureau chauffeur, and then mysteriously avoided my company to do his own private calling and keeping of appointments around town. That seemed only slightly odd to me.

Top, as he was called, would not come to the apartment for dinner that night. He said he was tired. So at my suggestion, we made a date to see the Buenos Aires stockyards, before lunch the next day.

The stockyards smelled of cattle, horses, manure, and hay. Top seemed preoccupied and annoyed. He asked to leave before we saw everything.

Then I took Top to lunch at La Tranquera for his first Argentine barbecue. He was distant, and I thought it was because he was tired and cold from walking around the stockyards in a drizzle. He wore his overcoat inside the restaurant. I explained about the strange meat parts Argentines served, including cow's udder and bull's testicles. Top ordered an ordinary steak. We didn't talk much during lunch. Then we walked outside into a windy, dust-blowing, cold afternoon to hail a taxi going downtown.

"Wait a second," Top said. "Do you know why I'm here?"

I was surprised. I thought he was there to tour stockyards.

"Sure," I said.

"Okay," he said. "This place is as good as any and I want to get it over with."

"Don't you want to go to the office or my apartment? It's pretty cold out here."

"It's fine," Top said.

He sat down at the sidewalk umbrella table. The umbrella had been taken down for the winter. I faced him.

"We've had a lot of correspondence," Top said, "about the bureau."

"I know," I said.

"You haven't answered most of my letters."

"Your letters said to do better work, and I did good work."

His voice was sharp.

"But you never answered me. When I write letters, I expect an answer."

"I'll do better in answering your letters," I said.

He tightened up his mouth.

"There's the question of how much it's costing to run the bureau. The general accounting department has about had enough of you with overdrawn checks and expense accounts that make people laugh."

He had me there.

I said something weak. "I'm getting that straightened out." But it was useless because he had me.

"I'm frankly sick and tired of it, too," he said.

There are moments, I guess, when they say your whole life passes in front of your eyes, and I assume the motorcycle rider had some of those moments between the time he swerved out from behind the truck until the sign guillotined his head off. When Top said that, I had my moments.

I didn't know exactly what was coming next, but I was scared.

"I'm going to bring you home," Top said.

"Why?" I said. Tears came into my eyes.

"I was going to recommend that you be fired . . . because there are people up there who think you're crooked with money. But I've changed my mind about that," he said.

He smiled at my tears and his own kindness for not firing me.

"When?" I said.

"Right away."

"Who will take my place down here?"

"Paul Montgomery will cover it and we'll use the stringer."

"Do I have to leave right away?" I asked.

"As soon as you can wind up," he said.

"I want to stay as long as I can. There are stories I can do I've never done. I think the bureau money problems are straight now. The books have been okay ever since I fired the other secretary."

"That was a mistake you made," Top said. "It cost nearly six thousand dollars for her severance pay. Did you know that?"

"Yes. It was worth it. She was working for everybody except the *Times*."

"It was a big mistake. That and not accounting for what you spend. I think that's straightened out now, from the looks of things," he said.

"It is," I said.

"And that apartment," Top said. "I heard about it. You know, people on the *Times* don't live in places like that. You know, it got very bad. I heard from the publisher upstairs on it," Top said.

"How?"

"I was at a cocktail party and when I went up to him, and we talked about my bureaus, he said, 'I hear you've got a bad one down in Buenos Aires.' "

"So why aren't you going to fire me?"

"Because I don't believe you're crooked."

"You don't?"

"No. I had two alternatives. To fire you for giving us a bad name, and probably making it stand up, or move you back to New York and put you on the metropolitan desk and tell you to look for a new job."

"I won't look for a new job," I said, with tears in my eyes. "I'll stay 'til hell freezes on the metropolitan desk until I show you and them I'm good."

Top believed me.

He chose an alternative he didn't have. He chose to go back to New York and argue that what I needed was more seasoning and maturity—as he put it—under a watchful eye in New York. If I promised to work and be good in New York, Top would try to spare me any more humiliation. He was as good as his word.

XXXVI

Reality is bee stings and baby farts.

Sir John Pop

"How are you?"

"Okay-ah."

"Have you got a minute?" I asked.

"Yah."

"Good, I wanted to ask you somethin'."

Eileen Shanahan didn't say anything.

"Who," I asked, "are the strongest, ah, women reporters, writers and so forth in Washington aside from yourself?"

"Oh, Christ," she said in a high falsetto, like a man trying to sound like a woman. "There are quite a lot."

"How would you . . . would you give me five?"

Her voice dropped back to normal low and gritty.

"Well, I don't know about five. Let me give you fifteen and winnow it down."

"Okay."

"You know, what do you mean by strongest?"

"I mean people——"

"——Most well established——"

"I just don't mean most well established, I mean intelligent, strong——" I said.

"You know——" she interrupted in the falsetto.

"Intelligent, strong, unafraid and . . ." I groped ". . . open."

"What do you mean 'open'?"

"Open-minded, unafraid—unafraid and unintimidated by being either women or in journalism."

"Well, you see, Barney, I think the question is a very wrongheaded question."

"Okay."

"There are *dozens* who fit that category. You make it sound like women in journalism in Washington are, are just a tiny little group and hardly any of 'em are terribly good."

"Well, I——"

"There are *dozens* and *dozens* and *dozens* of absolutely first-class women reporters, and news executives, increasingly, in Washington, who meet every description you have just given.''

''Well, for example.''

''Well, I need to know what you want to know for because I think the question is wrong-headed and potentially insulting.''

''Well I don't think it's potentially insulting. I mean I think it's . . . I . . . I've looked . . . I've been looking around . . . I'm doing a book on Washington.''

''Um-huh.''

''And Washington journalists, and I've been looking for *strong* . . . unafraid . . . and . . . ahhh . . . winning, let's put it that way—winning . . . female journalists.''

''For what purpose?''

''For what purpose?''

''Yeah.''

''To *write* about,'' I said. ''I mean, you know. To write about. Simply to write about.''

''Well, how many men are you gonna write about?''

''A dozen.''

''Well, if you only write about a dozen men, five women is about the right ratio. But I'll bet you——''

''Why?''

''Well, I mean, 'cause I think that's about what the ratio is.''

''Okay. Well, there'll be more than that and there'll be more women. I mean, I'll tell you what women I'm already writing about. Helen Thomas . . . ahhh . . . Christie Basham . . . ahhh . . . Betty Beale——''

''Shhhhi——'' Eileen said.

''Well, I knew you'd say that. But still, she's well known outside of Washington . . . ahhhm . . . ahhhm . . . who else is in here? I'm talking about major . . . well, two or three others at the networks——''

''What *men* are you writing about?''

I hesitated to say.

''Because to know whether you're going about this thing in the *proper* context, that is to reflect what the *real* world is, and in the real world . . . women are no longer in just a toehold position in journalism in Washington. Now, I don't wanna overstate that case and say there's no discrimination or anything like that and I'm really very wary of talking to you at *all* after the way you so totally misrepresented what I said in that Galbraith piece. I think that was an outrageous bit of *cheap* journalism.''

''Why?''

''Well, first of all you made me—you *hinted* or implied by juxtaposition that I'd *slept* with Galbraith, number one . . . and you hinted that Angie what's-her-name——''

''You know that that's foolishness——'' I said.

Eileen made a high-pitched yowl.

''No, it is *not* foolishness. . . .''

''Well, . . .''

''It is exactly what you did, I don't know whether——''

''Eileen——'' I said.

''I don't know whether——''

I said, ''Eileen, I know you, and I doubt that that was the case.''

She yowled again.

''You'd better *fucking* well *doubt* that it was the case, it's what you implied——''

''Well, I don't even think I implied it——'' I said.

''In addition to which. . . . You certainly did, and you——''

''Well, I never *thought* it, so I don't know how I could *possibly* imply it. I mean, I know you, I've seen you over a period of years, and I knew absolutely one hundred percent that it never even *occurred* to me that you'd either slept . . . or even intimated . . . or implied that you would ever do Galbraith any favor in the world.''

''Well, that ain't the way it came out in the book. I came out as some mindless . . . *groupie* . . . tugging at his . . . coatsleeves.''

I laughed at the image.

''I don't think so,'' I said.

''Well, *I* do, and so do the people who read it, and for the first time in my entire life, I, since I've been on the *Times,* I wrote a letter to the editor of the magazine about a piece. You also misquoted and misrepresented other people. Art Okun is too much a gentleman to do anything about it.''

I wondered why I never saw a letter printed in the magazine from Eileen or anyone else besides Galbraith himself.

''I gather from Okun that you just completely took half of what he said and not the other half, and that's just trashy, cheap stuff, so

I don't know whether I really wanna have any part of you doing another *trashy* cheap job about journalism, par-*tic*-ularly where it involves *women*. Women in journalism is a subject very dear to my heart. . . . I . . . women have made great strides in journalism, *especially* in this city, and there are many solidly entrenched, marvelously *professional* women, there are literally dozens *and* dozens . . . and I, I really——''

"Well . . . all I'm asking for is five," I said.

"Well, I don't want to give you *just* five," she screeched.

"How about fifteen and let me choose my own?"

"In terms of . . . I, I don't want to *help* you misrepresent the situation. I'm afraid that anything I do helps you misrepresent, since you seem to be a prize misrepresenter, based on the one piece of yours that I ever knew anything about . . . and saw what came out when you finished writing it."

"Um-hmmm," I said.

"There are dozens and dozens. There are women in *executive* positions . . . ah . . . on newspapers in Washington now—really *high* positions. Elsie Carper is an assistant managing editor of the *Post,* Mary Lou Beatty is assistant national news editor of the *Post*. Barbara Cohen is assistant city editor or metropolitan editor, whatever they call it, of the *Star;* Mary Lou Werner Forbes is state editor of the *Star,* which is a big job as you know. There are probably others."

"What about nationally?"

"National. Mary Lou Beatty, as I say, is, is——"

"I don't mean that. I mean in *national* journalism."

"All right, in national journalism there are dozens and dozens. I just got out my Washington Press Club directory that helped me . . . ahh . . . helped my *memory* on the matter—there are so many I just can't *name* a few. I mean there are people like, ahh, in the specialist field, like me, I'm economics, but in other specialty fields there are people like Charlotte Moulton of the Supreme Court for the United Press, who has made, has made, fifteen AP men . . . look bad over the years compared to her because she's so good. There are people like Bonnie Angelo of *Time*——"

"People tell me about her often." I said.

"She is . . . *stupendous!*"

"Why is she stupendous?"

The question made Eileen screech again.

"She's just—*whyisanybody* stupendous?"

"I——"

"She's *superb* at anything she does, she can do anything and she does it *all* superbly."

I paused to catch my breath after that one.

"There are people," Eileen went on, "like, you know, the national reporters on the *Post,* Susie McBee, Mary Russell. . . ."

"Um-huh."

"Ah, we've got four here in this bureau now, every one of them first class in my opinion."

"Who are the others except yourself?"

"Linda Charleton, ah, Maggie Hunter, and . . . Leslie Olsner now, who's doing legal stuff. She's only been here a few months and she's an absolute *smash!*"

"Oh, I know who she is. I knew her from New York," I said.

"Right, she's just absolutely super."

"Is she doing legal?"

"Yes."

"Um-hmm," I said.

"Why the hell don't you read the paper once in a while?"

"I haven't had much chance to read the *Times* lately," I said.

"Well, she may have got down here——"

"I know she was in New York doing legal things, and she's a lawyer I think, isn't she?" I asked.

"Yes, she is."

"She's an interesting girl, too. Who else."

"Awright, as I say, let me look through the . . . the list here . . . to check my memory because there are so *many*. It depends, there . . . there are *feature* writers, sort of the young breed of feature writers exemplified by Marlene Cimons, that's with a 'C,' on the *L. A. Times,* or Judy Bachrach on the *Post*. Myra McPherson *Segal,* who's on leave this year——"

"She I know——"

"She's just *super!*"

"How about Meg Greenfield?"

"*Stunning!* This has gotta be one of the most brilliant human beings, let alone women, in the United *States*."

"Um-hmm. I've talked to her."

"And she's given so much of the *sparkle* to that page, as well as its *depth*."

139

"What do you mean, 'sparkle'?"

"Well, there's wit and humor very often, in those *Post* editorials."

"Can you ever tell that it's hers?"

"I, I often . . . I have *learned* . . . ah, that when something really just breaks me up, I'll ask, and often when I ask I'll find out that it's . . . it's Meg. I mean as well as straight stuff, too, but I think that . . . Carol *Falk* of the *Wall Street Journal,* who's the only woman in that bureau, ahhh, just *first* class."

"How about yourself?"

She screeched, but it wasn't an angry screech.

"Of course . . . I said 'all four of us' here in the bureau."

"Did you know Soma Golden?"

"Do I *ever* know Soma Golden! I'm so thrilled that we hired her. She's in New York now."

"I talked to her at some length and I like her a *lot!*" I said.

"Yes, I do too," Eileen said.

"She, she . . . let me say something to you about her. She, from all of the ones that I've seen—and a lot of the ones you mentioned I don't know—some I do, of course, of all the ones I've seen, she was about the example of what I mean by unafraid and straightforward and open. And sharp."

"Well, I think almost everybody I named would be. . . ." Eileen said.

"Well, I talked to a couple of them, who have some real boundaries on their ability that comes from being women and not from just being people."

"Well . . . other things . . . someone like Carol Falk of the *Wall Street Journal*—the *Wall Street Journal* propos . . . imposes on everybody a lot of institutional restrictions on your expression and opinion even in conversation or, you know, being quoted, giving speeches, that kind of thing. Ah, and that's not women, that's the *Wall Street Journal.* Ah, and, there are people like Judy Randall, who's the science reporter for the *Star.*"

"How about in television, Eileen?"

"Let me . . . I was just thinking . . . Marilyn *Berger.*"

"She's at the *Post,* isn't she?"

"A diplomatic reporter at the *Post.* Marianne Means, who's the national political correspondent for Hearst, King Features. Who did you—TV? . . ."

"Television," I reminded her.

"Well, TV is a tough case. The discrimination has been so acute there. And they search, I think, often, I don't want to denounce anybody now *in* TV, but I think they look at the face first and the qualifications *second*. And someone like Cassie Mackin I would have rated as perhaps the absolute tops in TV, and she's in L. A. I guess, and there was some speculation, I *do* not know whether it is true, and that she was sent out of Washington because the White House hated her so, and in cowardly TV style they got her out of town. There are just all kinds of people. Bailey Morris of the *Star* you may not know by the name is a female, another economics writer."

"You've given me short shrift on television, Eileen."

"That's because there aren't very many. There really aren't very many. I'm impressed with this Leslie what's-her-name. . . ."

"Stahl."

"On CBS. I don't know her personally."

"Why are you impressed with her?"

"I know good reporting when I hear it, I think, and I saw her doing those stand-up fills during the Watergate hearings and stuff, and it was obvious to me she'd done her *homework*. And she was *solid*. I tell you somebody else who's really, really solid and was scoopin' the pack during the Watergate hearings is Martha Engel of the *Star,* who was one of their two top people on Watergate. She's a young woman, perhaps not thirty yet."

"Let me explain a problem to you," I said.

"Yeah."

"I have a difficult time in doing a *Star* or a *Post* or somebody like that simply because it is so Washington-oriented rather than national oriented."

"Well, why is the *L. A. Times* national and the *Washington Star* is not?"

"Well, who's on the *L.A. Times?*"

"Well, I just picked that out of the air."

"I don't know anybody on the *L. A. Times.*"

"There are two people, I named one. Marlene Cimons, who's a feature writer, and oh, what is the name of their legal reporter? Who's also a——"

Eileen turned to call, "Leslie! What's the name of the woman who does legal stuff for the *L. A. Times?*"

She turned back.

"Linda Mathews. She also is a lawyer. She's a Harvard graduate, a woman with a young baby, she's working full time. I mean I understand you don't want to over*load* it, but——"

"I can't overload it, and obviously I'm going to have to make a choice out of all of those that you gave me——"

"There aren't too many in TV. I think one of the most professional women in TV, but I think she feels the institutional constraints, and probably wouldn't be too open with you, is Audrey Dillman, who's the assignments editor for NBC news desk here."

"Do you know . . . what's-her-name?" I asked.

"Who?"

"Over at NBC . . . the woman who was executive producer or producer of Nightly News . . . her name's right out of my head now . . . but I mentioned it to you earlier——" I said.

"Oh, yeah, I don't really know her. I was on a panel with her once, and was most impressed, at the [*MORE*] counterconvention."

"Right, at the counterconvention."

"Yeah. Incidentally, you mentioned Helen Thomas at UPI, who's gotten a lot of *personal* publicity because she had to put her own name in the paper because of the Martha Mitchell phone calls . . . ah, equally, of equal caliber is Francis Llewyn of the AP."

"Um-hmm. I know. I've watched them both work. What is the name of the woman who used to be the flyer?"

"Oh, Faye Wells."

"What's she like?"

"Ah, she's a mush head."

"What about Sara McLendon?"

"Sara . . . Sara does not deserve the ridicule she gets."

"I think she works hard as hell," I said.

"She works hard as hell and very often she is asking a question that other people oughta ask, and just 'cause it's Sara people laugh. In fact——"

"I never laughed at her," I interrupted. "I think she's a tough gal and an interesting gal——"

"I do, too," Eileen said.

"I think she reports very well for who she reports for," I said.

"Well, I don't see her stuff, but just based on her questions I think she's often asking the right question when everybody else is being soft-minded," Eileen said.

"I do, too," I said.

"And if she were a man people wouldn't laugh at her," Eileen said.

"Absolutely not. I never laughed at her. I think she's an interesting woman," I said.

"Of course, you forgot Esther Van Wagner Percy, who I guess has run her own bureau for nigh on to fifty years."

"Let me ask you something else. How old are you?" I asked.

"Forty-nine."

"You're forty-nine. . . . How many *young* women are there coming up?" I asked.

"Oh, it's delightful. There are lots. I mean there are not as many as there *should* be, but if you have an impression of the women in the press corps as being all middle-aged, that isn't true."

"That's the impression from the list. When you talk about Miss Tufty, who's——"

"Well, she's gotta be damned near seventy-five," Eileen said.

"Right. She's up in the Dorothy McCardle range," I said.

"Or older. Older. I would be surprised. Esther has to be well over seventy."

"Right."

"But, no. I think the ones you will meet will run all ages, from about twenty-seven *up*."

"How old is Leslie?"

"Thirty."

"Leslie's thirty. So, probably in their mid-twenties up?"

"Yup."

"Why did you make that noise when I mentioned Betty Beale?" I asked.

"Because I think, even for the kind of stuff she does, which isn't my choice of a kind of journalism, but I realize that kind of reporting is . . . there's a demand for . . . but even *for* that kind of reporting, I just don't think she's a very accurate reporter."

"How about Sally Quinn?"

"Yichk! You know. I don't think their stuff is that good. I don't know. You probably shouldn't go on my judgment of that because I really hate that kind of reporting, true."

"How do you characterize that kind of reporting?"

"I don't know. Trash! It's not. . . . Am I being quoted?"

"Do you want to be?"

"I don't want to be quoted at all by you—ever! That is an absolute. I feel like I'm being very charitable even to talk to you, and I do not authorize any quotation whatsoever."

"Why do you talk to me then?"

"I don't know. Because I'm a boob and I find it difficult to be unpleasant."

"I've already quoted you in the book on one thing."

"Yeah, what was that?"

"You said, 'Are you the kind of slimy reporter that quotes what other reporters say?' That's a quote from you."

"Was that when you interviewed me about Galbraith? Well, I hope you gave the . . . I hope you give the *rest* of the quote!"

"What's the rest of it?"

"The rest of the quote is, 'Without *telling* them you're *going* to-ooo!' Now, that's what I *said* and that's what I *meant,* and it's a typical Collier cheap, misrepresentation to quote it any other way. I don't think I'll talk to you any more."

"Ah——"

"That's just really *low* and *lousy.*"

"What is low and lousy?"

"To take two-thirds of a quote like that, and barber it so it changes the whole meaning. That's a very good example that you just told me you're gonna quote me as saying. I *hope* you will have enough *integrity* to fix it the way I *said* it."

"Maybe you want me to not even put it in?"

"I prefer you not even to put it in."

"Let me think what else I was going to ask you about. . . . I'm overwhelmed by your hostility, for a minute. I just have to recover."

She screeched.

"Well, tough *shit!* You deserved it! You earned it!"

"I didn't earn your hostility," I said.

"Yes, you certainly did. Anybody who misrepresents what somebody says deserves the hostility they get. And that's what you did in the Galbraith piece and that is what you just admitted to me you intend to do again."

"No, I didn't intend to do it again," I said truthfully.

"Well, I trust you will *fix* that quote *then.*"

"Can I quote you, period? Can I quote you on everything you say?"

144

"No, you may not!"

"Do you tell that to your sources and the people you quote?"

"I believe *I* have a reputation for getting the quotes *right*."

"Well, I do, too," I said.

"No, you *don't,* 'cause I checked around after that piece on Galbraith and found out you had a terrible reputation which I hadn't been aware of."

"What was the reputation?"

"Just what I found reflected in that piece. That you were inaccurate and *sloppy*."

"In quotations?"

"Hmmm? . . . Generally."

"Just generally?" I asked.

"*Just generally!* I had people say to me, 'I'm astonished you didn't know that about him.' I heard the *Times* fired you . . . I don't know whether that's true or not."

"Did you hear that?" I asked.

"I did hear that."

I laughed.

"I never bothered to check to find out," Eileen responded.

"That's funny," I said. "Ah, it isn't true by the way. Just 'fyi' . . . for your information. . . . What else was I going to ask you? . . . What *else* did you hear? That's interesting to me what other slander——"

"People. I just absolutely blew up when I . . . when I read the Galbraith piece and I came to the office on Monday and mentioned to people that I had nearly called Frankel on Sunday. I was so mad and I decided I really ought to give myself a little time to cool off. And I hadn't known what a trashy writer you were, and people around here said, 'Oh, Christ, yes.' "

"Um-hmm," I said.

"And then I started hearing around town that, 'Boy, Collier really zonked you and made you look stupid and like a giggly schoolgirl et cetera and seemed to be implying you slept with Galbraith and the whole bit——' "

"You certainly do have friends who take you—who don't think much of you," I said.

"I have friends who think *very highly* of me and who were *incensed* at the way you presented me."

"Hmmm," I said.

"As was I. And who volunteered it. I have a *splendid* reputation as . . . you . . . may . . . know——"

"I know you have a good reputation for having a loud mouth," I said.

"Good-bye," and Eileen hung up.

In matters of reproduction,
I believe in the capitalist system,
and the communist system. I also
believe in the rhythm system.

Walden the Wolf

Soma Golden. She is the girl of a thousand dreams. She is a giant-
ess, a sad clown of a girl with a flaming bush of peachy hair growing in springs and corkscrews out of her pale white skull. She has
the arms of a fine athlete, the legs of a lightweight boxer, the confident walk and bearing of a man who is in excellent shape, and can
ski an expert slope. And on this body is grafted the head and mind
of a woman.

It is an entirely disconcerting thing to see.

Soma deals with herself in a way that is about as graceful as such
an odd matchup of mind and body can.

When she is on the job as a reporter and writer, she dresses up as
the clown in balloon dresses, with leather sandals on her shapely
feet, and a straightforward, man-to-man attitude. She is unshy to
walk up directly and gracefully to any man or woman and ask what
he or she is doing, and how to spell their name. She has the unhairy
guts it takes to be a reporter.

She can also talk and listen to men and women over a drink at the
bar.

She is not awed in Washington by public figures and men of high
office. Her father, a Russian-born doctor, told her, *"Remember!
Those men all wear underpants."*

How humble a man of high office can be imagined in his underpants.

Her mother, somehow, implanted in Soma a feminine face and
feminine graces with her hands. Soma holds a snifter of brandy with
her flexible face and head tilted back in to the lines of a picture hat
in a summer garden. There is a sparkle, something strong and something vulnerable, in her eye, and there is no doubt that she's a
woman inside her mind. Of course, some can tell right away if they
look at her queenly bosom.

Soma is the dream of women like Eileen Shanahan, who know in
their hearts that Soma could crack a little man's skull with her fist,

if she wanted to. It is a fantasy weak-minded women have. Big men would never need defending against, because they would respect her manly qualities and her good companionship, without noticing her sex, which is coincidental to a good man and woman relationship.

Poor Soma is a champion and doesn't mean to be, and doesn't really want to be and her secret is that she is terrifically female.

Women like Soma are usually mythical creatures and a girl who grows head and shoulders in her body above most men, and is blessed with both a strong father and mother, suffers bends and twistings of the mind when she bounces off into the world in a form most people of the world find laughable at first, too big, too gawky, too fat, too tall, too extreme among the almost exactly similar flock of ducklings.

She grew up in Washington with a capable head for schoolwork, and she learned her way through Radcliffe College, and she received a degree in economics. At Columbia she took a degree in journalism. She eventually found a job on *Business Week* magazine, as an economics reporter. In a few months she knew she could understand and write about economics as well as or better than most of her competition. She was not coy and not timid. Most reporters spend a lifetime trying not to be coy or timid, and few succeed. So Soma started out in front. Her ability to record facts accurately was superior, a skill only a few reporters bother to sharpen very often. Her manner of milking information from sources was worthy of any reporter who milks the teats of power in Washington.

So when Eileen Shanahan says, "Do I *ever* know Soma Golden," Eileen is talking about a dream woman.

Far down deep inside Soma is a woman who has not, to my knowledge, given birth to life. She has a desire to do so.

Soma said, "I'm happiest with a man. I give my best for men, and I like what men can get out of me."

No man has yet come along that can get better out of Soma than Soma can get out of herself alone, and when she left *Business Week* and took a job on the *New York Times* as an economics writer for a salary of $29,500 a year—which she was reluctant, but not unwilling, to talk about—she showed the kind of confidence in her worth that Meg Greenfield refused to; and Soma made none of the usual modest remarks about being overpaid that I heard from Dan Rather when he was being humble and down-among-the-common-folk.

Soma invited herself to the house in Vienna. There was no need to coax her. There were no excuses for not wanting to be looked at. She wasn't scared to the point of an upset stomach by exposing herself to the untrustworthy eyes of Barney Collier or the strange, funny, untamed eyes of Maggi Castelloe. Soma marched right in, with a young man photographer who taught photography as therapy in a private sanitorium where, at one time, Mrs. Graham's husband, Phil, was kept from hurting himself before he ended his life.

Soma and the photographer made a couple that was easy to get along with. Soma wanted to talk to me and she brought the photographer to talk photography to the photographer. Soma turned out to be very learned.

Her mind was trained to believe the scientific, the charts, the graphs, the statistical detail that measurers use to predict the future by the experiences of the past. She believed that economists produced accurate forecasts, in the same way people believed in the predictions of Jeane Dixon, a famous Washington seer.

Soma reported on economists' illusions, called forecasts, and for a while, she was in awe of them as people are awed by witches and wizards. Then her father told her, "Soma, they all wear underpants."

She was lonesome. Once, when she worked in New York, a man friend she knew asked her to listen to him, and he told her a story so enormously sad that the entire world of Soma Golden was turned dark by it. It enveloped her mind in a greasy, black smoke, a tale of a man's sadness. It caused her to scream inside her head. She couldn't work and couldn't think straight. She knew she needed a doctor's care, and she chose a psychiatrist. He was of the understanding friend-and-listener school of psychiatry. He helped Soma turn herself right-side out.

After that, she let her hair grow naturally.

The girl of Eileen Shanahan's dreams has left Washington again for New York, the scene of her worst depression. The *Times* promised her a by-line, which she had not had at *Business Week,* and a lot of freedom to write about economics.

I read her tea leaves and they said she would find the apartment she was looking for on the East Side. Soma said, "Oh, no, I'm a West Side kind of girl," by which she meant Jewish. The East Side was too swell for Soma.

I said, "You look and you'll find what you want on the East Side."

Soma smiled as if I were kidding.

"You'll also find a man. . . ." and I described him as very peculiar looking, and I saw a baby in the leaves, and it, too, was uncommon.

Soma said, "No, you're *wrong*," while she laughed and hoped I was right.

I saw a trip to China.

"Oh, good," Soma said.

I saw turmoil.

Soma did, too.

Maggi noticed that far in the back of Soma's mouth, where an upper tooth ought to have been, was a dark, empty space, that showed only when Soma tried to smile her most free, and could be felt by the tongue as an empty space that begs for explanation.

A message arrived indirectly from Soma a few months later that cast all of my predictions into doubt.

She found the place she was looking for on the West Side.

Always smile when your picture is being taken. It takes *years* off your age. Ha! Ha! Ha!

Perle Mesta

Betty Beale keeps chocolate candy kisses in the pouch of her cheek in her warm mouth and holds them there until they melt.

Her bedroom is bright and sunny and faces a garden where a mockingbird lives, and sings.

She is storky-legged, storky-nosed, sharp storky-eyed.

There is a streak of hard clay in her and a streak of hard coal and brittle glass. She was the daughter of a West Virginia man who came to Washington in the early part of the twentieth century and established his family. He became a vice-president of the American Security Trust bank. Her mother's father was a congressman from Tennessee.

Betty dutifully performed the chores demanded in the service of the Junior League and the societies to glorify America's early families. The *Washington Star* was the newspaper of such people, and Betty, who was not married, and showed no signs of desiring marriage, began to write about Washington parties for the *Star*.

Her strong point was that she knew most people at the parties by face and name. She was also completely acceptable and completely trustworthy to party hostesses. Betty knew how parties worked, and she knew where skeletons rattled, and she knew the politics of the people who gave the parties and those who came, and she knew enough not to blurt out something embarrassing she'd overheard, and to keep some things she observed strictly to herself. When Betty started to work in Washington, it was a more discreet place than it is today, a generation later. Indiscreet young women were rarely mentioned favorably in the society sections of those old newspapers. Almost never did indiscreet women write for them.

Before Betty went to work for the *Star,* she suffered some severe medical problems that she prefers not to talk about, and she was afraid she was not going to be able to work again or live an active life. Then, in 1945, the same year she went to the *Star,* she converted to Christian Science, a religion that takes hold of a person's mind and says, essentially, "Mind controls matter, or else God will."

It was both mind over matter and God's will that Betty recovered and became happier than anybody ever remembered her since she was a young girl.

I asked, "How old are you, Betty?"

"Oh, I can't say. It's against my religion," she said.

"You're kidding."

"No. It's against Christian Science to recall age. Age doesn't make a difference. It's how you feel . . . and I feel marvelous."

"Well, what year were you born?"

"Oh, come on! I won't recollect. But I'm *no chicken.*"

"Well, you've been married nearly five years. You celebrate *that* don't you?"

"Oh, yes." She turned her eyes toward heaven. "I do . . . *joyfully!*"

"Good."

"I met this beautiful handsome man, Barney," she said, "And he did the *one* thing that I wanted a man to do. He danced. He danced wonderfully—strong and handsome and very youthful, and I said to myself, 'Betty, you're going to get him.' "

Betty told how the odds against her were formidable. Washington is a city of wealthy widows. Most of them live in the section of the city where the streets have the letters N.W., for northwest, after them. Many live in elaborate settings, and many wear diamonds and emeralds over wrinkled skin. They hostess parties, and any available man, no matter what his age is, as long as he can stand up, doesn't smell bad, and will wear a tuxedo, is a potential catch for the widows.

Now and then, a fish other than the normal old mullet comes along, and George Kenneth Graeber, a year widowed, a representative for Union Carbide, came swimming along into the widowly pools.

It was November 16, 1968.

A married girl friend of Betty's called Betty at home from a cocktail party.

"Betty," she whispered. "You gotta come right over here. The most *divine* new man is here."

Betty said, "I've got to work tonight. I've got this Marc Chagall party to go to."

"Come on, Betty, this is a *live* one."

But Betty continued to be reluctant. There was some give and take and a few loud whispers, and Betty's friend put "George" on the telephone.

Betty and George chatted and to Betty's ears he sounded good enough to take a look at. The next night, they met between a cocktail party and a dinner party that Betty had to work.

George was astonishingly acceptable. Betty's eyes, which naturally pop a little, nearly bugged out.

He was fair, strong-faced, determined looking, and otherwise entirely satisfactory, and Betty thought to herself, "He's so good . . . I'll bet he can't dance."

Betty had a passion for dancing. She wasn't perfectly gracefully built, but her mind was strong enough to force her body to be graceful in a way it wasn't naturally. She had danced with many, many men, and none of the ones who measured up in the head seemed to be able to dance, and the ones who could dance like gigolos didn't have anything in the head.

George Graeber knew how to dance.

It was the athletic, precise, ballroom dancing of a businessman with a flair. It flowed with hours and hours of practice and self-control; and Betty was almost ecstatic. She had not expected at her age, whatever it was, to be swept violently off her feet, twirled in the air, dipped backward till her curls brushed the floor, cocked like slingshot in her partner's arm, and thrown across the floor in a spin.

In December, they were engaged. On New Year's Day it was announced that after many, many years of what seemed, to some people, eternal spinsterhood, Betty Beale was going to be married for the first time.

The announcement was to be an occasion of happiness for most of Betty's friends around the country, and therefore, she announced it in her column.

They were married on February 15, 1969.

Betty and George became a working partnership.

Betty said, "We work together brilliantly. When you have a column that covers official functions and parties, you have some influence. George is a representative of Union Carbide, not a lobbyist who has to register, but more just a representative of the company. He was a plant manager in Texas City and in the office in New York before he was transferred here.

"Somebody in my position can open doors right away . . . because I get invited to the right places, and I know an awful lot of people personally. And it's *ideal* for him. We go to some of the parties because of me, and some because of him. He does some of his work at the parties. He meets people and people immediately *love* him . . . and so George gets his invitations, and I get mine.

"Like some of the Cabinet wives will say, 'Betty, George is so attractive, so adorable. I *love* him!' And so we'll get invited where we want to go because of George, not me. And that's how it works out."

I asked, "What's love?" when I thought about how the Cabinet wives loved George.

"Love? Come on, Barney. If you're married and you don't know what love is I feel sorry——"

"I don't know what *you* mean. I think people think of love in a lot of different ways."

"Love . . . it means . . . wanting to *do* something for someone, trying to make them happy . . ."

"Is that so?" I asked.

"Yes. . . . It's funny," Betty said. "We were talking about that the other day, and I said something about us doings things 'fifty-fifty,' and George said that wasn't what makes a marriage successful as ours. What it takes, George said, is each one giving it *ninety* percent, and leaving only ten percent for the other one to do."

"That's one hundred and eighty percent," I said.

Betty laughed.

"That's right. That's why we are so good together."

XXXIX

I am a true believer in everything.
Therefore there are no contradictions.

Walden the Wolf

I telephoned Stew at home and Tish answered. She said Stew was asleep, and "a little bit low." I asked how she was, and she told me about their son Joe.

"Joe is not doing very well. We had another blow with that. I don't know if I told you. He had the equivalent of a stroke a couple months ago———"

"You told me about that and———"

"He's not in very good shape. He's . . . he's depressed, poor kid . . . he's only twenty-eight."

"Can he move anything?"

"Oh, sure. But see, what happened was, he made a rather rapid recovery and now the last part of the recovery is just kind of . . . not . . . nothing is getting any further along."

"What's left?"

"Numbness down his right side, and *extreme* fatigue."

"All over?"

"Yes. You see, he went back to work practically right away . . . half time."

"Didn't you say he worked for IBM or something?"

"No . . . he worked for a computer company, but a small one."

"Yes."

"He gets terribly tired," she said, and in a tiny voice she added, "and he denies it."

"Mentally or physically?" I asked.

"Physically and I *think,* mentally, 'cause he's worried."

"That's the problem."

"Really, that's the problem all around."

"Is he coming in?"

"No. They came for Thanksgiving. And I think that probably was a mistake because what he had written was that he hadn't seen anybody but Candy for a long while except the people at the office, which is different as you know."

"I wish it wasn't so low for you, Tish. I really do."

"Yeah. It's a bit of a bad time."

"I wish I could do something to lift your spirits a little bit. It's a funny kind of Christmas season."

"It's a very muted one," she said.

"It's very muted and very lonesome. It's——"

"It's a universal phenomenon," Tish said. "I've discovered it. I don't know . . . the whole kind of business about. . . . Oh, dear . . . the depression about the state of the country, the state of the government, it's gotten through to everybody."

XL

As I was going up the stair,
I met a man who wasn't there.
He wasn't there again today—
I wish to God he'd go away.

A Case

Once upon a time, there was born on Long Island in New York a boy by the name of Art Buchwald. His birth was greeted with pain in the Buchwald family because his mother died not long after he cried his first cries of life. He might have been a pretty baby, but nobody noticed because of the sadness that filled the Buchwald house.

Art's father's trade was upholstery. He also made window draperies. He was good at his trade, but he did not earn much money. He was afraid he couldn't keep his family together without his wife's love and helping hand. He sent Art and his three sisters to foster homes.

Art never had anyone dependable around who loved him from the time he first cried.

The first foster home Art remembers was two German women who were Seventh Day Adventists. They both were nurses. They taught him everything he knew about sin. It was a sin to wet his pants, it was a sin to overeat, it was a sin to sass back, it was a sin to laugh too loud. Fun seemed like a sin.

One of Art's sisters lived with him, but it was still very lonely. They were taught to believe in Jesus Christ. Art's father believed in his own religion, which was Jewish. It would have been a Jewish sin, never to be forgiven by God, if Art's father let his son be raised up believing in sins that weren't Jewish. Art's father stopped paying the Seventh Day Adventist nurses, and little Arty was moved in with distant relatives.

It was also lonely. Art was always afraid of what bad thing would happen next. He never knew which things he did and thought about were sins, and which things weren't sins, because he had been taught the sins of two religions and together, if all the Commandments are kept, every living breath a person takes is taken in sin. To make it worse, it says in the old Bible that, "the sins of the father shall be visited upon the sons." So all of Art's father's sins, sins

Art never knew about, fell on his shoulders. Why are the sins of fathers not visited upon their daughters? As far as I know, there is no religion in the world that visits a mother's sins on her children. Mothers and girls can sin without the Lord making it too tough on them, because the Lord is a loving old gentleman.

Art was one of those boys about whom people said, "He'll never amount to anything." He was a shirttail boy because nobody cared enough about him to get him to tuck his shirttails in. One day he did a very shirttail thing. He roller-skated all the way from the house he was staying in in Hollis, Long Island, which is twenty miles from New York, into New York, in the heavy traffic. He was ten years old. He spent the whole day walking around the Franklin Simon department store. He said hello to his flabbergasted sister, who worked there, and he bragged to anyone who would listen. His sister gave him carfare back home. When the people he was living with found out where he had been, they said, "Arty, you'll grow up to be a bum. You'll *never amount* to *anything!*"

They said Art was a *wild* kid, and the people who tried to keep him kvitched at him. Kvitch is a word that means nagging, whining, hurting complaints like, "You're a slob," or "You let some wee-wee splash on the toilet seat," or "I'm tired, you do it," or "It's too hot to bother making food," or "You just can't go," and "You're a little bum and you'll grow up to be a *big* bum." It was kvitch, kvitch, kvitch, kvitch.

Anyway, they kvitched so much at Art that they almost drove him insane. His brain was sick and tired of listening to all the kvitching, which after a while makes you feel as bad as a very bad stomachache, with a lot of going to the bathroom. Art tried not to listen, but it was a stomachache that never stopped.

There is only one way to work when you stay around kvitchers and have a stomachache that won't go away, and that's to hide yourself away in a back room of your brain, and try to forget how much it hurts. If you have to go to the bathroom six times an hour, you act as if it's only to wash your hands. After a while, people will think you are a very clean person. They don't know that you only wash your hands, and not your face. But that's how you have to do it if you walk around with a stomachache caused by too many kvitches.

Kvitchers are worse than cigarettes, whiskey, Mississippi gamblers, ladies who do bad things in Paris . . . and the only thing worse than kvitch is when kvitchers get together.

You may, someday, hear in common speech the word kvetch, which sounds like kvitch, but is not. The difference is that kvitch is poisonous, and comes from the fangs of kvitchers. A kvetch is like a ball of sticky brown dirt. If you swallow a kvetch you may want to throw up, but you rarely die from it.

But you shouldn't get serious in the middle of a sad story.

Art, you remember, was going insane with the kvitches, and he had to find some way to live among kvitchers, but not to swallow too many kvitches. He decided that the best way was to be different people at different times.

There was the Art who never had a mother, and nobody dependable ever around to love him, and who lived among the kvitches. And there was the Art Buchwald who went to school and could make even the teachers laugh.

Art would get up in front of the class and say:

"I'm Art Buchwald. I am going to present a play written and directed by Art Buchwald. All the actors are Art Buchwald."

And he would present a play. One play was about a girl in his class who looked down her nose at Art.

Art found out in school that he had a gift. His gift was being able to look at people, see what they are, and then imitate them so perfectly that people knew what Art saw was true. He was very good at doing the little girl who looked down her nose. He went on and did other people. He looked at all of his classmates and saw exactly what they were, and when he wrote a play in which he imitated them, practically everybody laughed because it was true and Art was funny.

"Even the teachers laughed," Art said to himself. Not a fake laugh. A real laugh.

After a while, Art knew that he could use his gift to make people laugh, and people who laugh at you usually don't hurt you. But beware of people who laugh *with* you.

Art thought to himself, and said:

"I'll never argue with somebody. I'll just smile and listen, but I'll never come out and fight 'em. But then, when they think I'm gone, I'll come back and *stab* 'em."

"You will?" I asked, for the record. But I believed him.

"Yeah," he said. "I'll never *kill* anybody. I'll just stab 'em to hurt 'em and get 'em back."

But both at school and at home, there were kvitches, like some people go home and find rats and cockroaches walking on their bed.

There was a great writer named Ernest Hemingway, who once wrote: "What is the best training for a good writer?" His answer was, "An unhappy childhood."

Art thought that he had an unhappy childhood and that meant that he was certain to be a good writer. He thought it was better than the window drapery business. He was going to go to France, drink wine, go out with beautiful girls, and do wonderful, exciting, adventurous things as a great writer in Paris.

Art's father decided to take back his three girls and Art from their foster homes and make them live with him. Art had seen his father only on Sundays and sometimes for longer during all those years, and now Art was strong and looked ready to go to work. Was Art going to be a writer, or was he going to be a bum?

Was he going to Paris? Or was he going to stay on Long Island? Was it adventure, or torture with an everlasting stomachache caused by the kvitches?

He decided to run away from his father's home.

Like any fifteen-year-old boy at the time would have done, he joined the United States Marines.

It was not easy joining the marines in 1942—if you were fifteen years old. You had to get the signature of your father, and Art's father was on Long Island and Art had run away as far, believe it or not, as Charlotte, North Carolina.

Art ran out of the Marine Corps office where they had demanded his father's or guardian's signature. He ran down the stairs and onto the sidewalk where he spotted, staggering down the street, an old, unshaven man who was holding an empty bottle of wine in one hand and holding onto a wall with the other.

"You need some wine?" Art asked the bum.

"Yeah," the old man croaked like a frog.

"First you gotta come with me," Art said.

"Okay, if you give me some money for wine."

"I got plenty of money," Art said.

He took the old man by the shoulder and pulled him down the street. Art had to find a notary public who would believe the old drunken bum was his father. Everybody in the neighborhood knew the drunk, and nobody had ever heard of him having a son. But Art had heard how you can fool people if you gave them money, so he decided to fool the notary public, who had to swear a legal oath that he knew, with his own eyes, that the old drunk truly was Art's father.

The notary public wasn't fooled at first.

He took one look at the old man and knew who he was. So Art gave the notary some money, and the notary agreed to be fooled, and to let Art steady the bum's hand while he signed Art's father's name to the letter.

True to his word, Art gave the old man money to buy wine. And the marines took Art.

That was the first good adventure that happened to Art Buchwald, who was on his way to Paris to become a great writer.

XLI

One of the only two loonies
I ever saw thought her mate
was a peacock. The other
thought his mate was a white swan.
Their first offspring brought
them down to earth, but she
was so unusual people could
hardly believe it.

Duc de la Roche de Balloon

One day Art said to me as he dealt out the gin rummy cards, "Barney, in the newspaper business, we all have deadlines . . . and my psychiatrist said, 'Deadlines are little climaxes.' So I figured that newspapermen like us want little climaxes all the time, like every day, or every other day, or three times a week, when you get older."

"Yeah?" I said.

He dealt some more cards. I could not keep my mind on the cards. He was telling such a good story all the time.

I heard him talk about how he committed suicide—almost.

He was home from Paris. People were telling him he could never compete with the "heavies" in Washington. The bad feelings were ganging up on him. People were boring. And he almost cracked.

When he felt he was going to jump out of the window of a building and watch himself hit the pavement, he asked to be admitted to a hospital with bars on the windows and nurses to watch open rooms all night, and only electric razors, and orderlies who know how to hold a brawny man down and tie him in a straitjacket.

He was checked in.

The worst part was at night. In the daytime Art felt . . . okay.

At night he looked down into the great dark and saw whatever he saw.

It lasted three weeks. Then it went away.

When it went away, Art made up his mind it would *never* come back. He bit his lips with determination.

By now I had forgotten that Art had picked up the nine of clubs. So I threw him an eight of clubs and he knocked on one. He always played a conservative game. He almost never ginned when he could knock.

Many years later, when I visited Art at the scene of his slaughters, he had the same office and the same old photographs, and the same lamp advertising a beer on the wall, and the same infuriated letters from readers framed on the walls of his little outer office, where a different but equally loyal and dedicated secretary was unavoidably off that day.

I asked Art about his suicide ideas. He said, "Well, Barney, I tell my friends about how it feels if they get really depressed. I tell them about my psychiatrist. I tell them to get a psychiatrist, too."

"Well," I said. "How tall a building were you thinking of jumping off?"

The crack winked.

"A one-story building," Art said.

"From the basement window, no doubt," I said.

"Yes," Art said.

He added one more bit of detail for good measure. He said, "Ya know somethin' else? I came back to the office and sat down at the typewriter like I do, and I couldn't write.

"Well, I got scared. So I tried again, but I couldn't write. So I started fiddling around in my desk, and I opened this drawer right here—" he opened the top right-hand drawer of his desk, "—right here where I keep them now, and I found this cigar."

He pulled a cigar out of the drawer, and waved it.

"So I put the cigar in my mouth and I turned back to the typewriter, and I could write."

XLII

A handin' man's learned too much about rope.

A Texas saying

It is eight thirty in the morning.

"Jean, get me a cup of coffee, would ya?" Dan calls. His voice on the telephone is groggy with sleep.

An inaudible voice in the background.

"Coffee!" he shouts. Then he says in a pleasing voice, "Go ahead, Barn."

"Are you sure I should get you before you get your coffee?"

"You bet, because I'd like to get finished."

"Okay, I can understand that. So would I."

"Well . . . oh . . . I've gotta travel today," Dan says. "I've got to go to Duke tonight."

"Duke? Whatcha doin' in Duke?" I ask.

"Yeah. Ah . . . um. It's a long story and you want to know . . . ah. [With reluctance] Sandy Vanocur is doing something down there—I gather what he's doing is making seminars and teaching something—and he asked me to, as a favor to him, go down and make a speech, and . . . [Sigh!] . . . I couldn't do it and had to cancel it, and I rescheduled it for today."

"Is Sander going to be there?"

"No. . . . Well, I don't know whether he's going to be there or not, actually. When I took it on I thought he was. But, it's been kind of *strange,* but I gather that what happened was that one of the side benefits to them taking him on was that, you know, he could *get* people to come down for him. So I don't *mind* doin' it, it's just that you don't like to take on ah. . . ." (And the words drain away into breathy inaudibility.)

"Who do you speak to?" I ask.

"I don't have any idea. I assume that it's, ah, you know, sort of an assembly kind of thing. It's at eight, but I've got to leave at two thirty or three . . . *But!* Let's get on with the project! What can I help you with?"

"All right. It's hard shuffling all this damned paper," I say.

I shuffled papers for what seems a long time, thirty-eight seconds, to allow Dan's head to start working. The silence is broken only by a grumbling sound I make that says I'm not able to find what I'm looking for. At the forty-five-second mark I say:

"How's Sander doing?"

"I don't know. I haven't seen him. His wife was *very* ill for a while."

"She's got it again," I say.

He gave no indication he knew "it" was cancer in the abdomen.

"You haven't seen him lately, you mean?" I ask.

"No," Dan says.

"Oh. I've talked to him recently 'cause I'm doing something about him, too. . . . She's in the hospital now and she's——"

He interrupts.

"Well, that's what I'd heard, she was in the hospital again so I haven't busted my dropped him a note."

There is no space or pause between the "my" and "dropped" in Dan's remark.

Dan's tongue moves so fast you must catch his turnabouts in mid-word if you want to know how he makes a twist of emphasis or flipflops completely away from an idea that does not seem to please.

"I saw you appeared in the paper again on Sunday," I say.

"Ahhh . . . a *cartoon* you mean?" Dan says. "Cartoon" is the first wide-awake word he says.

"Yeah, yeah," he continues. He coughs twice, clears his throat, and adds: "That's the one that only makes me a hero with my kid, you know. You know, television all the time. It doesn't mean anything to 'em——"

"I don't blame 'em," I say. "That's important—to be in the cartoons!" I am pleased for Dan.

Dan acts as if I am mocking cartoons. He doesn't know cartoons are the source of my inspiration in matters of reality and philosophy.

"Oh, yeah, you bet. . . ." he says, with a cautious lack of enthusiasm. Then, tentatively, he says, "That's a big thing. . . . I don't know him . . . Trudeau." Trudeau is the cartoonist of the comic strip "Doonesbury," where Dan appeared.

I laugh to think that it would be fun to appear in a cartoon—if I appeared as some kind of creature I wanted to be. I wondered if I'd ever have enough self-confidence to become a worm, or a bat, or a slug on a rock, or a skunk, or any of the crawly, nibbling, creepy,

gnawing, biting, stinging, decay-eating loathesome things that car-
toonists can make of a man with his imagination working low down
enough. Trudeau portrayed Dan as a miniature hero, and who can
ask for more than that from the pen of a cartoonist?

"He's pretty good," I say. "I enjoy him." I try to make it clear
I'm not baiting him.

"Oh, he's super!" Dan says with a little less caution.

"Just a second, I've got to let Buckeye in," I say. "I work out in
the office, and if I don't let Buckeye in, he's our dog, he raises
hell. . . .

Dan chuckles a dry ha-ha-ha. "Wakes up all the neighbors?" is
all he says.

"Go 'way, Buckeye. Go 'way. . . . *No* . . . he just stands up
on the door and keeps, and refuses to . . . refuses to go away.
Some days he smells like hell because he goes chasing the horses
and . . . chasing . . . running through the horse manure."

Dan quickly elevates the subject matter.

"I was very interested to see the other day, I've forgotten—I
think it was O'Neill—who said that he could not imagine. . . . No,
it wasn't O'Neill, it was ah, Yeats . . . said he could not——"

"Who was it?" I ask.

"Ahhh . . ." A self-annoyed sigh. "It was . . . maybe it was.
. . . Wel–l–l . . . it *was* Yeats . . . said, that *anyway,* the point
was that that he could not imagine living in a place where there
were not animals—which I'd never thought of before—as a kind of
'circle of environment.' "

"Who? . . . Yates who?"

"Ahhh . . . I forgot the guy's first name. . . . It was a writing
. . . ya know, the guy was talking about *life* . . . and the 'circle of
environment,' and the point was he was raised in a rural environment. And it's one of the things in the city, you go to New York
and you say, 'Jesus Christ, why do all these people have these
dogs?' Which never had occurred to me. What he said was that,
'For some people, as a matter of fact for many people, it's part of a
circle of your environment. It's necessary to have animals around.'
Ummm! I'm not sure he's even true . . . I can't remember the
guy's first name."

"I don't know," I say. "We lived in the city for a long time, up
on Capitol Hill, and Buckeye came to the door one night; two little
Black boys brought over a box and there were two little puppies in

it. . . . This was before Maggi and I had Kate. I took a look at them and picked one. I said, 'How much?' and they said, 'Three dollars apiece,' so we picked one and said we'll test him out for the night and see whether we want him or not. And once you bring a puppy into the house it's got to be a very unusual puppy not to worm his way into your affection. And I, I hate to admit—"

I think for a few seconds about the reasons why I bought Buckeye.

"—and he did, and we got Buckeye, and we *enjoyed* having an animal."

"You know," Dan says, "as matter of fact, that's a very interesting point. We had, when we lived around the corner from you, on Thirty-fourth? Was it?"

"Yeah . . . I lived on R and you lived on Thirty-fourth——"

"Thirty-fourth. Well, we moved to London. Well, we had a puppy that somebody had brought down on pretty much the same basis. . . . I can't remember how we got it, but it was something similar to that, somebody brought it by. Anyway, the point of it was, we had tried to give it away and tried to get somebody to take it, and the time came to *move* . . . a-a-and . . . it was *my* job to take that dog to the pound . . . because we——"

"Why was it *your* job?" I ask.

"Well, simply because . . . you know, it was time to *move*."

"Right," I say.

"And Jean wasn't going to take the job . . . and the kids do something . . . anyway, you know, I mumble mumble mumble. . . ." Into a hurting nothing.

He snaps back.

"Jean and I talked about it and there just was *no* alternative. We couldn't get anybody to take it and it was time to go, and we couldn't take it with us because as you know England has this law that——"

"Six months in quarantine," I say.

"Six months or somethin'. . . . Well, anyway! I got in the car to take 'im to the pound and it bothered my conscience so that *damned* dog, that. . . ."

Dan starts to talk with a big grin on all his words. He says:

"I took . . . I remember, I took a piece of Scotch tape and I Scotch-taped a . . . twenty dollar bill to his collar—and put him on a doorstep with a note. It said, 'I'm moving and I was told to take this dog to the pound, but I don't have the heart. If you've got the heart to take him in, he'll pay his own way for a while. Godspeed.' And I *drove* off.''

''Where'd you put him?'' I ask.

''On a doorstep on the *east* side of Wisconsin. You know?''

The east side of Wisconsin is the more established side of Georgetown.

''Uh-huh.''

''I just . . . I was in the car and I *could not* take that dog to the pound.''

''Do you know what happened to him?''

''I don't have any idea.''

''Would he stay on the doorstep?''

''No, he was in a box. I put him in a box.''

''Just in a regular box?''

''Yeah, in a cardboard box, which I was supposed to take him to the pound in . . . but I had this vision of him in the pound . . . nobody would claim him. . . . But it's all to your point that they do have a way of worming their way into . . . I don't have any idea of what happened to him.''

XLIII

Thank the candle that burns until dawn.

Transylvanian saying

I was too early and unbeautifully married to a girl who thought my role in life was to be a good and honest provider. I was a very good provider, although not honest, and she performed very reluctant services, which is a frequent man-woman combination. I resented it, and she, at first, was sorry, she said, about it. And then it got so the more I provided, the less she serviced, and after a long, long, long time of this, and two children who hitched on to that unhappy wagon, I got the message into my brain that I was being cheated, by an expert, and that if I didn't finally quit I'd be sliced three ways and served to the family as squab. She caught a lawyer she "secretaried" for who was paid $60,000 a year, which was a modest good living in Manhattan, in comparison to the $22,000, and all I could steal, that I was making at the *Times*. I know he was making $60,000 because she left his confidential tax statement hidden in a place in the apartment where I would be sure to find it. Money was the root of our problem, and in the end, right through her lawyer-friend's offer, while he was still married to someone else, to adopt the children, it was money.

The oldest boy never knew what to believe. He didn't know if his father loved him or not because he'd been taught by his mother that no man who isn't a good provider, and didn't serve his country in the army, is worthy of the name "Daddy."

He had been completely enthralled by the lawyer, down to the point where on one visit to see his Washington daddy, he made notes on the back of a three-by-five card containing a transcript that he had dreamed up took place in a courtroom, where "Mr. Collier" is being cross-examined about how much money in stocks and bonds are listed in the name of Taylor Collier. (Whose alias in real life was his baseball idol, Al Kaline.) Taylor thought his Washington daddy had never bought stocks in his name.

The other one, the one I never tried to please, but who was pleased just being close to me and putting his head on my arm, talked to me one day on the telephone from New York, a rare and wonderful thing when it happened. Adam had only one thing to say, and he tried very hard to say it without anyone else hearing. He was afraid Taylor was on the other line, and every time he heard a click he would say, "Taylor, hang up, I'm talking to daddy." And the click would click again, as if a distant extension had been quietly, detectively sneaked back on its cradle, or the button delicately pushed down.

Finally, he said it fast. "I don't care what they say, daddy, I love you."

I was reasonably hopeful then that Adam would survive, and know what love is, and be able to take love no matter how sometimes it hurt.

That's when I agreed to adoption, in my mind. I felt it hurt Taylor to be exposed to me, whom he couldn't depend on to love him with things provided. And Adam would love me anyway, if his mind was very strong with love, as it seemed to be.

It hurt to lose each of them; I am sorry for Taylor because he has doubts about me, and therefore, doubts about himself. I'm sure Adam misses me, if he's still alive. I was under an agreement that I would make no attempt to contact the children from the moment I agreed to adoption until adoption was final.

I obeyed the agreement scrupulously, and I have never entered their life to my knowledge since, except perhaps in their thoughts, happy or sad.

And one day I sat in a Washington courtroom, it was a warm spring day, and a Negro judge read the order, looked questioningly at me. He asked me my name.

I was sitting in the witness chair, on his left and below him, so that I had to look up to see his eyes.

I said, "Barnard Collier."

He said the court in New York demanded that I be asked nine questions in open court to be made part of the record of adoption according to New York law.

He saw I was clearly going to go through with it, so he proceeded. I can't recall all of the questions, but the first several were name, address, and so forth, and one of them, I think, was, "Are you of sound mind?" and I perjured myself, of course. The other one was, approximately, "Do you understand that this day constitutes your day in court on this matter of adoption, and that you'll have no other legal recourse?" And I said yes.

Then he made me repeat my relinquishment of both children, by name, and I was through.

I left court legally relieved of legal responsibility of two male children, and I thought, "I hope one day we can be good friends. I hope they don't grow up too damned moral to be my friends. I hope Taylor isn't a junky looking for love. I hope one day they turn up as free friends on my doorstep, not wanting anything. I hope I can be their friend."

I shook the lawyer's hand and walked to the car and drove home feeling lighter than I had in years and years and years.

My first family, the one I had learned so many lessons from, and had made dozens of mistakes with, was held together in the end by Beatriz, the Chilean cook I brought back with me from Buenos Aires. She had a peasant grandmother's love, which she gave to me, and she lavished on Adam. Adam would crawl into bed with Beatriz and cuddle next to her warm, solid, soft body, and he crawled in bed with her whenever he was frightened at night, which was any night he could get away with it, and Beatriz didn't have a cold or bad trouble with her liver.

Taylor suffered his fears inside his head, and almost all alone, and his feelings hurt him so badly that he invented one story after another, and became one fictional character after another, and he settled pretty hard on Al Kaline at my last sight of him.

There's more, but the point of all this is Jean Rather.

She is the size and shape of a small cheerleader, with a cheerleader's set, toothy smile that says, "Yeah, team, come on, let's win!" through wins and defeats and ties and moral victories and inglorious slaughters and what few championships there are, considering all the tremendous effort.

Under the glistening-eyed cheer, with the set smile and the soft-waved cheerleader's hair, and lightweight cheerleader body, she had an afraid something that attracted my protectiveness, and before I knew it the cheerleader had Dan and me, two of the most promising young men in Washington, wrapped around her little finger.

She was my first encounter with cheerleaders; I was never good in sports at school, so I was green in the cheerleader department.

Jean was, first and foremost, cheerful. Beverly was too scared of me to be cheerful. She was afraid I was some kind of sex maniac, whose lust was a mechanical necessity she would avoid as often as possible. Her first line of defense was almost always wearing underpants to bed. Her second line of defense was telling me that I must have a rotten tooth in my mouth. Her third was mentioning the checkbook. And then came the crying, and the trying, and the not enjoying, and the inevitable simulation, and my inevitable wanderings to a cheerleader, the wife of my rival, who was on his way toward making $200,000 a year, in my inflated vision, and when I took a crush on Jean, I took a heavy crush.

When Dan was away, I played "daddy" to the little Rather children, although they called me Uncle Barnard. I was hardly ever Barney Collier then. Always Barnard Law Collier or Barnard L. Collier, or Uncle Barnard.

I did the best I could to be a friend to Jean, and the best I could do was one memorable warm night, with a moon clear and white above the trees on Thirty-fourth Street, I walked outside her bedroom window, back and forth, at one o'clock in the morning, sadly, downheartedly, pacing like a forlorn lover walking back and forth beneath a balcony. That's going pretty far for cheerfulness, but I was cheer starved in Washington and Jean was a smile when even an unfree and not always genuine smile was better than imprisoned fright.

Jean spoke to me twice in her robe at the front door, and then Jean whispered out of the upstairs window, "Good night, Barnard."

My dreams of love drifted away in Washington's sultry, magnolia-scented air.

A lot of water passed under the bridge after that. Dan and Jean went to London and Rome and came back. I left for Argentina, and I didn't forget her cheerfulness. Jean sent me a note, with a stick-figure smile on it, that said, "I miss you." I called her in London. Then feelings flickered low and lower as the crush melted with distance. One night it went out.

Later.

"Where did you meet Jean?" I asked Dan.

"I met her in Houston. At a radio station where I worked. She came . . . her sister worked there. Jean's sister worked at the radio station, and Jean came there to fill in on a temporary basis——"

"How old was Jean?"

"I don't remember. I'd have to figure it out. She was about twenty."

"How old were you?"

"I was what . . . twenty . . . four? I believe that's right. Yeah. Anyway, she came as a fill-in. She was 'between jobs.' And her sister worked there and she came in and filled in. . . . Then she got on there, and she got a regular job there, and she worked there and I'd say about a year before we were married. Not a year. Nine months."

"What sort of personality did she have?"

"Well . . . *exactly* the same kind of personality she has now. . . . I suppose that's not precisely correct, is it? I suppose not exactly, but as I remember it it's exactly as it is now."

"Which is what?"

"Well, you know. . . . You'd be in a better position to judge that," he said.

"I don't know. I'm not. I really wouldn't be in a better position to judge it," I said.

"Well, I mean to *describe* it. Not to judge it, to describe it. It was very, *extremely* happy, a great deal of the time. And even when she wasn't happy, you know, the ability to not be down. A great smile . . . very persona . . ."

"Is that what it is? The ability not to be down?"

"Well, I don't know 'That's what it is.' I don't know what you mean by that. I think that's a very essential part of her personality. . . . A distinguishing mark of her personality. But she was —I'm groping for a word here—vibrant and bubbly. . . . I don't mean bubbly in a giggly way."

Dan paused to grope for another word.

"She was joyful, all the time, which . . . you know, keeping in mind this radio station was an old, very staid place, both physically and spiritually."

"What do you mean?" I laughed.

"Well, it was located in the Rice Hotel. Which is a huge old hotel, as a matter of fact, the best hotel in town in those days. But it was still a rather dark, dreary decor, and the radio station was literally a floor of the hotel. So physically it was a dreary place and it was also a very old station. It'd been in business since the early thirties I think."

"How many watts?"

"Fifty thousand."

"What were its call letters?"

"KTRH. So, also, it was owned by the Jones interests, Jessie Jones interests, and it had a lot of older people there, which is very unusual for a radio station . . . the broadcasting business being a business of high mobility, chicken-today, feathers-tomorrow business in general. It's rare to see anybody over . . . forty . . . particularly in the lower echelons of radio. That's changed a little now. The business has stabilized, some, and settled down a little. Not much, but a little. But at this station there were an unusually high number—'' he chose his words very, very carefully ''—of 'older' people . . . because the Jones company prided itself, they were very big on giving people security at the end, but not a great deal of pay out front. It was a matter of . . . company philosophy.''

"Um-hmm.''

"And as a result of that they kept employees for a long time. But anyway, she stood out all the more in contrast because of that.''

"How about you? You weren't very old yourself.''

"No. I can't remember, but I don't have much doubt I was the youngest person on the staff.''

"What was your job then?''

"I was in the news department. I came there as a reporter and writer and broadcaster, but heavier on the front two. I mean in those days I was not . . . a good broadcaster.''

"What was your problem?''

"For one thing, I'd been out of it awhile. Remember, I'd gone away to the service, and although I hadn't stayed long, I was a little out of practice. Secondly, all of my experience was at small stations up to then, and I'd worked at KSAM in Huntsville, but that's the rough equivalent of jumping from about class D baseball to double A. It was just an awfully big jump in terms of broadcasting. . . . On the other hand they didn't have anybody who was . . . accustomed to reporting. I'll tell you, Barney, it was at the stage when this station was a basic 'rip-and-read' station. That is where they hired big voices to come in and simply cut the news wire and read it. And the competitive pressure for what you and I know as street reporting—covering city hall and county courthouse and the police beat—had built on then to a point where they had to enlarge the news operation and get into the street reporting business. And that's the reason they hired me. So, at that stage, although I did some broadcasting, most of my day was taken up with writing and reporting. My job basically was to come in, *be* there, at five o'clock in the morning, and what broadcasting I did I did mostly during the farm broadcast period.''

"Which is——''

"Five to about seven. At these big, fifty-kilowatt stations in a rural area——"

"Yeah, I know. Michigan was WJR."

"Yeah. Right. You read the grain reports and cotton futures——"

"That's the nicest part of the morning," I said truthfully.

Dan laughed halfway sincerely, two ha-has.

"Well, also because . . . I'd get momentum for the day and write a newscast somebody else would read at seven o'clock——"

"What time did you get up in the morning?"

"Three thirty."

"That was fun."

"It'd probably kill me now. I don't know. I did that for a long time. I did that for six years."

"From what years to what years?"

"I did that from fifty-four 'til I got the job at the television station which was in sixty."

"What happened to you during that time?"

"A lot of things happened. Among other things, I got married."

XLIV

I think, therefore
I am never sure.

Dr. Watson

"It seems to me you've made your mark through diligence," I said to Dan.

"I'd agree with that," he said.

"And a good-looking face."

"I wouldn't argue with that either. I don't say that immodestly, but dealing with reality. The diligence, however, was done frequently at the sacrifice of my family."

"Are you reasonably well-to-do now?"

"Reasonably. That's always a comparative. Certainly by the standards of what I had for goals originally."

"What kind of goals did you have?"

"When I started out it was a goal to make ten thousand dollars a year. That hasn't been that long ago."

"When was it?"

"I can remember interviewing for a job in 1956 and the guy asked me what my goal was in terms of material things, and I told him I wanted to make ten thousand a year, and own both a car and boat. By boat I meant an outboard motor boat. So by those standards, yes."

"What do you own now?"

"Not a hell of a lot. I own a house."

"In Washington?"

"Yeah. An automobile."

"What kind of car?"

"A Fiat. Own a reasonable amount of stocks, which is in a trust, which is one of the bows you make to people who are always clamoring to politicians to make known their financial dealings. I assumed that one of these days someone is going to say that to me, so I do it that way. I don't own a great deal."

"Why do you put it in trust?"

"Basically in a blind trust so that no one can say, 'Rather ran a story favorable to the oil business because he owns X number of shares of Exxon.' If I pulled in everything I've got, including insurance, which I have considerable of——"

"Who so much insurance?"

"Frankly, because when I was young I didn't know much about it and I fell for the line, you know a fella has to have a good deal of insurance to protect his family in case something happened to him. . . . But *net* worth, I'd be amazed if I have altogether more than one hundred and fifty thousand. That includes the house, which is most of it, as it is with most people."

"What about your salary? Is it pretty good by network standards?"

"Yes, it is. But people have a really distorted view of what network salaries are," Dan said.

I said, "Most people judge network salaries by the Sander Vanocur hassle, where he was getting eighty thousand or eighty-five thousand dollars from public television, to 'match' the kind of salary he was making at NBC, and he wasn't *that* important a correspondent at NBC."

"That's right," Dan said. "It's based on that, and the fact that Cronkite and Huntley-Brinkley salaries are usually said to be three hundred thousand or two hundred and fifty thousand—and above. I don't think most people are making anywhere *near* that. I know I'm not. I don't intend to tell you what I make, but you can pretty much figure it out."

"Give me a hint so I'll have some idea."

"Well, I make fifteen dollars an hour. I figured that out," Dan chuckled.

"Twenty-four hours a day?" I asked.

Dan laughed.

"No, but the range at CBS, which is the best paying of the networks, I could be wrong about that but I don't think so . . . I don't think we've got anybody except Walter who makes above a hundred thousand and if we do I'm mad as hell about it, I'll tell you that."

"Not Roger? Not anybody?"

"I would think Roger would come as close as anybody, but as I say, I just don't think anybody in the news division does."

"How about more than fifty?"

"In the news division, I think we've got, let me count, half dozen or fewer who do better than fifty."

"You're one of them?"

"Well, I'm not going to answer that, but I'll let you draw your own conclusions."

"How about better than seventy-five?"

"We might have two, and I'm *not* one of them."

"It is a distorted picture," I said.

"I know it is," Dan said.

"Does that mean total annual salary? Does that include additions like bonuses and speeches and extras like that?" I asked.

"That's the total for me. Gross. Now, if one chose to do so, if you really pushed it on the lecture circuit, you could make one hundred. But what that means is that you have to spend at least twelve nights away from home."

"What do you mean by 'one hundred'?"

"One hundred thousand. Let's assume a person is at seventy-five, which I've said to you I'm not. But if you were at seventy-five and make twelve speeches at two thousand dollars apiece, which is another twenty-four, you could do it. But with agent fees you'd probably have to make fifteen. But you earn every penny of that."

"Do you make many speeches?"

"Not any more. I did it at one time when I first came back from Vietnam. I got intrigued; it always looks easy. Somebody says, 'I'll give you two thousand dollars to make a speech.' Boy, I'll be there. I booked an awful lot of speeches. Maybe twenty speeches. Not all at two thousand dollars apiece I should hasten to add. At that time, the rate for me was much lower. It was eight or nine hundred dollars. But I did a lot of them in sixty-seven. But I found at the end of the year I was one beat dog, A, and, B, that not a great deal of the money had stuck."

"Where'd it go?" I asked.

"I wish I knew. If you find the answer call me collect. You know, some of it went to expenses; you had to get there and get back. Some of it went as agency fees. Then you get smarter as you go along and ask for your price, plus expenses . . . but you don't do that in the beginning because you're afraid they won't pay you. And then taxes take a hell of a lot."

"So you're not a millionaire?"

"No, and I never expect to be," Dan said.

"Do you spend much personally?"

"Very little. We're not a money-oriented family. Anybody who knows me reasonably well would say, 'I don't see any sign of expensive taste or that he does a hell of a lot.' Jean and I both say, 'We should cut loose and *do* something. Do a little more.' Probably the only two extravagances I can think of, which are not extravagances, we go home reasonably often, to Texas, which is an expensive proposition for us. I feel strongly about it: one, to keep my own sense of place, sense of roots, and more important to give the kids a sense of belonging.''

''Why do you feel that way?'' I asked.

''About wanting that, you mean? I suppose it has been an asset to me to have that sense of place.''

''What is the place? Where do you call home?''

''About a hundred and seventy-five or eighty miles between Houston and Smithville. Jean's home, you know, is in Winchester, which is near Smithville, and my home is in the Heights of Houston. Those are the two places that are home. But I know that if I find myself feeling that I don't know exactly who I am or what I am, then if I look back and think about, 'Awright, think about home and who you know, what their standards are, what their values are,' then I can get myself on the track. It isn't to say that my standards and values are still the same as theirs, 'cause they are not. But it does get my mind and my heart pointed in the right direction.''

''Where is your heart?''

''In terms of place that's where it is. It's never been anywhere else.''

''On that road? In the Heights, in Winchester, where?'' I asked.

''Yeah. In the Heights and in Winchester. My heart is on the fourteen hundred block of Prince Street.''

''That house still exists?''

''Yes.''

''What sort of place is Smithfield?'' I asked.

''It's incredibly green for one thing. Hot. Heat everywhere. Quiet. Not Walden Pond quiet. People are around. But certainly by Washington or anything around here, it's quiet. There's a water. The river is very wide there.''

''What grows there?''

''Trees grow there. Pecan trees.''

''Any crops?''

''Cotton, cattle.''

''That's Jean's father's house?'' I asked.

''Right.''

''When you go back in your mind and you feel those values and feelings of back then, what are they?'' I asked.

"That covers a lot of territory. . . . Part of it, I suppose is being honest with yourself, and I'm not all that good at that."

"What do you mean?"

"Facing things as they are. Not having pretentions, or saying, 'Wait a minute, don't be something you aren't.' "

"Have you ever tried to be something you aren't?" I asked.

"Oh, hell, yes. I've been the route. I mean everybody tries to be something they aren't. I've tried to be a smart son of a bitch for one thing."

"When was that?"

"Sometimes I think almost constantly."

"What do you mean, 'smart'?"

"You know, intelligent. I know something. I've been to school. I read the *New York Review of Books* and by God I'm pretty intelligent. Well, I can almost hear somebody at home say, *'Bullshit!* Nobody in this neighborhood has ever been intelligent.' It's just a way of kind of bringing yourself . . . down. I remember when my brother got into Rice, which is a big thing in our family, and it was no small accomplishment. Rice has a reputation justified as being the best school in that part of the country. Very small school and everybody who goes there has to have a straight-A average. But he got a football scholarship. Somebody, I don't know . . . it wasn't my father . . . *I* may have said it . . . Don is getting in Rice, and it wasn't said to hurt, it was just said matter-of-factly. 'Wouldn't you know that the first fella from our neighborhood to get into Rice would get in with his back and not with his head!' "

We laughed.

"That's a *truth,*" Dan said. "You could read the great books and you could read the *New York Review of Books* all you want, but you get where you are by getting up early and getting after it. Those are vast oversimplifications, but those are the sort of things I think about. And I also think, 'What would somebody at home think of that?' I say to myself, 'I want to do right and the problem is to recognize what's right.' So I begin by saying, 'What would people at home think about it?' I mean, 'Would they think that's the right thing to do?' Now I *don't* say, if the answer is, 'They wouldn't like that,' that doesn't mean don't do it. But that's a starting place."

"Have you assumed yourself to be things that you are not, aside from smart?" I asked.

"I don't want to come off too strongly on that. I have a reasonable amount of intelligence. But it's easy, particularly in this business, where people say, 'Gee, how did you get so brilliant in such a short time?' ''

"Does anybody ever say that?" I asked.

"Yeah."

"Will Bill Small say that to you?"

"No, Bill Small will not say that to me. He generally says, 'How could you remain so stupid for so long?' . . . No, you often make a speech at some college, and that's one of the things I do reasonably well, and then you handle questions for twenty-five minutes, do that reasonably well, and you come away and a history professor will say, *'God,* it's nice to have somebody as brilliant as you.' Well, you can inhale that stuff. And sometimes I do."

"What's it smell like?"

"It's very heady, very heady. It smells very good. That's the temptation of it. You start believing that, you are in trouble. So it's not a matter of saying, 'Look, I'm just a stupid country boy.' I mean, that isn't true. But it's very nice when you have what a sense of place gives you. You say, 'Well, wait a minute. Just think about who you are and what you are and keep yourself on even keel.' ''

"So that's who you want to think about first before you make your decision."

"Right. I frequently catch myself thinking, 'Boy, I have to work hard. Boy, I *really* have to work hard.' Then I find myself literally thinking, 'Shit, man, you don't know what hard work is. I mean, think about Mr. Hoyt or Mr. Sykes who live on our street. They *really* work hard.' So then I can say to myself, 'What the hell are you feeling sorry for yourself for working hard? This is duck soup.' ''

"Does a guy like Bill Small appreciate that?"

"I think so. I don't mean to question that. Yes. He does."

"How?"

"Let's say he wants me to do something on Sunday. Let's say he wants me to come in on Sunday and do 'Face the Nation.' Okay. It's no big deal, it's a morning shot. And I'll say, 'Bill, I've really been working hard lately,' and Bill'll look at me and say, 'Come on, man, what do you mean hard work?' Small's the best man I ever worked for . . . With Small, if you make a mistake he'll defend you fiercely to anyone above you, or on the outside. And he'll take the hide off you himself."

"What does that mean?"

"He'll punish you if he thinks you made a mistake," Dan said.

"How does a man like that punish you?"

"Well . . . a lot of different ways. He can take a broadcast away from you. He has the power to do that. He can change your assignment. He could make you work extra days."

"Has he ever punished you?"

"Yeah. Particularly when I first came here."

"How were you punished then?"

"In all of those ways."

"For what offenses?"

"Sometimes sloppiness on the story. He can't *stand* that; he just can't abide that. You know, something would turn out to be wrong, and you'd say, 'I'm sorry, I thought that was right . . .' Well, you know. He'd say: 'You thought what? What the hell you mean "think"? *We don't think around here. We gotta know!*' And then he says, 'Well, who did you call? Could you have made *three* more telephone calls and perhaps one of those three . . .' and that sort of thing. Also Small was very good about saying, 'Listen, if you want to become a dashing, swinging Playboy of the Western World, that's your business. But. . . .' "

"Is that what you wanted to be?"

"No. That was his lecture."

"Have you learned anything about yourself?" I asked.

"Yeah. . . . What I've learned . . . I don't know about this year, but the last year and a half or two. I always felt there was a limitlessness of my own energy, and my capacity for work was unknown. And I've reached the outer extremities of that."

"Have you?"

"I think so. I could be wrong about that, but for the first time, I can ever recall, I found myself thinking it, this year. Saying, 'Well, gee, I never thought I'd see the day, but I think I'm at or near absolutely full throttle.' "

"When are you most relaxed?" I asked.

"When I'm with the children."

"Is that just going out with the children?"

"No, in almost any circumstances. If they're home, and we're home, and do something very easy. Play."

"Why do the children relax you so much?"

"I don't know the answer to that, Barney. I really don't know.

Part of it is that I don't fear them at all. They don't demand a great deal.''

"Are you as relaxed with Jean?"

"I'm relaxed with her, but probably not as much as with the children, no. First of all she is adult. Full-grown adult. It's more difficult to relax around adults——''

"Why?"

"I think it would be the same thing with her. It's much easier for her to relax around the children. As a family unit, if I'm ever relaxed, that's when I'm relaxed.''

"You know, Dan," I said. "I'm always looking for a champion. You know dramatists are always looking for champions. They're fun to find. I want to know if you're ever going to be a champion and not a runner-up?''

"That's a very good point," Dan said. "I think in those terms myself.''

"Do you?" I asked.

"I do, and more recently, I don't mean in just the last few weeks or months, I mean the last several years, there's an awful lot goes into that. First of all is recognizing what a real champion is. We all think we know what a champion is, but then you see one and you say, 'I thought that was what a champion is, but it's not really.' ''

"What is a champion to you?" I asked.

"Well, again, Barn, I don't know. I do know my perception of a champion has changed.''

"What did you think it was to start?''

"This goes back a long way. Simply that you got on *top*. Then you get down to, 'What is on top?' ''

"Are you on top?" I asked.

"No.''

"So you're not a champion yet.''

"No. I'd agree with that.''

"When will you be on top?''

"If I had the ability of being utterly honest with myself—which I do not have. And I know very few people—I'm not sure I know anybody—but very few people I'd even think could be honest with themselves. That would be one mark. Another would be to be at peace with yourself. That is with a minimum of conflicts. I know one *always* has to have conflicts with himself. It's one thing to be truthful with yourself. It's another thing to be at peace with the truth. They're two separate things there. Other marks of a champion would be——''

"Do you think you have a chance?" I asked.

"I don't know. I think I've got a shot," Dan said, as if he meant it.

"You do have a shot?" I asked to be sure.

"Yes," he said.

"Are we being honest?" I asked.

"I'm being as honest as I possibly can. What's changed is knowing how *few* people really have a shot," Dan said.

"How will you know when it happens? Will your career suddenly blossom? Will you go off in the mountains and become a hermit?" I asked.

Dan laughed a happy laugh at that last thought.

"I don't know. I do think this is one of the differences, between a champion and not being a champion. This, parenthetically, is Jean's great strength. She's known this for God knows how long. And I didn't. That is that a career doesn't pull you into being a champion."

"Did you ever think it did?" I asked.

"Most of the time. For a very long time I did. . . . So the mark of a champion is *not* the career, and the person pulls the career and the career doesn't pull the person. Do you follow me?" Dan asked.

"I follow you," I said, "but I don't know if you believe it. It sounds like something Jean might say, but it doesn't sound like something that you believe in your heart."

"I'll buy that," Dan said. "And you see, that's where we are . . . in *this* discussion. For a long, long time, ten, twelve years, I said to myself, 'Bullshit, that simply is not true, I don't believe that.' Now, I'm at the point of reexamining and have been for several years, saying, 'You know, that *may* be true.' Now, that's where I am. Saying, 'That may be true.' So if you ask do I really believe that, I'd have to say in all candor, 'Not yet.' ''

XLV

And so ended the Age of Reason;
And yet, the sun rose the next morning.

The Gorgon Sisters

So I went to see Bill Small, who managed the most important television news stars in Washington, as CBS's bureau chief. He had managed the stars and the bureau for ten years, a very long time to stay in one place in the television business. I believed Bill was staying in Washington instead of going to New York because he was so good. I believed Washington was the center of the world and Manhattan was an island. He, I expected, would be *one* man who saw reality without distortion and could look himself in the eye every morning and see *exactly* what was standing in front of his mirror.

I was in Bill Small's office one day when Chuck Chester, a gray-haired man who was technical manager of the bureau, walked in.

Bill said: "This is Chuck Chester—he's my conscience, since I don't have one."

"You never said that before," Chuck said.

"Which part?" Bill asked. I had to go back in my mind to figure out what Bill meant.

Bill had a forehead that overhung his eyes as suspensefully as a ledge about ready to fall. His blue eyes crouched in the dark shadows below, and prayed that the ledge wouldn't fall.

He was a little bit concerned about his memory. He didn't remember now quite exactly as much as he used to. He depended now on experience, and wariness, and worry.

I asked Bill, "How much can you remember?"

"Ninety . . . maybe . . . eighty-five percent."

He pointed to his forehead. "Not like when I was young."

"How old are you?"

"Forty-seven."

Bill had the morning's *Washington Post* spread open on his desk. It was open to the page with the bridge column.

"You play bridge?" I asked.

"Yeah," Bill said, looking up from the page.

"Master's points?"

"No–o–o. . . . Social bridge."

"Good?"

"Not that good, but I play pretty good."

"With who?"

"With my wife, Gish."

"Anybody else?"

"No."

"Do you read the column every day?"

"Yes . . . there's a good story I can tell you about that. . . . I read about it years and years ago . . . in your old paper. The *Herald Tribune.*"

"There were a lot of good stories in the *Trib,*" I said.

"Well, this one was by some dame—I can't remember her name . . . but she was good—had it in her column.

"It's about a bridge bum who was on a ship playing high-stakes bridge. He was down to the last hand before he was wiped out . . . and he saw it was lost. So he took a black queen—I think the queen of clubs—and slipped it under a caviar sandwich . . . and *ate* it. . . . The bad hand was a misdeal, because when they got to the end, they found the queen of clubs was missing."

I watched as Bill munched in his dreams on a cardboard queen of clubs, smeared with pearly black caviar.

I asked, "Did you ever use the black queen convention?"

"In life? No. . . ." he said.

Over a Chinese lunch one afternoon, Bill had described his father as "a shitty baker." Now, in his office, I reminded him of the phrase.

"You must have misunderstood," Bill said.

"I didn't," I said. "You said he was a 'shitty baker' and those were your own harsh words—and I couldn't figure out why you were so harsh on him."

"If I said that then I didn't mean he baked shitty bread—which he did. I meant that he didn't run the bakery right. He didn't *manage* right."

"Did he own the bakery?"

"Yes."

"Did he make the dough?"

"He didn't get in there with his hands and make it, no."

Bill didn't think of dough as money. He thought of dough as bread.

My eyes saw a fat man with dough on his hands and flour on his shoes standing with his shoulders pinched and his arms crossed in front of a stainless steel vault with a protective, defiant, miserly scowl on his Bill Small face.

I wanted to know about his only bridge partner.

Bill tried to tell me about Gish in two riddles.

I forget the details of the second riddle, but I recall the word "shit" in the last line. I recall the first.

In the days when television was first experimenting with mobile cameras, a TV station in Texas advertised that it was going to be "first" with the news, because now it had the capability to send a live TV camera in a truck to the live news scene.

One day, as the truck was cruising around town, its crew heard on the police radio band of a robbery a few blocks away. The TV team arrived on the scene minutes after the armed robber had run away, and before the police arrived. The excited television reporter called to tell the manager of his good fortune. The station manager, overcome with enthusiasm about the "scoop," ordered the remote sound and picture to be put live on the air.

The reporter poked the microphone at the liquor store salesman's face, and asked what the robber looked like. The liquor store man said it was a "Nigra," and gave the rest of the man's description.

The reporter pushed his luck and asked the man another question.

"Did he say anything?" the reporter asked.

"Yeah," the liquor man said. "He said, 'Gimme all your money!' "

"And what did you say?" the reporter said.

"I didn't say nuthin'. I gave the black motherfucker all the money and he ran like hell."

That was the end of the riddle.

I said:

"So what the hell does that have to do with Gish?"

Bill shot me an exasperated look about my dense head, and told me the second riddle, about the other bad word.

Even after the second riddle, I still didn't understand about Gish. So I told Bill one morning a few weeks later, that I was going to call Gish and talk to her. I'd worked and worked on the riddles and couldn't solve them.

"You won't do that," Bill said.

"Why not?" I asked.

"Because I said *not*," Bill said.

"Do you speak for you or do you speak for Gish?"

"I speak for me . . . and I speak for Gish, in this case."

"Well, I can't imagine what those stories you told me are saying about Gish, so I'm going to ask her. I don't think you really think you speak for her. Do you *really?*"

"What the hell!" Bill said. "Bar-*ney*. . . . Do you really believe in that women's lib shit?"

"No," I said, "but I do believe in people having their own minds . . . women, too."

He made a sighing noise. I explained:

"You know, I heard you one day talk to someone on the phone about a miniature TV camera, and you apparently weren't anxious to go to a lot of trouble to produce one for somebody. So you said, 'Look, if they'll be satisfied with a picture of the gear and not the gear, send them a picture.' I don't want a picture of Gish," I said.

I looked up William J. Small in the telephone book, and called it. Gish answered.

Gish had a strong voice. At first, she used it to weakly parrot Bill's line about me not writing about her—only about him.

I thought, "She sounds dutiful enough. What do those two stories mean?"

I fought to keep her on the line. Finally she said, "I'll tell you just one thing, one incident, that tells about Bill and me. Bill got a big promotion at work and Fred Friendly—the big shot then in New York—called up at the house to congratulate Bill about it, and he and Bill chitchatted for a while, and then he told Bill he wanted to talk to *me*. Bill hesitated a little bit. I didn't want to talk to him, and then Friendly insisted, and Bill handed me the phone.

" 'Hello, Gish,' Friendly said. I said, 'Hello.' He said, 'I want you to know you'll have another man in the house now that Bill's got this big, new job.' He was trying to get me to say, 'Oh, wonderful.' But I said, 'Mr. Friendly, I *have* a man in my house, and as far as I'm concerned, CBS is the *enemy* in this house.' "

So I'd solved the riddle. Bill was trying to tell me that Gish calls every black queen a spade.

XLVI

Hate is the will to survive
all alone.

G. G. Gander

As a manager, Bill said, "Talent is easy. You bring them in, talk to them quietly, lay down the law if you have to, and if there's a *real* problem, and they get on their high horse . . . I take 'em to lunch. A lunch always does it."

"Always?" I asked.

"Almost always," Bill said.

"When doesn't it?"

"When I've failed."

"What do you mean?"

"I mean nobody I cared about has left CBS to go somewhere else since I took over the bureau ten years ago."

"Nobody? *No* failures?"

"Well. . . . Well, there was Harry Reasoner, who went to ABC, but he dealt with New York. . . . He was New York's, even here in the bureau . . . he was a friend of mine, and I liked him, but I don't take responsibility for that."

"Nobody else?"

"No."

"Can you keep it up?"

"I hope so," he said.

On the technical side, Chuck Chester acted as Bill's "right-hand man."

Technicians are hard to deal with. You can't take an electrician's union man to lunch at Sans Souci like talent. If you do, the electricians start sniffing when your lunch guest gets back to the union hall and somebody passes wind loudly, and says, "Hummm!! . . . I smell a sweetheart!"

You have to be a far deadlier negotiator with electricians than with news talent, mostly because the technician works to a closer tolerance than talent, and must do his job *just* right, within the limits of a machine far less elastic than even Dan Rather's imagination. It is cruel, hard, exacting body and head work, for which only money—not love, or free lunches—can pay.

Talent learns to laugh off its mistakes and still play the game until it gets better, or quits trying. But a light man never laughs when the lights go out, a cameraman won't chuckle, "Heh, heh, heh," when he doesn't get anything acceptable on his film, and a soundman who lets the tape run out on a tape recorder at all the most crucial moments is not worth the powder to blow him to hell, and he never laughs, because he does not exist, except in nightmares and fairy tales of reality.

Technicians who work for proud and competent managers don't let the tape run out at all the crucial moments . . . and technicians forgive Bill's arrogance about technical matters, which he knows about only from asking. When a technician inevitably loses his or her concentration, and misses the right situation, Bill will tell him or her so in a low voice, and take the blame for poor management himself. Technicians respect him for it. Bill works for their respect; while he has a positive talent for managing "stars," he has to stretch his mind to deal with people who call a sweetheart a sweetheart in very poetic terms.

But once, in one of his less modest moments, which technicians would kindly ignore, Bill said, "I went to the University of Chicago. It was the last place my mind was *really* stretched."

Each weekday morning at about nine o'clock the bureau chiefs of CBS, NBC, and ABC held a conference telephone call on the day's news. Bill took unto himself more authority than either of the other two bureau chiefs wanted, because of his knowledge of what Bill calls "the technical problems." He explained that one day, when the bureau chiefs were discussing the problem of setting up cameras and communications at a news scene, a technical problem arose that the NBC bureau chief sluffed off, and told Bill to sluff off.

Bill said angrily, "He told me that bureau chiefs weren't supposed to know about things like that. He told me to leave decisions like that to technicians who knew what they were doing. I told the guy, 'I know about technical things, and I make decisions like that.' " And he added for me, "With Chuck Chester, my technical man."

Then Bill said, "You know, I used to remember instantly what the back doors of every major hotel in Washington looked like, because we had to know how far we could stretch our cables for press conferences. I can still see them in my head."

"Can you see the back door of the Sheraton-Carlton?" I asked.

"No, but I have a picture in my head of the exact lengths and dimensions of dozens of rooms, hallways, loading docks, alleys, and side corridors of the Statler Hilton, across the street. . . . But it's not as much fun to know all that now.''

"Why not?" I asked.

"Because I've been doing it so long a boredom sets in.''

Bill went on with his day while I sat and kept my eyes and ears open.

Bill asked his secretary to place a call to the CBS booth at the White House. He quietly read the rundown on the evening plans for radio and television coverage.

"Leslie Stahl, keep your hands to yourself, will do radio with Pierpoint," he said.

His daughter called to ask his advice about buying a suitcase for college. Bill talked to her quietly, with an occasional sigh. A little later the dark, curly-headed girl entered his office hesitantly, went back out, and then returned with a brown, businesslike, Lark model suitcase. She handed it to him to see if he approved. He did.

"It's just like the ones we have at home," he explained later. "She shopped all morning, and bought one just like the ones we have at home.''

I can't recall the girl's name, but Bill called her "The Brain Surgeon.''

"Why?" I asked.

Bill grinned.

"Because she will jump in and do *anything,* even if she doesn't know a thing about what she's doing.''

He answered a call from Dick Salant, the president of CBS News.

Bill picked up his telephone and said, "Hi.'' He sat hunched over his desk, the telephone close to his mouth and ear, and he spoke in a confidential voice so low that if your mind was interrupted by a single thought, other than listening to what Bill was saying, you couldn't have heard what he said.

The conversation was about Bill's predictions of the news that day in Washington. Salant probed to be the first in New York to know what would go on in Washington. The main question seemed to be, "Would President Nixon announce his resignation that night?" The day was excited and tense in the political world of Washington, but in Bill's office, it was as calm as a treacherous deep pool.

Bill lowered his volume to a very delicate place where he was still perfectly audible on the other side of the line. He expressed himself in an extremely well-modulated voice. His voice had been trained as a television newscaster for years in Louisville, Kentucky, and in Chicago.

"It's a ten-million-to-one shot on 'abdiction,' " Bill said.

There was now good-natured conversation about Eric Sevareid. Bill called him "The Big Fella."

"He's sleeping now," Bill said. "In a little while, I'll go in and massage his back."

The call concluded on a talk-to-you-later note.

It was shortly after five o'clock. Bill toured the newsroom. Wherever he walked, people got on their toes. I saw Eric Sevareid's image appear on a color television monitor. He was in the studio with a camera focused on him. He was preparing to record his evening commentary.

Eric was seated in front of a backdrop the color of a cloudless blue sky. He was expertly lighted not to emphasize his wrinkles. His face was a pancake tan. His distinguished hair was white. His eyes were dark, sad, and anxious as they looked at his script. He silently mouthed some of the words, and wrung his hands as if to warm them.

"It's quiet," Bill said, when he returned to his office.

For dinner, Bill put together a party of himself, Eric Sevareid, Roger Mudd, Don Richardson, who was his sidekick and "shotgun," Dan Rather, an ungainly girl, and me.

The party went to a dark Italian restaurant two blocks away. The ungainly girl said she would "powder up" and be late.

Two square tables were pulled together to make room for seven. That left one chair inevitably on the crack between the tables.

The single seats at the ends of the now rectangular table were quickly occupied by Dan and Roger Mudd. On the side with only two chairs sat Bill, next to Don. Bill was sitting closest to Roger. Eric sat across from Bill, and I sat across from Don. The empty chair between Eric and me sat on the crack.

I sensed something wrong. Dan sensed something wrong. Eric knew something was wrong. So did Bill. So did Don.

"The girl can't sit in that seat," Don said.

"Why not?" I asked.

"She just can't," Don said.

The shotgun had started things moving.

"It's a little close in here," Eric said. He scraped the legs of his chair on the stone floor.

They were after Dan first.

He perked up to listen.

"I don't like this chair," Eric said. "Floor's a little uneven. Hurts my back."

Don offered to trade places.

"No, no," Eric said. He scraped again.

Dan listened.

"I can't sit here," Eric complained.

Roger Mudd took his face out of the menu. He took a quick look, made a funny face, grunted to himself, put his face back in the menu, and reached for his cold martini.

Eric creaked his back bones. Dan could stand it no longer.

"Eric, why don't you take my seat?" Dan offered, from his end of the table.

"All right," Eric accepted.

There was a scuffling and scratching of chairs, and Eric loomed up to take the seat at Dan's end of the table. Dan held the chair for Eric.

Now the game was played against me. The goal was to move me out of my seat so that Dan would not have to sit beneath Roger Mudd any more than Eric had. And Dan could not sit on the crack.

I sat stubbornly.

Dan stood. Eric sat triumphant. Dan looked down at me, and I pretended to ignore him.

Roger looked up with a silly smile on his face, as if he didn't know what was going on in the world. He knew enough to know there was no peace, but he didn't understand why there was so much war. War interfered with him.

The girl arrived. I said, "Dan sit down here, and let the girl sit over there."

I moved over one chair.

"I don't mind sitting with my plate on the crack," I announced. "I'm just here to look."

Dan sat down gratefully at Eric's left elbow.

There *are* a few openings in the lunatic fringe.

Thomas Jackson

Bill told me that if I wanted to do a book about the press, I should concentrate on "stars people know" . . . and not someone behind the scenes. Then, he said, "Have you talked to other people about me? I suppose you have. And they've told you what a cocksucker I am."

So I asked, "Do they really say that about you?"

He hesitated. "Sure they do. . . . Don't they?"

I said, "Is that what you think they think of you? It's so graphic, and I've come across people who don't like you, and they say it's because you're hard on them or smart-alecky sometimes, but nobody's ever described you to me that way, although I haven't asked too many people about you. . . . Are you?" I asked.

He said, "*Shit,* Barney, what kind of a question is that?"

I said, " 'Shit.' That's another one of your favorite words. How come?"

He grinned and seemed ready to play a little bit, and then he backed away. "Whaddaya mean?" he asked, as if I'd made a hearing mistake.

I said, " 'Shit' is one of your favorite words, and I wondered why you used it so often, and why you used it in association with your father and Gish?"

He clamped his lips and shook his head.

He said, "Ask me something else. What else do you want to know?"

A few weeks later, I called him to check some facts. He said, "I've been thinking about it, and you've asked questions about my family, and other off-base questions. What the hell are you doing, Barney?"

"A book," I said.

Bill insisted that we "talk" about how I was "using" the conversations we had had.

I said, "I can't tell you because I'm not sure yet myself." He pressed me again to talk. I told him the one thing that I found impressive about him. "You don't say, 'appointment,' you say 'commitment,' and you're one of the few people I've met in the

Washington news business who commits himself and knows what a commitment means."

Bill made an agreeable sound. Still, he insisted that we meet for lunch, downtown, near his office. He said, "I have to stay close, in case of trouble. We can discuss the matter."

I said, "I think you're a nice guy. I don't want to tell you any more than that. You shouldn't ask any more than that. I don't want you to buy my lunch for nothing."

Bill said, "You make too big a thing out of lunch."

I said, "You told me how you use lunches to get your business with 'talent' taken care of."

He said, "Shit, let's have lunch at one o'clock and we'll talk it over." To pacify him, I agreed. But I said, "It won't make you feel any better." He said, "One o'clock."

Now I have been accused of making too big a thing out of lunch. But Bill insisted that I make myself presentable and drive twenty miles into the city to eat lunch with him. I don't want anyone to think that I'm being fictional, or even bending the truth, when I say the following. I arrived at the CBS building. I took the elevator directly to the newsroom floor to Bill's office without stopping to announce my arrival through the switchboard operator in the lobby. An elderly secretary said, "*Oh!* Mr. Collier. Ah. You didn't get the message? Downstairs with the operators?"

"What message?"

"Mr. Small left a message that he was going to lunch."

"Yes, with me," I said.

"No. With somebody else."

"You mean with somebody else, and for me to join him?"

"No. I mean with somebody else. He said for you to grab a bite around here. He'll pay for it in the cafeteria or something. And he'll be back by one thirty."

I laughed. I had gained wisdom.

A young, Black secretary also laughed. She was pleased to see I wasn't angry or upset. She was sassy, and she smiled what we used to call a "shit-eating grin," and said, "I'm sure he'll be back at exactly one thirty, and he'll have an explanation."

I said, "Excuses." The sassy girl said, "Yeah, they call 'em explanations around here."

Bill's explanation was that a CBS corporate vice-president, who outranked him, had, some time between the time I left home and arrived in Washington . . . about thirty minutes, asked Bill to join him for lunch.

I said, "How come you didn't tell him you already *had* a lunch?"

Bill said, "I did. I said, 'Can I bring him along?' But he wasn't keen about it, so I said, 'Well, the guy'—meaning you—'would probably be bored anyway.' So I left you a note downstairs with the switchboard."

In the next few days, an announcement was made that Bill was going to New York to take over almost all network news operations there, and he left Washington the next morning.

XLVIII

My dollies would not play with me.
They simply stared their
Silly stares.
It made me wild to pull
Their hair.
I kissed them very
Quietly
And walked outdoors
And kicked a tree.

From A Golden Book of Children's Verses

"And *here* . . . is Eric Sevareid."
  He tries so hard to be serious that it nearly cracks his makeup.
  He is at his best in tragedy.
  He is a consummate actor.
  He told me one afternoon about his fear of impending death. How his money is running out. But how his life is running out first.
  He looked at me tragically, and said slowly, in a voice of doom, "Two of my best friends . . . have died of shotgun blasts."
  Eric looked beautiful. His voice was beautiful. His hair was combed back and silvery white. His face was composed in a death-like mask with rouge for highlighting. He spoke in a voice barely above a funeral parlor whisper. He looked deep into mourning, his eyes almost tearing, but there was, under it all, hidden down some-where in his toes . . . a secret laugh. It came out as a tiny star you could see in his eye when I asked him who killed himself with a shotgun, and why.
  He waited a decent length of time before he delivered the news. He looked me in the eye, and his eyes were brimming with unshed tears.
  "Ernest Hemingway and Phil Graham," he said, and one long-fingered hand brushed with delicate agony across his right profile.
  "They were two men I respected most in my life," he said softly.
  "I didn't know Phil used a shotgun," I said.
  "Yes. He might have blown his head off."
  "Hemingway blew his head off," I said.

"I know."

"I wonder why they blow their heads off?" I asked.

"They were in deep depressions," Eric said. He leaned forward confidentially. "Phil was a manic-depressive," he said, in a hushed voice.

I said, "Eric, my father tried to commit suicide."

"He did?" Eric said. His voice turned bored.

"Yes," I said.

Eric's body drooped down in his seat and he turned his head away to listen with the back of his right ear.

"Tried to drink carbolic acid," I said.

That captured his attention. He turned back.

"Twice!" I said.

"Twice?" he said. He made a gargle in his throat. Can you imagine what a couple of swallows of red carbolic acid would do to the vocal cords of Eric Sevareid?

And what with Walter Cronkite already losing his voice, maybe to a dreadful vocal cord disease.

"Went up in the closet in my bedroom where all his old chemicals were stored. My mother caught him both times before he put the bottle to his lips. He was looking for punishment."

Eric rubbed his hands in front of him as if he were cold as ice and his shoulder bones ached and his feet were freezing, and he put a tortured look on his face, and he said: "Barney, I'd prefer a shotgun."

Now, in a less commonly seen role, I saw Eric playing a cowboy in from the plains of North Dakota.

He sat in a window seat, with the raw sunlight on his face, his arms leaning on the table in friendly, plainsman, face-to-face fashion, and he told me a Lyndon Johnson story in an accent so precisely Lyndon Johnson's that I forgot Eric was Eric and he turned for several moments into Lyndon, with the drawl so wonderful and lifelike that I put my chin in my hands and listened like a child.

It was a story about how President Johnson used to reward his Secretary of Defense . . . by patting him like a good dog, and how Lyndon would watch as his Secretary of Defense hung back after a Cabinet meeting, fooling with his briefcase, until Lyndon noticed him and patted him. Eric made Lyndon live.

Eric was completely in another world when he did Lyndon. He

saw the President in his head. Whenever he spoke the name "Lyndon," his eyes got a clever, almost femininely playful mood in them. He sprawled in his chair, and started talking from a position pushed far back, with his chin down in his chest and the Johnson drawl kind of sneakily coming out his mouth, as if he could turn the Texas act off any second and be an Easterner, if he ever absolutely needed to.

And when Eric finished Lyndon's story, he sat back and looked at his audience to see if they were still hypnotized.

I was swaying back and forth, listening to every word, and when he stopped, I was still waiting for the next one.

He gave a small, satisfied smile as the spotlight of the sun dimmed behind a fortuitous cloud, and it was in my heart to clap my hands, but I resisted in the crowded restaurant.

Then, I watched as Eric melted into the role of Eric the Poet.

Eric made a steeple with his elbows on the table and twined his fingers in front of his nose.

"I think you're a poet, Eric," I said.

"You do?" His eyes got a tiny starry light in them, and his body squirmed a little bit with pleasure in his seat.

"Yes. An electronic poet," I said.

"You do?"

"Yes. You write poetry in whatever time it takes to put together two minutes or so on the air."

"About four hundred to eight hundred words. Mostly four hundred," Eric said.

"That's wonderful. A really *rigid* form. Just like the Elizabethans. Only you have to do it for television and it's not really written down."

"*I write my own,*" Eric said. He looked offended at the notion that someone else wrote the poetry Eric performed.

And then at his office, he played a role women love.

I saw Eric in his office at the CBS bureau. It's the biggest office in the news department.

Eric's door was closed and his private secretary said Eric was writing. She made a face that meant he was too busy to be disturbed.

"I'll come back," I said.

The second time she said, "He's still working."

The third time she looked up at me with a pleading look on her face and said, "Look, he's sleeping. Do you think it's *really* important enough to wake him up?"

"Absolutely not," I said.

The fourth time Eric was awake and elegantly arranged behind his desk. His long fingers gracefully lit a cigarette. He sat with his chair turned about one-third to the right, so that his left profile showed. It's the same one you always see on television.

A warm, practiced smile crossed his mouth and his eyes were overburdened with sorrow, but brave.

"How are you?" he asked.

"Fine," I said. "How are you?"

"Feeling a little better."

"You weren't well?" I asked.

"Oh, you didn't know? Oh, yes, last weekend."

"Too bad."

"It's getting better."

"How's Cristina?" I asked.

"Well. Very well."

"She is the bubbliest little girl we've seen. She was great fun and we enjoyed her."

His face drooped down.

"Kate enjoyed playing with her, too," I said.

Eric's face drooped so badly I thought he was in pain.

"It's very hard," he said. "Very hard."

"What's hard?" I asked.

"The blow to Cristina. . . . Her mother . . . going away."

Love to her was freedom;
Love to him was chains.

de Balloon

At home Eric is daddy. To Cristina.

His little girl doesn't call him Eric or Dad. He's daddy, little d, because no man she can twist so easily around her forefinger truly has the Big Daddy feeling. She is a little bit condescending to her daddy, as if he didn't quite understand what was going on in the world, no matter how famous he is on television.

She seldom talks about her mother, or looks very sad that her mother is in Italy, or seems in the least deprived of food and clothing and mother love. She is fat-full of daddy love, as much as she wants almost any time she wants it, and she'll climb all over Eric and flirt with him and kiss and hug and maul him, and listen to his stories lovingly, and fall asleep in his arms, and she'll be too scared at night to sleep alone, so she will sleep in her daddy's room until her fears of what Eric calls "her mother leaving" are gone away.

When Eric, along with his good friend Scotty Reston, had helped me piece the story all together, it came out, more or less, that his first wife had grown mentally unwell, and after treatments of various kinds for what seemed, after menopause, an unstable personality, she became what Scotty Reston called "unmanageable." Eric and his first wife were divorced; they had two almost-grown men children. His first wife, whom Eric refers to as "a beautiful woman," and whom Scotty refers to as, "A *huge*, a *big* woman, very strong and hard to handle," lived after the divorce in a "cabin" near Warrenton, Virginia, owned by Eric, until she died. Scotty said she would check her own "high" and "low" periods and when she was feeling high she would come into town, get new medicine, and retreat back to the mountains.

"I was a little upset with him for deserting her," Scotty said.

Meanwhile, Eric, when he was about fifty-one, discovered in Italy, a dark-haired, dark-eyed, Cuban-Spanish woman, whose mother was once a prima donna at La Scala, and married her. They produced Cristina when "mumble"—as Eric sounds, instead of referring to his wife's name—was twenty years younger than he. They lived together eight years before they were separated.

"Mumble" moved to the seacoast of Italy, with her younger friends.

Cristina turned into the theatrical image of Eric and "mumble." Cristina is a double dose of drama. She has mischief in her eyes, and when she and her daddy are together, she aims it at needling him.

So one day, Cristina says, "I love math more than my daddy," and another day she musses up his hair when his picture is being taken. Not just once, but three times. The best he will do is say, with a big frown on his face, "Stop it, Cristina, I'm asking you."

And then he holds her hand.

At the end of his performance with Cristina, Eric nods, knowing that she has outstarred him. He knows it, yet he puts up with it, as any man presenting a lively new act must, even if he's a big ham himself.

Later, I asked again, about "mumble."

Eric was grave.

"You must *not* . . . this is *not* for. . . . Christina. . . . She *must* not be hurt. The woman—her mother—has a problem. We were in Italy to see her this summer. It is . . . ."

The burden of responsibility for still another "sick" wife settled on Eric's head.

He sighed, manfully, tragically . . . but down in the toes of his handsomely moccasined, narrow, graceful feet, there was a laugh.

L

Life is a fatal thrill.

Shag Common

Washington reporters learn to live a roller coaster. There is hardly a chance for them to catch their breath before the moods of the morning telephone calls run them up, the calls in the afternoon plunge them down, and the unreturned calls leave them hanging in anxious suspense. To a Washington reporter, the telephone is more addictive than tobacco, more important than a lover, and more respected than a husband or wife. A Washington reporter knows where the nearest telephone is at *all* times. The saying is, "What the hell good is the story if it's not on the editor's desk?" So a reporter either carries dimes for pay phones or dashes into innocent people's homes or offices calling, "Can I use your phone? Can I use your phone? Gotta call the desk!"

He leaves a trail of many thank yous, and seldom any dimes.

A telephone stampede is Washington's bullfight.

In the Senate Office Building, there are only two or three public telephones at the end of certain corridors on each floor. When a big story about a senator breaks, a herd of reporters enter a senator's office and completely overwhelm the staff of young people. The young people walk around in a daze. Certain reporters ask to use the office telephone line—on a "friendly basis." The rest, when the press conference is over, stampede to the public phones.

The ones who are slow-witted or clumsy lose the race. They fret and pop in and out of innocent offices calling, "Can I use your phone? Can I use your phone? Gotta call the desk!"

A few reporters somehow developed a sense of moral indignation about begging for telephones, and they stand like suffering saints outside the telephone booths, a dime clutched in their fist until it is hot and wet, their mouth dry as old smoke, their stomach churning green bile, their bladder and bowels aching to be emptied. A telephone call is far more demanding than the calls of nature.

There are newly important people who look down their noses at the telephone stampede, the reporter swarms, the scurriers, the loud noises they make, the rude, poking, probing, stinging, venemous questions they ask, and the peering eyes and prying ears of cameras and microphones bristling like porcupine quills all pointing in the same direction.

They say, "The press isn't deadly. It's too funny looking, too clumsy, and disorganized, too common and ugly to be deadly."

They say, "The press can wound you, but it can't kill you. Nobody in the Washington Press Corps is deadly."

True, if you were backed up against the wall with your hands down in defeat, there isn't an individual member of the Washington Press Corps who would put you out of your misery by yanking a blade across your throat and letting you bleed to death in a graceful hurry.

But, when the press, the collected beast with all its eyes and ears and fangs and bristling quills, waddles and scurries down the street heading for your house, plan, unless you are a fool, to protect yourself and your family. In the long run, the beast will be as deadly as a kvitch.

The press takes your words and ideas and image and passes them through the mechanisms of a series of human and mechanical minds, and every mechanism bends a little, twists a little, chops off a little, adds a little, mixes up a little, and dims down a little. Your body and your personality are sucked up by the lenses and shrunk down to the size of an insect walking across a picture tube. If you fancy yourself great, the press automatically edits you down to size. Only if you know you are a fool to expose yourself to the press, can the press not hurt you. But few people are strong enough to know their own foolishness. Instead, they strut about in full pomp and glory in front of the press and the press picks them up, smushes them down to bite size and swallows them whole, and it hardly bothers to burp over its little meal of your great and wise person.

If you are newly important and your mirror looks back at you in the morning and says, "You, master [or mistress, as the case may be] are the fairest and the brightest and the *coolest* of them all!" then you have a lot to worry about when the press comes waddling and scurrying down the street after you.

On the other hand, if you have very few shames to hide and understand what a fool you are for facing the beast in the first place, and you know for what you are facing it, then the press scrubs you raw with its rough tongues and puts a few itchy claw marks into your fool's flesh. It won't often eat you. But it's a lot of things if you take it seriously, including a cannibal.

LI

When a lucky roll comes along, bet your head off, if you've got the guts.

Mlle. de Balloon

Maxine is Washington's telephone queen.

Maxine is the daughter of a Kentucky mining-town lawyer named M, for Millard, F, for Fillmore, Hall . . . and his initials tell it all. That's how he ran for office, as "M. F. Hall," and maybe Maxine never knew what kind of a feller her daddy was, but the miners did.

The eastern part of Kentucky, where Maxine grew up, is so tough that people walk through the forest and tell you, "See that rock here. That's where ol' good Harry Bessie caught it clean in the head with a twenty-gauge shotgun from behind that rock 'cross the road. Wait'n for him . . . *all night long* 'til he come by drunk and wasn't lookin' 'round careful, and *Flammm!* his head's found next mornin' all over the trees and people say, 'Harry never could hold his likker; only half a jug an' he loses sight who his enemies is.' " That's pretty tough country, and Maxine grew up there and saw her daddy go to work in the morning at the courthouse strapped into a bullet-proof vest, because miners and mine owners sometimes didn't see eye-to-eye, and as a lawyer, her daddy sometimes had clients whose enemies didn't draw the fine line between a man and his mouth-piece.

Maxine came out of it a scrapper, a biter, a scratcher, and a digger. When Maxine digs in, she says, "Aaacharrgh!" and thrusts with wrist and shoulder behind it. When she aims, she aims at the vital organs, and you don't have to worry that the enemy is going to be a pitty-pat wounded in the pride; Maxine gets them in their passion, if she can.

Maxine's strength is the telephone. She taught herself on the newspaper she worked on for a while in Tennessee, and as a reporter in Washington, how to make the telephone an extension of her mind. It is not an easy business to master. Let me explain in detective story terms.

You want to find a man named Ronald Lodico, who lived twenty years ago in Nyack, New York, fathered a boy child who never saw him after he was five, and is looking desperately for him. That's all you know. Your problem is to find the missing father for his son by using the telephone. Or to determine, beyond doubt, that the father is unreachable because he's dead. The deadline is twenty-four hours.

That sounds like a very difficult problem, and it is. But if the father is alive, and you make it worth her while, let's say a $10,000 sable coat if she does it, Maxine will find the father or his fate on the telephone. If there were such a contest between Maxine and any other reporter now working in the world, I'd give you ten dollars for every one you bet that Maxine wins. The window closes in two minutes. All the suckers bet in the last two minutes.

First, Maxine thinks of the telephone first. She learned long ago that legwork and reporting are not married to each other. With a knowledge of the world's telephone systems, and especially the American one, she can put her mind extension into the most remote and unlikely corners of the earth, without leaving her telephone seat.

Second, Maxine has a first-rate telephone voice, and a first-class telephone ear. Both are exceedingly important for a telephone queen.

Her voice is high, and high frequency carries a lot of information in a brief time. You can talk to Maxine for three minutes, and have been messaged thirty times, about one message every six seconds, which is astonishingly fast for a normal human voice. That's because Maxine and her mind are capable of a rather difficult skill: sending a tentacle of her mind down the telephone lines and into the speaking party's head.

When the speaking party speaks, Maxine can listen to all the significant and telling nuances of voice and inflection, hear the tone, and see through the other party's eyes things such as the color of the handkerchief in the party's back pocket. That's not an exaggeration. The ear of a telephone champion is alert to sighs and breath catches and changes of thought pattern. A champion's ear is especially alert for signs of cooperativeness, which is to be exploited, or restlessness, which signals lack of complete communication with the other party.

Maxine knows how to convince men in police departments almost anywhere in the United States, perhaps in the world, to help her hunt down a fact or a person. She knows detective talk and the detective mind, and she knows how men in police departments can be charmed, flattered, and made to feel proud of themselves for helping her to dig up a piece of information.

A telephone champion learns to use the power of the press in hundreds of clever ways; the power comes mostly because unsung people, no matter where in the world, like to think of their names in print or of their cooperation having helped to make a newspaper story. The press still provides a tiny slice of immortality for people beyond their birth, marriage, and death notices. No telephone champion can ever forget the power of promised immortality.

One day I asked:

"Maxine, are you the fastest in town on the telephone?"

For the record, I quote:

"I can beat anybody," Maxine said.

I believed her, of course, as my odds earlier prove.

When she is on the telephone, Maxine concentrates completely. Her eyes, which are a blue green like the salt of copper and sulphuric acid, are starey. Her pupils, in any light or darkness, barely quiver open or closed a notch. Her skin is unbaked bisquit dough, and her mouth is a red-hot cinnamon candy. The only dent in her face is a small scar on her right forehead, a souvenir of a fall into a coal bucket when she was two years old. A small bump on her right cheek looks like a permanent tear. She is small in size.

Now consider her training.

It is almost perfect for an investigator, which is what telephone champs receive their crown for. She says, proudly, "I am a lawyer's daughter. I knew my way around the courthouse with my daddy when I was a little girl. I know how to look up things in courthouses, and I know who to go to to find out vital records, and I know what the clerks in these offices are like, and how to get them to go after something for me. I know how to talk to people so they'll get in their cars and drive five miles down the road to find if somebody who doesn't have a telephone is at home, and bring them in in the car to the telephone where I can talk to them. Give me a telephone, and I'll get what I want." Which is a mouthful.

"Have you ever come across anyone as good as you?" I asked.

"No," she said. "I'm looking for somebody good to help me. I've tested a lot of 'em, and most of them don't know what they're doing."

"Men or women?" I asked.

"Mostly men. Only *one* has really seemed to have a talent, and I'm testing him right now. If he can find the person I'm looking for, who has some Watergate information I want, then I'll hire him. He's had almost a week and he hasn't done it yet, but if he does it in a few days more, I'll grab him because he's better than most anybody I've seen."

"If you put *your* mind to it, Maxine, how long would it take you?"

She answered seriously, as I had expected.

"If I had unlimited resources, I could do it, or anything else like it, I mean finding out something or locating something, within twenty-four hours."

"What do you mean," I asked, "about unlimited resources?"

"I mean, I could telephone anywhere in the world as many times as I had to, as often as I needed to, without anyone questioning it," she said.

"How would you rate people out in the other parts of the paper or other people you've seen work? Like Bob Woodward and Carl Bernstein, for example?"

Maxine said, "I respect Woodward and Bernstein's work. And I know a lot of it was accomplished by telephone."

LII

To one who thinks, life is a comedy; to one who feels, it is a tragedy.

H. Walpole

The first time I saw Bob Woodward's face was in the *Post* newsroom, walking down an aisle. It was a boy's face, a well-mannered, nicely taught, midwestern American face, not too dark and not truly fair, unpocked and unblemished except wind-reddened and rosy-cheeked, with a longish round nose and eyes a swimming-hole brown that pulled back from a hard look and grew timid and then, as soon as the regret about being afraid reached Bob's sophisticated brain, the eyes turned and stood their ground. But fear always came first, followed by bravery, and then a certain shy sweetness, like high school boys get in their eyes, when, with their precocious wit and wisdom, they have managed to talk the panties off Miss Potato, the young English drama teacher.

Then I saw Berstein, Carl, and I was astonished by him. He was something let out of a cage, and he was not a boy. Whatever he was was full-grown and dark as a silhouette against a jungle sky. His hair was black with strands of gray, and it fell to his shoulders with matted pointy separations like half a dozen tails. His face was pitted, it seemed all over, a complexion that had suffered humiliation. His forehead seemed an inch high because his hairline appeared exaggeratedly low, and his black eyebrows ran together like two colliding locomotives at the bridge of his nose. Neither his nose nor mouth seemed terribly important, just existent in his face. His eyes are deep brown and they are unstable, unmanageable, not entirely tamed eyes, and, unlike Bob, Carl's eyes say that he has done things that a moralist would truly be ashamed to dream of.

Carl and Bob were brought together like most couples, by accident. Bob was no longer living with a wife and neither was Carl. It happened one day that Harry Rosenfeld needed a good local reporter to handle the story of a burglary at the headquarters of the Democratic National Committee at the Watergate office building. Harry, who found Bob a hard worker and an excellent pupil, gave him the story, which meant to Harry that he was going to get a careful, well-checked, logically put-together, well-researched job, and that any matters of credibility would be reasonably easy to sustain in an argument.

Bob was the son of a Republican judge. He was a Yale man. He was not a radical thinker. He dressed like a young businessman, typed on his typewriter without loosening his necktie, didn't raise his voice too loudly in a disagreement, had just the right streak of brooding unsureness in him, so that his cockiness would never get out of control, and enough collegiate charm to handle himself among civilized people.

Carl was not among Harry's favorites. Harry doesn't even like to talk about Carl, and the way Carl looks, and his personal habits do not meet Harry's standards of good taste. Harry sees Carl as the weak link in the chain of credibility from the news sources through the team of Woodward and Bernstein, to Harry as metropolitan editor, to Ben Bradlee, when he's at the office, and finally through Mrs. Graham, if the decision is critical enough, and into the torpedo tubes of the *Post*. But Carl possessed, according to both Harry and Bob, the ability to . . . "write." Both Harry and Bob used the word "write" in different ways.

To Harry, "write" means to simply get the words down on paper in a mechanical way, like concrete mixers mix concrete. This result from the writer, in Harry's eyes, then goes to the editor to mold, shape, rework, tighten, expand, and exercise artistic editorial craftsmanship, until he has sculptured the most perfect missile possible from the concrete information at hand.

Nevertheless, writers are required in Harry's world as hard laborers are needed on construction jobs, and Carl Bernstein was "loaned" to Harry's use by the editor in charge of reporting Virginia news. Carl was assigned to writing what newspapers call background material. This is the part of the story that contains information available in the newspaper clip files or elsewhere. For a better than mediocre writer it is almost always elsewhere.

After a while, as a story grows and grows, as the Watergate story did, there is no longer "hard" news available every day, and if a story is to be kept alive, it must be kept alive by fancy footwork, new twists on old themes, extreme close-ups of detail, but never once losing track of the main theme, which in the case of Woodward and Bernstein, as Harry continually reminded, was the chain of evidence leading to the White House.

Pretty soon, the writer and the reporter who have the most ambition and talent bubble to the top. They spot each other, and they know they are going to be more successful together than ever they are apart. Trust comes almost naturally out of such relationships with the writer always being a little more trustful of the reporter than the reporter is of the writer.

Bob explained how he and Carl think together. He did it by drawing a diagram with his finger on the tabletop in the *Post* cafeteria.

He said, "I'm very good on getting the facts straight and my mind works in a logical, step-by-step way, like links. But Carl doesn't think like that. He thinks like this. . . ."

Bob drew with his forefinger a main island of thought that represented what was known about the story factually, down pat and most of it printable. Then he drew little circular islands offshore.

He said, "What I'll do, is build a chain of facts, one by one from the main island of facts. At the same time, Carl's mind, in a kind of Voltairean sense, has jumped to one of the islands, that nobody is even sure exists, and he starts building up facts, and somehow—"

He drew a line from the shore of the big island and one from the shore of the small one.

"—they meet . . . and we've put it together," Bob said.

He talked with a tone of gladness and wonder when he explained the seascape of the Woodward-Bernstein mind, and there was no doubt at all that he appreciated Carl's talents and wanted to keep him for a writer.

"So Carl really writes good?" I said, to get it on the record.

"Well," Bob said.

The schoolboy in him popped out all over. He was making me aware that I had used incorrect grammar, but I could hardly believe that he was so teachery as to correct me a second time. So I waited for a minute of chatting to go by and said, "He really writes good then, doesn't he?" And Bob said right back, like Miss Potato used to do, "He writes *well*, not he writes *good*."

I grinned at him and said, "Thank you, I don't write too good myself."

Then I asked him about his social life.

His former wife, he'd told me, was a very "smart" girl he had known since he was a boy, and who was smarter than he was at college, and is smarter still. She lives in California and was teaching a class on the politics of women's liberation at a college. He spoke of her very carefully and gave the impression that if there was any fault in the breakup of their marriage, it was his, and he was sorry for it. There was a feeling in the air that he doubted his own mental ability in the realms of free thinking.

So I asked him, "What is intelligence?"

"What kind of question is that?" he said, as if I were asking him something I ought to have discovered in the *How and Why* books when I was eight.

"What is your definition of intelligence?" I saw I had to explain my question. So I said, "Andre Malraux in *Man's Fate* has his characters define intelligence. The answers are of interest to me for the book."

The references to a classic work appeared to have convinced him, and he said, "Intelligence is the ability to make independent judgment."

I asked him to explain further.

"Well, if I'm in a room and ten people are in it and nine of them say yes, I won't be afraid to say, 'I don't think so.' "

"Can you be the one who says, 'I think such-and-such,' and stand up against the nine who don't?"

"Of course," he said.

I told him, "Why I asked was that the philosopher in *Man's Fate* said that a man's definition of intelligence reflects his desire, and now I know your true desire."

He smiled rather freely, for him, and said, "Yes, it is."

Bob remembered a tense, somehow bland but tainted childhood in a small town where his mother and father divorced when he was twelve and soon remarried others. Bob lived with his father and a woman he didn't like, "who made a mess of my little brother," Bob said, and was a wicked stepmother in the brooding Gothic way women can be in midwestern American towns. His mother married a jollier man than his stern-feeling father, and less a judge than a friend.

I started then to call him *You and Bob.*

It passed him by the first time I said it and the second time he took note of it and decided to himself he wouldn't let it pass the third time, and when the third time I said "You and Bob" when I referred to him, he said, as if I were an extremely forgetful child, "I'm Bob, the *other* one's Carl."

But that wasn't how I saw him split. I saw him split between the

You of his father and the Bob of his mother, so You and Bob was one in the same and Carl was a third party.

Bob once tried to write a novel. He described it as "brooding and dark," about four characters who merge into a single character at the end of the book. It was too brooding to sell and it broke his confidence as a fiction writer while he was still in college.

Then he went into the navy and he remembers it as a time of despising the military discipline, but never thinking seriously of deserting to Canada or breaking out of his four-year commitment. He was a ship communications officer, a post that takes commands and repeats them, and he described his method of getting along as being "friendly and understanding to everybody," of trying to figure them out but not make any enemies, of playing himself a little bit aloof and apart, but not unreachable, and of spending almost every free moment reading hundreds of books of important literature (no mention of trash) so as to cultivate his scholastic mind during the boredom of a sailor's life at sea. The only fun was four hours a day when Bob stood on the bridge and watched the sea and the compass, and in case of emergency, he could give commands to the engine room. Those four hours, in the darkness of night mostly, in the salt air, Bob had his only chance to exercise any independent judgment that could result in a command, and when I asked him what his job as an officer was, he said: "Steering the ship."

Bob was standing on the bridge in command, in a dream that fairly burst out of his head. The other dream was Bob the swordsman.

Before he and Carl became partners, Bob was a very dependable one-woman-at-a-time man, and the soapy smell of sinlessness was on him, with cheating not necessarily a sin.

Now, proud of his accomplishment, Bob said, "I've got three girl friends."

He saw me smile. He said, "Yeah, I owe it to Carl."

I asked, "What are they like?"

Bob described them by profession . . . a teacher and two reporters. And then I said, "What are they like as women?" And he described their hair, one of them having long hair that he said reminded him of a "hippie." He was uncomfortable describing women, almost to the point of blushing.

"Don't you want to ask their names?" Bob asked, as if I'd forgotten something essential.

"Not if you don't want to mention them," I said.

"That's a difference between you and me," Bob said. "I'd have asked."

And he made a scratching movement on the table with his thumb and forefinger as if he were taking down notes.

My own question would have been, "Why not nine or ten girls?" but I knew Bob would think I was being silly.

Carl did not want me looking at him. For all the untamedness, he is still shy. The limelight is bad for his complexion, and he knows it. Alone, without the boyish charm of Bob, Carl would be unacceptable in the eyes of men like Harry, who believes in logic, virtue, revenge, and judgment. Carl is a name to be growled as it is; before he teamed up with Bob his name was growled with even less respect.

LIII

The search for meaning is best accomplished with the nose.

P. T. S. Bocaccio

Clark Mollenhoff is angry with himself. When Clark is angry, the noise that comes out is loud trumpeting. He stands up at a televised press conference and yells "Mr. President" so thunderously and repeatedly, only Sara McLendon in her prime as a women's army sergeant might have gotten more attention.

Clark is angry because he was conned, he was flimflammed, he was hoodwinked, he was buttered up and jerked around in the White House after he left his newspaper job to become what was called, "The President's Ombudsman." It was a hick's dream. Clark dreamed it, and when he woke up he found he'd also . . . *lived* it. Clark Mollenhoff, the winner of a Pulitzer Prize for investigative reporting of labor racketeering on a national scale in 1958, found himself naked in a strange city, sick and humiliated.

The way the White House fights is to strip people of their pride. It's a psychological warfare game, and everybody plays it on one level or another, and the White House plays it on a national level. The pride of the press in Washington is that it understands how power works and that it's close to the men who have the most power. There's an attracting electricity about Washington's gigantic power that takes hold of a man like Clark Mollenhoff. He wants some of it for himself. He wants the smell of power inside the White House. Power is a clean, good smell to him. He wants to touch power's trappings; the seat in the presidential helicopter that once he rubbed his pants against, the wonderful old room in the Executive Office Building that once was his noble headquarters; the corridor trivia of Washington politics discussed in knowing, winking, highly confidential tones by men who are sure they know what's going on. It makes Clark's head swim to think about knowing all those secrets, to be on the inside looking out instead of the outside looking in.

So, the White House invited Clark in, and gave him the title of Special Assistant to the President, a political appointment with a salary of $28,000 a year. They convinced Clark, with arms over his shoulder and winks, and some shared little secrets that he wasn't *ever* to reveal, that Clark Mollenhoff, (drumroll in the distance), from Fort Meyer (boooom!) Iowa (the corn state), a lawyer (trumpets blare!) (da-da-da-da-da-da-da-da-da-*tum!*) as well as a Pulitzer Prize winning journalist (the entire brass section and all percussionists join in for a Ta-TUM!) is joining the staff of the White House as . . . Ta-ta-ta-ta-ta-ta-T-U-U-U-U-M! . . . The President's Ombudsman!

God, what a dream!

Big old Clark Mollenhoff, who wears red pants and blue blazers and knows every telephone booth in the Senate Office Building from standing in them talking with the desk until he had puddles in his shoes, is now ensconced in the White House and vicinity.

Clark decided that it was about time that he himself undertook a civic responsibility, as agonizing as such a decision was, and work for the American people in a role in which he could offer a unique background of probing into men's crooked affairs.

Clark combined the minds of a detective, a prosecutor, a judge, and a moral philosopher of the plains, and a hidden quality as a minor poet. He was a unique American man, a member of a vanishing breed, The Old Work Horse.

This is a poem Clark had printed on parchment paper and signs for admirers. Mine is signed, "From the Old Work Horse, Clark R. Mollenhoff," in a big, easy to read hand.

THE
OLD
WORK
HORSE

A curry comb, an old check rein,
The curb bit for the bay—
The farm horse ghosts still linger there
In shadows bare and gray.

The big black's hair is matted in
The brush upon the wall.
The mane hair of a young roan mare
Clings to the single stall.

The unused harness rots away,
And hames are turned to rust.

The empty manger gathers chaff;
The grain box fills with dust.

The double-trees and neck yoke lie
Unnoticed in the shed,
Except when curious children's hands
Stir memory of the dead.

The massive-bodied sorrels and roans
No longer fill the stalls.
The quiet is no longer pierced
With trumpet stallion calls.

Some stalls are rigged for feeding calves.
Pigs desecrate the box
Where broad-beamed Belgians stood and munched
With straw up to their hocks.

On down the road, five miles or so,
An old team walks the lane—
The remnant of the massive power
That plowed this rolling plain.

From the Old Work Horse,
CLARK R. MOLLENHOFF

"The Old Work Horse" was going to the White House for the most patriotic of reasons, when the White House got through with him. His mission, the White House people said, was to poke around inside the government and detect, with his sensitive old nose for news, where the next scandal might break out, especially if the scandal might hurt the Republican Party. Clark was to have a free hand and good access to the President. He was an early warning device. If complaints came in about a bad or dirty job some tentacle of the government was performing, Clark was supposed to hunt down the facts, correct the situation, and keep it from turning into a major embarrassment in the press. It was a dream job.

Clark trotted off on his way, deep in a hick's dream, and he was happy. There was more trivia than he ever imagined in the White House corridors. He gobbled it up like sugar lumps. He sat down and wrote memos to the President, and almost every memo was stopped before it got there, by a careful system of screens and filters controlled by the President's chief of staff.

The memos were newspaper stories; they read just like his column would have read if he had been writing a column. He found little scandals everywhere he looked, practically one a day, and he was allowed to nose around discreetly and look into them. He was buddy-buddy with the press secretary, who began to tell him lies. Clark was not a man you could tell a secret to, but he asked a lot of questions people tried to answer somehow. It began slowly to dawn on Clark that he was being made to appear ridiculous.

He had been stripped of his newspaper column in Des Moines, which made him a famous man in Iowa, and his freedom of speech had been stolen away by the obvious chains of working for the President. His trumpet stallion call made hardly a peep.

They'd reduced the old work horse into a plucked Sans Souci squab, which was called in the White House, a pigeon. Just then he woke up from the hick's dream and he was, as he says, "Goddamned mad!!"

His character was saved by a lucky brain tumor, because life is full of wonderful oxymoronic experiences.

The tumor was sitting right on his memory bank.

Memory was Clark's professional strong point. He remembered names, telephone numbers, newspaper articles, lines from presidential speeches, addresses, song lyrics, and apt quotations from plays and poems. He went on stage at the Gridiron Club spoof dinners, where old and respected members of the Washington Press Corps gather with their guests to watch musical skits about politicians. But one day, Clark couldn't remember his lines. He blanked out.

Then he gave a speech in Iowa, and in the middle of it he blanked out again. He simply left the track and disappeared into an empty part of his head, and then snapped back again, very upset and flustered, and *scared*. It was just a matter of a second or two that he was gone, and even a good friend of his in the audience didn't detect anything except perhaps a slight pause, and maybe a little bit of surprise and fear on Clark's face, but nothing serious. Clark was an excellent speaker and most men stutter and pause and hem and haw a lot more than he ever did.

But Clark knew he was getting sick and that the trouble was in his brain. Over the next few weeks, he lapsed again and he went to doctors. The doctors said he was getting older and that the brain begins to deteriorate after a certain age, like the rest of the body, and that pieces of his memory were simply drying up and flaking off like oak leaves in the fall. They didn't find anything else wrong.

It took doctors at the Mayo Clinic several days to locate the tumor with a machine that Clark describes as "a superscope."

"The tumor was as big as a grapefruit," Clark said.

I said, "How the hell did the Washington doctors miss it then?"

"I don't know," Clark said. "But the Mayo doctors were just great."

The brain tumor, his awakening from the hick's dream, and his return to the *Des Moines Register* all happened within a year's time. Clark wore a wig over his head. He was made the *Register*'s Washington bureau chief. He started acting very odd.

If his fellow reporters were asking sharp questions, Clark would hammer questions aimed at cracking a man's skull. If the press secretary, his old buddy-buddy, tried to ignore him at the White House briefing, Clark would make barnyard noises until he simply had to be recognized. No other reporter at the White House, except Sara and Bob Pierpoint, made noises half so insistent.

He began to intrude his big body and his indignant voice and made even more of a spectacle of himself than before.

Word was spread that Clark was out of his mind.

I said, "Clark, they say you're crazy, insane, ever since the brain operation. Is it true?"

"What do you think?" Clark asked.

"If being loud and aggressive and pushy and a little bit obnoxious means you're insane, I might agree."

"I've always been that way," Clark said.

"I thought so," I said.

"No different now," Clark smiled.

"Then I don't believe you're out of your mind."

"Good," Clark agreed.

The brain tumor didn't change the shape or the form of Clark's world so much that he sees things upside down or anything drastic like that. He still shivers with excitement when the idea of big offices in High Government comes into his head. He is aching to be let inside again to play in the corridors of power, to know the inside-inside trivia, to send letters to high school friends with "The White House" engraved across the top.

However, since the brain operation, Clark's memory about politicians is short. He can look back, even in the face of Watergate, and say, "I went into government knowing full well. I was no virgin. I had covered the Congress and investigated. I had seen the reality. . . .

"I worked for the President. I had the right to memo him. I memoed him every day. I wrote memos to Haldeman and Ehrlichman—but I was not confined to that. Why didn't I go in and see him directly? A gnat couldn't get in unless he went through the secretariat."

He calls the White House, "Over There," as if the grass was greener over there. He wants to get back. This time on friendlier terms with the President. He can be persuaded to use his unique blend of talents as a Pulitzer Prize winning journalist and lawyer to serve the public good. Of the politicians who are exercising their nimble fingers waiting to pluck him, Sen. "Scoop" Jackson of Washington State has the first crack. Clark admires him for his fast mind and his politeness, his toughness and self-control. Senator Jackson shakes Clark's hand and talks to him confidentially. Clark trots around after the senator with a look of open enthusiasm on his face. He sings Scoop's praises to people sitting next to him at press conferences.

It's a dirty, sinful, stinking, ugly, unscrupulous, low-down, mean, and rotten trick to pull on the Old Work Horse again. Take pity, for Clark's sake, on a sweet and trying man.

But what's the use of asking for pity from a politician? Clark is ready for a hick's dream again and if you watch carefully in the corridors of power, you will see a politician with his arm around Clark's shoulder, and his mouth not too far away from Clark's ear.

LIV

I get high on honeysuckle.

de Balloon

Tiny men who succeed in a world of giants learn to perform illusions to make themselves appear much larger than they are. They do it by carefully devising shifts of perspective so that bigger men are fooled by their eyes.

Larry Spivak is a tiny creature. Larry wears doll's suits and doll's neckties, and a doll's eyeglasses in front of glassy blue eyes; but to fool us, on his doll's feet he wears doll-sized elevator shoes.

So, when I first saw him, he looked like a giant, and when he told me how he used to box in college, "and was good at it," I thought he was probably a heavyweight.

One afternoon, I was waiting outside the "Meet the Press" office and I saw Larry and his tiny gray-haired wife walking in the hotel lobby—their backs very straight, arm-in-arm, her gray hair combed very neatly into rolls, her coat hanging matronly below her knees, and Larry, brisk, bowlegged, and feisty, parading next to her.

Larry learned about the perspective of fairness by being so tiny. He found out about David and Goliath as soon as he learned that giants can squash little guys if little guys don't watch out.

He was lucky to have a good brain. He outsmarted the giants in school, and in the playground he dreamed he was strong as a madman and meaner than a fiend. When he woke up a few humiliating times from *that* dream, Larry realized that David didn't murder Goliath between the eyes with his little fist, but instead he used a hurled stone—a little bit of what the Hebrews called, "using your tuchus," as they touched their head. Using his head, Larry saw the concept that fairness expanded tiny guys to the equal of big guys, and he decided to promote fairness wherever he went.

Naturally, he was drawn to one of the great strongholds of American fairness, the press.

The mottoes of the press were:

I. The pen is mightier than the sword.
II. He who holds a pen is at war.
III. The pen owns the last word.

Armed with those mottoes, and the weapon of the pen, the press lived in fortress of fairness in a forest of swords. The fortress walls were made of the parchment on which the First Amendment was written.

"When I was a small boy," Larry said, "I would see fights in the street when a big boy was hitting a little boy—and I had to run over and help the little guy."

"Why?" I asked.

"I don't know," he said.

"Is it your Jewish background?"

"Maybe," he said, "but I just *had* to."

"Did you win?"

"I won my share."

"Did you lose?"

"Almost never."

"Sometimes?"

"Sometimes."

"Did it hurt?"

Larry smiled.

"I don't remember. But I always preferred a fair fight."

His early career was with *Antiques Magazine,* and later as an administrator and editor of *American Mercury* magazine, when it was the rage of the 1930s. He was dedicated to careful business from the start, and he earned a reputation as a man who kept his appointments as well as his word, a very unusual combination in American journalism. It was a reputation that set him so far apart from his colleagues that he chose to think of himself as a "producer" rather than as a journalist.

His "Meet the Press" was born on the radio in 1945, when Larry was forty-five years old. It went to television in 1947, at a time when television was still two or three years away from the living rooms of most of the people.

The concept of the program was simple and evangelical: To bring to as many Americans as possible—on a Sunday afternoon when their minds were receptive and relaxed—a thirty-minute program that embodied the messages of fairness.

"It's the most important part of the show," Larry said. "Fairness explains why we've lasted so long. Americans are fair-minded and we take pains to keep the show that way."

Larry has set down several rules over the years for his staff to follow.

"One," he said, "is that we can't ever allow the *implication* or the *appearance* of unfairness—even if we aren't actually being unfair."

Larry and his staff are careful to warn the journalist panelists on "Meet the Press" not to ask "clever" questions that cause a guest to blush with shame or squirm with embarrassment. Larry's guests are treated as guests might be in his own apartment—they are subjected to brainy, informed, occasionally sarcastic or blunt questioning, without wounding too deeply or personally.

Larry is very careful about every detail of his show. If you *watch* it intently next time, you will see that the set is extraordinarily simple for the eye. A long desk behind which four newspeople sit, and a small desk behind which the moderator sits with his guest. Larry is the moderator for fifty weeks a year, barring bad health—or his eventual retirement.

The guest is always the most important and newsworthy man or woman Larry can engage each week. Here is where his good business sense and his reputation as a fair promoter serve him well. A newsworthy guest is usually in a ticklish spot in his political life—a newsworthy guest is often on the defensive and can't mount a killing attack against unfair treatment—unfair interrogators could get the goods on a guest. A guest doesn't want to face unsheathed daggers and worry about sneaky stabs in the back—a guest wants to know the members of the press will act like gentlemen and not untamed beasts—a guest wants what he has to say said without deadly snipers picking his words to death—a guest knows that the doctrine of fairness protects unscrupulous men—that kind of guest will gladly appear with the spirit of fairness to "Meet the Press." It may outnumber him, but it will not hurt him, if he doesn't hurt himself.

The guest, unless he is extremely, mortally weak and about to die anyway, can walk away from a "Meet the Press" matchup with a triumph, or at least a draw, every time. The four panelists are not paid a cent for their participation in the match, because news people, you will find, will fight fairer for recognition than for money. They amble off the stage, pleased and satisfied with their appearance, smug in the warm thought that their faces have been seen by millions of people and their voices were heard asking jabbing questions. Larry leaves the stage, where he has acted the part of the toughest fair questioner of them all, assured that he will continue as long as he works and lives to round up the most important guests in the news for his show, whose reputation for fairness has spread its doctrine around the world.

In other countries, the press is unprotected by a parchment fortress, so Larry is careful that "Meet the Press" is as fair as ever with leaders who aren't accustomed to an American press.

"I warn them," Larry said, "that they won't be given the questions in advance and we won't take special care of them in the scenery or the questioning. I suggest they be prepared for some difficult ones. By now, they all understand."

American guests are treated as if they ought to know what they are doing when they get in front of the cameras. They are aware that without any tricks, other than some pancake makeup, and perhaps some powder and rouge, they will be cut down to democratic size by the television cameras that shrink all men to the size of a mouse, and can expand a mouse to the size of men. Only a mercury wit, a silver tongue, or a golden spirit can save giants from the humiliation of being dwarfed by the magic of television.

Little people, on the other hand, are happy to see their image expanded. With their head filling the entire screen, there is no easy way to determine a person's physical size.

LV

The grave's a fine and private place,
But none, I think, do there embrace.

Andrew Marvell

It's nine o'clock in the morning. Ben Bradlee hasn't had any restful sleep in so long he can't remember the last time.

I say, "You look tired."

"I am," he says.

"Your left eye is drooping."

"I know. It's a nerve inflammation. I noticed it a year ago. I thought it was a brain tumor or a stroke. The doctors said no, but they put me on warning about my health."

He puts his feet up on his desk. He wears a small-sized loafer that isn't polished. He says, "I was on the bathroom floor throwing up all night."

He makes it sound glamorous.

I ask, "Was Sally with you?"

"No, she went back to New York."

"Then you were alone."

"Yeah. And I had to get up this morning to take my kid to school."

"Your children are living with your wife?"

"Yeah . . . but I go over there and pick 'em up in the morning."

"Why?"

"I get to see 'em that way."

"None of them live with you?"

"No." And then he says, "Barney, I want to keep away from that."

"Are they making it hard on you, Ben?" I ask.

"Sure they are," he says.

I ask, "Who's doing it to you?"

"You know who," he says.

"No, who?"

"All the ones in Sans Souci. All over town. It's the *big* topic. It was in *Newsday* and *Time* in New York. People in the business. I can't go into a bar in New York without people knowing about it."

"What do they say?"

"Nasty things. You know. What you'd expect."

"Doesn't anybody wish you well?"

He shakes his head.

"How about your friends?"

"Yeah, my friends."

"Do you have any friends?"

"*Of course* I have friends."

"A lot of friends?"

"No. Not a lot."

I say, "They've really got you by the balls, eh, Ben?"

He says, "Huh?"

"I mean you throw up all night and then run to your wife's home to run the children to school and then run the ship all day until your eye droops, and then live with Sally Quinn on the weekends, and you're fifty-one years old."

He puts a cigarette between his lips.

I say, "Do you love her?"

He says, "I think so."

"Are you and your wife separated?"

"I've got lawyers, and my wife's got lawyers."

"Sounds messy."

"It is."

"You going to have to give a lot up?"

He nods.

I say, "It looks as if you don't want to give so much up, for Sally."

"I don't know yet."

"You going to keep the children?"

"No, but I won't have any trouble visiting them."

"And paying for them."

"Yeah, paying for them."

I say, "You think you love Sally. Why?"

And Ben says, "You know, Barney. . . . Her brightness, her freshness, her charm."

The telephone rings. It's an old-time Washington lawyer who often calls to chat with Ben for a few minutes.

Ben tells the man, "I was on the bathroom floor throwing up all night."

Ben's face grows concerned as he listens to the response, and he stammers, "Oh, no, no, it's not serious. It's just something tainted I ate. Something temporary. Don't worry."

226

If I had the time,
I'd write you a short letter.

Montmorence Pimm

The next announcement about Sally Quinn said she was leaving CBS by mutual agreement and that Sally was going to work in the Washington bureau of the *New York Times*.

The next announcement a few days before she was supposed to go to work for the *Times* said that she was going instead back to the *Post*.

As usual, the announcement was made in the *Post* "Style" section, where the headline on the story said, "Sally Quinn Back in Style."

The gossips were thrilled. One story that circulated in the *Post* was especially telling.

"She even drives his car."

Everything good in life
Comes as a complete surprise.

August Adrian

If you see words as I do, the pictures of them that you get in your head become very vivid.

Take *c-o-c-k-s-u-c-k-e-r* for example.

I see a man who looks like Bill Small, with the head of a rooster in his mouth. He looks choked and upset.

When the word *s-h-i-t* comes out of a person's mouth, I can see the word sometimes as big as hippopotamus droppings, and sometimes like little mouse calling cards the size of rye seeds.

So when I was talking to Marvin Kalb, and he told me Henry Kissinger was a *tuchus lekker,* I saw a picture of Henry Kissinger bending over to lick the nose of a desert donkey, while a smiling crowd of Arabs in the background watched.

I believed *tuchus lekker* was the way Marvin saw the man he was writing a book about. Then a year passed by.

One afternoon in Marvin's house I asked, "Now that you know him even better, and he comes to your house for dinner, and you're two months from finishing your book about him, do you still think he's a *tuchus lekker?*"

Marvin said, "Christ, Barney, what the hell kind of pronunciation is that?"

I said, "I don't know. It's the way I learned it."

"*Tookus* lekker. *Tookus* lekker," he said.

"Mine has a Spanish accent to it. From Galicia."

Marvin gave a knowing nod of recognition, with his chin pulled into his neck and his lips pursed.

Marvin had explained to me a year before how he ranks the Jews he knows.

There are German Jews, according to Marvin, "who have the ability to kill."

And there are Russian Jews, who Marvin described as "court jesters, ones to act the fool, to entertain."

Marvin said Kalb was a Russian name.

So I said, "You mean *you* could never kill?"

Marvin reviewed the idea in his mind and said, "No, I don't

think so. We Russians weren't made to kill. We dance and write.''

He asked me where my parents came from, and I told him my mother's father and mother were from somewhere near Kiev, near a city now called Dnepropetrovsk, and my father's parents came from a place I don't know, and he never named to me, but described it by saying, ''It was one of those little places on the border between Germany and Poland that was German one day and Polish the next.''

Marvin nodded. I hadn't mentioned any Spanish heritage.

I went back to his idea of German Jews.

''Do you think Kissinger can kill?''

Marvin said, ''I'm not sure.''

''Could you imagine him ordering *other* people to kill?''

''Sure,'' Marvin said.

''But *you* couldn't kill,'' I said, to see if he'd changed his mind.

''No,'' he said.

I said, ''Do you feel so purely Russian in your soul?''

''Yes.''

''What happens when a Jew is part Russian and part German, and part something else?'' I asked.

''He's in trouble,'' Marvin said.

Marvin and his older brother, Bernard, who is commonly known as Bernie, were writing the Kissinger book together.

When I saw Marvin and Bernie together in Marvin's house, I asked them, ''Do you trust each other?''

Marvin exploded with, ''How can you *ask* a question like that? What kind of question is that? You obviously don't know *anything* about us if you ask a question like that!''

''I don't,'' I said, ''that's what I want to find out about, so I ask questions.''

''But that's a wrong kind of question,'' Marvin said. ''Brothers *trust* each other. What brothers don't trust each other?''

''In the Bible there are two famous ones,'' I said.

''I don't mean in olden times. I mean in modern times.''

''I don't trust my brothers, and they don't trust me,'' I said.

''Well, that's possible,'' Bernie said. ''But we do trust each other completely.''

Marvin's house was pale and quiet.

Bernie's house was a world of fun. Phyllis Kalb called the house, ''The Mushroom.''

A roly-poly Oriental woman, with a gold tooth, answered Bernie's doorbell. Then she ran in little steps to find him for me. She called, "Mas-tuh! Mas-tuh! Mas-tuh!"

Four happy Balinese masks, each about the size of a two-year-old baby's face, hung in a row on the side of the stairs facing the front door . . . as greeters.

Bernie's love of beauty and grace filled the first floor. His collection of Oriental bowls and carvings and furniture was most obvious. He displayed the bowls simply and proudly in a special room on shelves he built himself. He does not want other people handling his treasures.

We were talking about Bernie's journalism career, first with the radio station of the *New York Times,* then as a *Times* reporter on a ship off the South Pole and finally a *Times* correspondent in Asia, after which CBS hired him. Bernie loves and misses Asia.

Bernie hopes to go back to Asia.

Twinkle, Bernie's and Phyllis's seven-year-old daughter, ran into the living room where we were talking and threw her arms around her daddy's neck and kissed him.

He said, "Careful, Twinkie, you don't want to break anything." But she almost tripped into the coffee table in her delight at seeing him. Twinkie ran upstairs to play.

Phyllis, plump and juicy, came in with tea and cream-filled cookies, but she left when Bernie said he wanted to do all the talking.

"It's *his* house," she said. "And it's his collection."

A few minutes later, Tanah, the oldest of his four daughters, who was blossoming into a young woman, a little bit shyly walked in to kiss him.

They exchanged a few serious words, befitting the girl's more mature mood.

But Bernie couldn't stand the seriousness, and I enjoy remembering the scene.

He reached out for his daughter's hand as she was walking away, pulled it to his lips, and kissed the back of it, loudly. She smiled shyly from the kiss, and then Bernie patted her firm, rounding bottom, two gentle pats, and Bernie turned to me with a look of true delight in his eyes, and said, *"Delicious!"*

LVIII

People who can hear are embarrassed
in front of deaf people,
because when they speak they get
the feeling of talking behind the deaf person's
back.

Walden the Wolf

Mike Waters has a cathedral in his head, the nose of a flying but-
tress, the beard and moustache of a Flemish bounder, and the spirit
of an Irish heaven. This kind of character isn't professional in the
warlike sense, and instead of fighting he's dreaming and fretting and
writing poetry, while Watergate is exploding, liberated women are
attacking from every direction, prices are rising, and the world is
coming apart. He's only vaguely interested. He'll take a peek to
know what's going on in the outside world. Then he turns away
from the blood and corruption, and to the world of a god with a
deep bass drum voice, ordering his angels—each night—to produce,
stage, direct, and manage, with a cast of thousands . . . the sunset.

It is lucky that a spirit like Waters's is hitched to a sturdy, feet-on-
the-ground, substantial, black-eyed, black-haired, strong-faced
mother named Susan Stamberg.

Where Mike is slumped, Susan is straight-backed; when Mike
comes to the microphone fretting, seconds before being late, with a
just-completed idea in his head and still scribbling on his script,
Susan is meticulously prepared, and she is concerned whether other
people are prepared. On many occasions, just before their daily
broadcast starts, Susan has the time to take a lipstick out of her
purse and apply it to her ample lips for her radio listeners.

Susan does brass-knuckle work; most of the time Mike flies
around the action like a kite.

It's unlikely a better matched male and female couple exists in
the American radio business.

Radio requires imagination, and "All Things Considered" is an
imaginative hour-and-a-half-a-day program produced by National
Public Radio.

Cleve Mathews, the producer, was just slightly wild-eyed. He
seemed on the surface to be perfectly suited for the life of mediocre
accomplishment on the foreign desk of the *New York Times*. He was

231

a man I'd sent messages to from Buenos Aires, and who sent messages back. A man without a personality of a sort you are attracted to or repelled by, a face among the faces, just slightly wild-eyed. At an age when most American men are burning out, there is a rare breed of man who begins to blossom forth, and whose mind begins to stretch again, and they pop out of their shells like seventeen-year locusts and sing and sing and sing.

That's what happened to Cleve. At the age of forty-four, when he had advanced and was perfectly secure as an associate news editor in the Washington bureau of the *Times,* he picked up and left. He took a cut in pay to administer and produce for National Public Radio—a radio network that gets its money from the Congress and is, therefore, as jittery about money as any ransom victim. Cleve was no longer able to look ten years into the future and see comfortable retirement on a *Times* pension.

Cleve and I met unexpectedly in his office at NPR. He remembered my problems in Buenos Aires, the ones that scandalized the New York office, and he was still enough of a *Times* man to be a little leery of irresponsibility. For my part, I remembered his face, and the slightly wild eyes, and the name Cleve, and his tense bearing, but I wasn't at first sure it was from the *Times* or somewhere else, perhaps *Time* magazine or the old *Herald Tribune.* He said something about the *Times,* and then I knew for sure . . . but he wasn't the same Cleve I remembered.

He was trying to hide it under his old *Times* cloak of white-shirted respectability, but here was a man who was as happy with his work as a child at sunrise.

He said, after a while, when we had gotten to know each other as people instead of Barnard Law Collier, the bad South American by-line, and Cleve, the guy on the other end of service messages.

He said, "Barney, we never talked with each other about my ideas about news and stuff, but I used to talk with guys in bars and talked about news concepts and new ways of covering the same old story, and now I've got a chance to try most of my ideas out, and it's *fun.* You asked if I was having fun, and yes, I'm having fun."

One of the surest signs that Cleve was having fun was that Cleve said he and his wife, who for many years had almost nothing truly stimulating to discuss with one another, were now eager to talk to each other any time they could find time. And they worked hard to find the time. Cleve's youngest son, Rich, who was twenty years old, had studied and practiced himself into one of the most promising giant rope sculpture artists in the country, and he chose to live at home in a studio on the third floor of Cleve's house—a decision that was an honor to his father's and mother's understanding. The gallerylike lobby and alcove of NPR's offices were hung with his son's serious work, all of which had the presence of museum pieces in a strange, predestined way. Cleve had no false pride about his son's work; it was true pride.

I asked, "Cleve, could you have developed so much freedom of mind at the *Times?*"

Cleve said, "I don't think so. I never had anything really my own there. This has a lot of headaches, and a lot of risks, but it's my own."

LIX

When you see a field full of beautiful, wild flowers, look for a bulldozer.

John Dear

At first, Connie Chung appeared more than pretty. Then, as the bindings and strictures, the pushing and pulling of television took their toll on her mind, she descended to pretty, and then to not so pretty, and then she wilted under the strain, and her freshness took refuge in a small corner inside her and she was stripped to a girl with speechless eyes and false eyelashes and curly hair from a beauty parlor.

This is a terrible process.

Believe me, when I saw her in the CBS studio in August of 1973, she was a graceful, feminine creature, and there was a spring to her walk, and a gentle and understanding quality to her voice and an air about her that said, "I am working hard and enjoying looking at life."

She was a curiosity beyond most curiosities in the television business.

Connie, underneath her cosmetics, is a pure Chinese girl. Her skin is the color of precious ivory. Her Chinese name is Precious Ivory Chung. In her own memory, Connie remembers her father telling her that her Chinese name meant, "The Melodious White Keys on the Piano." Then Connie would have been Melodious White Keys on the Piano Chung, which may be too long and difficult for a television news career, but sounds wonderful in the imagination. Connie has been convinced to be something she is not, in front of millions of people, and the masquerade shows itself on her skin, in a blemish or an ulcer on her precious ivory, and on television, where she will pretend to have no feelings.

I looked closely at Connie's eye makeup.

She learned to use eye makeup from her next oldest sister, Maimie. Maimie's mind is hard where Connie's is soft and pliable; and the shrewd, hard approach to life is, in Maimie's imagination, the way to get ahead in American life.

Connie is the youngest daughter and the only one in a family of five daughters who found a way to avoid becoming married and to make a name for herself. Her oldest sister married a Chinese chemist, a good, suitable marriage, and she and her husband run a Chinese restaurant in Kissimmee, Florida. Her next two sisters married military men, both Chinese. One is a colonel in the American army and the other is the only Chinese commander of an American navy ship of the line, a destroyer. Maimie is a different story. Her life was somehow infected with the confusion between the old Chinese ways her older sisters followed, and what freedom of choice women can enjoy in America. She married a Chinese boy as usual, but then entirely unusually, the marriage ended in divorce and she married the first white man in the Chung family for many, many, many— maybe infinitely back into Chinese history—many years. Maimie and her new husband, a Canadian employed by IBM, produced a half-white Chinese baby, the overwhelming joy of his grandparents, Mr. and Mrs. Chung.

Connie became famous, but she was not so overwhelmed by her fame that she moved away from her parents' home. She stayed home because, if she left, her mother and father would miss her too much for her to bear.

When I asked him, Connie's father agreed that Connie may be the most famous Chinese face in the mind of non-Chinese Americans, next to Mao-tse Tung, and perhaps, in some places, his equal.

Mr. Chung is a proud father. He cares about Connie's beauty and he will examine her face, with the care of a great collector of precious objects, in the hope of finding no marks or blemishes. When he finds an imperfection, he is saddened. He is very afraid that his damaged heart will stop beating too soon.

Behind Connie's eye makeup, I saw a girl who dreams that she was not born in Washington, where she *was* born, but in a Pan American airliner, over the Pacific Ocean, with the plane flying toward Washington from Peking. She would be, therefore, either a citizen of the air, or of China—with a tinge of American, because the plane is American. But she dreams she is not a special category of Chinese, who are born away from the mainland of China. They are called, in outcasting Chinese words, *Hwa-chow,* for foreigners.

And Connie is also a foreigner in America, despite her American citizenship, because her heart is in China.

Her American name, Connie, was arrived at completely frivolously. It was decided that Maimie needed an American name if she was going to grow up in America. Mr. Chung had been on the losing side in the war Mao-tse Tung won in China, and he decided to exile himself in the United States. He was working in the embassy of Chiang Kai-shek in Washington when he decided that exile was the only way. He took a United States government job that made use of his administrative ability with paperwork, and his Chinese skill with numbers. The Chungs didn't know how long it would be before they could go back to China, but it was practical to give a young child a name Americans could easily pronounce. The older daughters picked up a copy of *Photoplay* magazine from a table, and opened it to a photograph of Constance Moore. And so, Precious Ivory had an American name.

The naming copy of *Photoplay* has been kept as a Chung family memento.

Connie grew up near Washington and was sent to public schools and the University of Maryland, and the Americanization of a pure Chinese girl took place and her Chineseness was good in one way, because it called immediate attention to her, which she enjoyed, and it also set her apart, which she did not so much enjoy. It is much more comfortable in America to blend, and round Chinese eyes, which Connie still thinks "are right off the boat," don't blend well in America. She was excited when Maimie had the courage to experiment with eyebrow pencil and eye liner. In high school, Connie was finally permitted to take lessons from Maimie in how to make her round eyes, with their stubby Chinese lashes and almost no eyebrows look like the eyes of most American girls, with a slanted fold in their eyelids and eyebrows that rise and fall and arch. Once she started painting her eyes, Connie would not appear unpainted in the company of other than her most intimate family.

Her voice also has been made up. It is a good, strong, clear voice, but on television, it has only one tone.

Chinese is a singing language, and to know how to speak it is to know how to sing very complicated songs. So Connie can sing her speech, but instead she has been molded to mimic the American newscasters continuously "objective" tone and expression.

The one time Connie dared a free smile with a television camera focused on her, she heard in her earphone the voice of the producer in the control room shouting, "Stop that smiling!" The producer told her later that news was, "Serious."

Connie, at twenty-seven, was convinced that the way to the top in a television career was to pace herself, to learn the rules of the business, discover who has the real power, be their friend, and make them a friend of the family. It was old Chinese philosophy. When Bill Small came to dinner at the Chung house, he brought his wife, and those of his children who were available, and also a relative from Chicago.

But for all the philosophy behind her, Connie Chung had decided not to be herself, Melodious White Keys on the Piano, and the television camera was completely unforgiving. It diminished her breeze of freshness to "a novelty," in Bill Small's words.

LX

Dawn't fahk mit bawses!

Ada Gerlovin

Another spring came, and hideous dreams.

A black-uniformed man came to me one day and said, "We have your wife and daughter. We have come to break you."

He took me down to a clean-smelling, white torture chamber and said, "You will be allowed a single escape from madness. You see against the wall there. Your wife and daughter are tied and their heads so arranged that a small space, perhaps the size of a half-dollar, still remains between their eyes."

I looked and there they were, Maggi and Kate. Maggi on the right and Kate on the left, looking at me frightened and sidewise, and the sadness was so deep and dark that memories of joy and gladness and laughter crowded into my mind and I began to cry. And then they began to cry. And we sobbed silently together, our minds connected by memories of daffodils and roses, and cake parties; and the black-uniformed man stood to the side, disrespectful, counting a most painful time to let the hurt sink in.

Then he said:

"I here hand you a pistol."

He put a lightweight pistol, long-barrelled like a target gun, in my hand. I wanted to drop it, but I held on.

"It is filled with bullets," he said; and I thought, "Why?"

"You may have as many shots as you like," he said.

He looked like an American and he talked like an American. A college-educated American, with no particular face, and a flat, competent accent.

I held the gun in my hand and I did not think of turning it on him immediately and killing him. I knew he was not alone, and eyes were looking through peepholes. I waited for him to say something instead of killing him and not listening to the voice of reason and compromise. I listened, and he said:

"We will let you free if you succeed in the following."

"All of us?" I asked. I knew it made no difference. I wanted to hear the empty promise. It was a matter of hope.

"All of you," he said. Maggi's tears poured down her cheeks. She knew it was an empty promise and she was crying at my hope in the midst of hopelessness. I could feel her mind say, "He still hopes, the poor fool, I love his hope."

The black-uniformed man said:

"You may use as many bullets as you like. If you succeed in hitting the small silvery spot between the eyes of your wife and daughter, you may all go free."

There was a long pause in his voice while it sunk in, and then he said, "Or as many of you as there are left."

Tears came fresh into my eyes. I remembered a red dress and a dancing walk and the hammock in the trees and the New Year's Alligator, and a cabin in the West Virginia mountains, the old stream, Kate's baby feet, Maggi's arms around my shoulders, a summer garden, flying balloons and a birthday cake ballerina, and then the black-uniformed man prodded me in the ribs with a finger.

"Make up your mind," he said. "We haven't got all day to wait."

I thought of shamrock leaves that are three hearts on the same stalk and how two close up to sleep at night and one remains awake. I thought of zebras and Buckeye the dog ("Where is he?" I wondered. "Escaped, I hope!") and "Goodnight Moon," a stubbed toe in New York, and a banked car track near Atlanta, and a small-checked shirt, and the black-uniformed man prodded me again.

I gripped the pistol hard, as if I were about to shoot him, but I held my hand.

"Indecision here is simply prolonging the agony," I thought.

"Can I hit the target between their eyes in the hope of an empty promise? No."

I decided what I would have to do.

I took aim, praying that the barrel hadn't been tampered with, and I did what had to be done. I pulled the trigger as I looked directly into Maggi's eyes and said, "We will be free, we will dance."

And both our eyes were full of tears as the explosion cracked in the room, and the black-uniformed man held his crotch and jumped up and down and screamed with laughter at the red silk flag on the metal rod that poked out of the gun barrel. There was one word on the flag: "Pip!"

LXI

Don't you know anything?
Don't you know the most unctuous preachers
have the most Devil in them?

Esther Wulf

I don't want you to believe the truths that follow about the Reverend Lester Kinsolving are true in the "human" sense of what is true, meaning that every human has similar experiences, and if you hit a true artistic chord it will ring the bell of truth in every human head and heart. I knew very early there were creatures in the world who looked human but whose bells of truth didn't ring the same as everyone else's, and who were entirely unconcerned about an artist's mania for similar experience; they knew humans act essentially like sheep, and the creatures understood this, as wolves understood about sheep, and when a wolf dresses in a sheep's clothing, he puts on the turned-around collar of a priest and leads his flock, one by one, into his hungry, salivating, big-toothed jaws. Humans will sing hymns of complete nonsense, done up in solemn but joyful chorus, sometimes raising the intensity of a single word, like "Hallelujah," into vast extremes of musical piousness, and it is the dream of humans to have the entire population of the world, the rich and the poor, the lions and the mice, every living creature and all of the dead, singing, with their eyes upraised to the heavens, "Hallelujah! Hall-le-lu-yah, hall-ay-luh-yah, halayluhya, ha-le-lu-uuuuuu-*yah!*" until the heavens rock with their singing and the Lord smiles down upon them and gives them peace. Amen.

But those are human prayers. On the other hand, there are creatures who pray first for blood, and then for lust, and then for luck, and then gold, and these are not well spoken of among the murmurings of human voices.

Now I want to narrow this theology down to a priest by the name of Lester Kinsolving, the only man who appears in the White House press room as a journalist, on a regular basis, with the audacity to wear his collar turned around. This audacity, all by itself, sets him apart from the crowd of civilians who claim to be objective reporters. I didn't notice Kinsolving right away because I was concentrating on the human beings, and when I concentrate on humans, I don't bother to notice if there are any other creatures working the same flock. I figure there's enough to go around and a rival creature has to climb down my back before I'll bother to notice him. I notice angels a little more readily, because they are rare and I'd say that out of the sixty to seventy Washington journalists I saw and talked to, three angels, Carl Rowan, a Black angel, protected by two big, black dogs, Jack Anderson, a white angel, protected by one of the surviving Gorgon Sisters, and Mike Waters, a white angel, unprotected, were all I saw.

When I finally got around to noticing Les, I recognized him right away for the devourer of life that he is.

It is a common, human, everyday illusion to see in a priest something fatherly, something pastoral, something free from sin and evil. The turned collar is a magic ring. It is as magic as a police dog's badge.

However, what came out of Lester Kinsolving's eyes was desire for life. Not a shred of fear, no apologies, no denials, no unspeakable gaps of thought, no deviations, and almost no limits to the wildness of his ideas.

I do a disservice to Les's creature to describe him manwise, but manwise, Lester Kinsolving is about as tall as a short basketball player, bony white and hairy-legged, and when I saw him at his house, he wore basketball shoes, short socks, baggy pants, and a knitted sweater.

I called him at home about sunset on a Saturday.

I said, "This is Barney Collier. I'm writing a book. We have a photograph of you I think is excellent. It shows you at work. I've called once before, and you were out of town . . . and now the time for the end of the book is getting near, and at the end of the book I want a man of God. . . . A priest."

"Well, I'm flattered," Kinsolving said.

"I'd like to speak to you, if I can, as soon as possible," I said.

"I'm going on a business trip tonight. I've got to sell the column. But I'll be back, sometime early next week."

I allowed a pause that could be interpreted as desperate need . . . and the disappointment that a man of God could tell a dying man to wait for an appointment.

"How about coming over tonight," Kinsolving finally said. "And if you can, bring the pictures with you."

I told him that I was calling from the nearby supermarket in Vienna. I knew he lived just down the road.

I knew he wanted to see a rare photograph of a priest working in the open, and not just lying back and waiting in the darkness of a church for stray lambs to come along.

Kinsolving told me stories. He told me about watching as priests stole from the church, and he told me about his first stab at journalism—a four-page, legal-sized bulletin he called "The Crucifer," which means someone who bears a cross. It was soon nicknamed, "The Crucifier," which means someone who worries and torments.

He published the salaries of pastors and assistant pastors in his Episcopal diocese, of San Francisco, and showed that the pastors took three times more salary than the assistants. He opposed the death penalty and openly debated about it. He called a state legislator who favored death "an idiot." He had been a prison chaplain, and witnessed electrocutions. Now he wrote a column about Washington and religion for nearly three hundred newspapers around the country.

Kinsolving works mostly at the White House.

One day, President Nixon gave his personal support to a bill in Congress reestablishing the death penalty for some crimes. Kinsolving asked the President's spokesman of the day whether the President had any preference as to the way a criminal ought to be executed. "Firing squad, electric chair, or gas—or perhaps the guillotine?"

There was tittering among most of the other White House press.

The President's spokesman said he would inquire of the President. The President did not answer.

I wondered about the question myself. How would I prefer to be executed? And my mind always tells me, "Barney, you would prefer *not* to be executed." And I say, "Oh, yes, I know, but a man must do his duty sometimes, and sometimes that ends up badly. And with a manly sternness of purpose a man must march to the executioner, a cigarette in his lips, a drink of brandy warming his insides and numbing his imagination, with dreams of God and country and political purpose in his clear, unmasked eyes."

And I remembered, in the vividness of just escaped life, the betrayed look of someone in a motorcycle helmet who learned the last lesson there is to learn about death, which is how it feels.

Then I noticed the hand-drawn sign of the cross on Kinsolving's office wall. Under it was the benediction I was looking for: "Bless This Mess."

LXII

A bell rings
When we are born.
A bell rings
To call us to supper.
A bell rings
For us to answer the telephone.
A bell rings
When an idea hits us.
A bell rings
When the typewriter nears the end
Of the line.
A bell rings
When we die.

From "Do You Answer When It Rings?"

Life is a free spirit inside Jack Anderson's pudgy, undistinguished, and durable body.

I said, "Jack, if the Mormons believe that a free spirit is trapped in a piece of machinery called the body, they ought not fear the death of the body, because their spirit can be free again for the next adventure."

We were at Jack's dining room table looking at each other directly in the eyes.

"That's right," Jack said.

"But do they fear?"

"Yes. Every man fears."

"Why?"

"Because a man might be condemned to a terrible life."

"On earth?"

"Yes. And, of course, nobody knows what happens after life on earth. Maybe *that* will be terrible. Some people don't want to take the chance."

"They like what they've got, so they stay down here and run the machinery," I said.

I imagined myself down in the engine room of the universe stoking coal.

"That's right," Jack said.

Suddenly, Jack was a big white angel with his wings folded, temporarily, inside his human arms.

With the strength of my imagination, I was lifted with Jack, high in the sky, high above the spires of the new Mormon tabernacle near Georgia Avenue, far above the clouds, and into the gentle rocking blackness of life in endless space.

I was alone.

I was afraid.

I didn't want the blackness, gentle and rocking or not. Not yet.

I wanted red balloons, sweet potato smells, a warm kiss, the clean crunch of new snow, a beautiful smile.

I wanted to be an earthbound creature until I was sure that my love would fly with me. I was afraid I'd never be sure. I'd fear the death of my body because I might be condemned to a lonely afterlife without my love. I was damned and cursed by my unmadeup mind.

Jack knew it. He stared at me puzzled, trying to figure out which way I'd jump. He wasn't sure I wouln't fly one day. Dark things can also be angels.

Most, but not all, angels are guarded either by black vicious dogs or one of the two remaining Gorgon Sisters. Medusa Gorgon was killed by Perseus. Jack is guarded by Opel Gorgon, who goes under the name, only a very slight alias, of Opel Ginn. Her stare turns mortals to stone, and her mouth, if you get close enough, tears flesh. She masquerades as Jack's secretary, and for public purposes, she is entitled an editor of *Parade* magazine.

Opel has been faithful solely to Jack for nearly twenty years, ever since Jack moved out of Drew Pearson's office to strike out on his own while continuing to serve Drew. The details of how Jack and Drew cared for each other until Drew died has been distorted into a menial and shabby story by the kvitchers, who should be turned to salt. The fact is that now Drew is dead, and Jack inherited Drew's column.

Sometimes, Jack gets his wings sooty. In 1972 Jack told his listeners on television that an American senator, who was already wounded by the disclosure of his mental record, including shock treatments, also had a hidden record of drunken-driving arrests.

The information was hot as fire. He had been told that proof of the hidden record was available, but not for a few days. However,

Jack was warned by his "unimpeachable source" that one other journalist in Washington had received the same hot information, and was preparing to publish it in her column the next day. The other was Maxine the Telephone Queen.

Jack made a greedy, mortal error. He rushed to his television program and blurted out the unchecked news. It was too hot to sit on for his column, because Maxine might publish it in her column, which would come out before his.

The story of the drunk-driving arrests was a lie.

But after he realized it, Jack stalled for time, in the human hope that the awful lie would be miraculously true instead of sickeningly false.

Finally, Jack decided to confess to his people, eye-to-eye on television.

Jack's people are unforgiving of hidden sins, but very forgiving of confessed ones. So Jack was allowed to shake off his grimy, soot-blackened wings, bathe his face and skin of the perspiring he'd done down near where Maxine lives, dress up in clean white, and climb back to the clouds.

After that, Jack put on a display of unsurpassed brilliance. He seemed to wave his hand and astonishing revelations drifted out of closed offices and locked vaults of the government, even out of the iron mausoleum of the White House, fluttered across Lafayette Park to 1620 K Street, blew up on a breeze to the ninth floor, and puffed in through an open window.

Jack called them documents. Every one of them revealed to newly believing people that the government was telling them one thing and doing another. He revealed the hidden actions of the government during the fighting between India and Pakistan; he revealed how time after time a corporation of men was more influential with the government than any individual was with the government. He revealed greed and treachery at the pinnacles of human society. His revelations shocked American moralists, many of whom wrote or spoke as members of the press. The moralists were convinced of the existence of right and wrong, and the moralists believed in the idea that a mature human who doesn't know the difference between right and wrong is dangerously insane.

Jack's revelations out-dazzled his brief descent into the coal mines of the human condition, and his full restoration was nearly complete. But not completely. There remained a very little bit of something sooty and when a child saw it, a child said, "Euooou."

Back at his dinner table, Jack said, "We simply learn to use our bodies."

"Do our bodies belong to us?"

"We occupy them for a lifetime," Jack said.

"How do we get them?"

"Children are free to choose their parents," Jack said.

"Are you sure?" I asked.

". . . Yes . . ." he said.

"I believe that, too," I said. "And some are lucky and some aren't."

Jack turned to look at his wife at the other end of the table.

Her shape was sturdy and strong, and she is dark where Jack is light. He said, "She believes about children more than I do."

Mrs. Anderson seemed surprised that Jack had any doubts about it. Theirs was a vision of a world with infinite choice. A world that seems unreal to people who measure time in milliseconds, instead of lifetimes.

From the photographs on the mantel, nine good-looking children had made their decision to join the Jack Anderson family. The girls looked healthy and unblemished and headstrong, and the boys looked a little less headstrong, but by no means weaklings. Only Lance Anderson was strange, and perhaps even misunderstood. Lance was twenty-two, and he didn't seem to be able to do much of anything with precision of thought, a characteristic that Jack described as "lacking confidence."

To me, Lance looked like an artist whose mind was always elsewhere, and I could see it hurt Jack to see Lance struggling in the real world, and it was the only hurt I saw in Jack.

The life in the Anderson house lived with noise and food smells and a kind of happy disorder of magazines, old sneakers, letters for mailing and letters received scattered around open, a big piano that was played, a living room fireplace that worked, and which Jack built a fire in, a back porch playroom with a bare tile floor that milk can be spilled on and wiped up without any tears, dogs, bicycles, a tube of "Sunscreen" suntan cream, which my eye picked out immediately because my father had invented its name and formula, a small television set with a football game on it, a Chinese girl, who acts like part of the family, stirring in a black frying pan with chop-sticks, and Jack in tropical-weight white trousers, white soft shoes, and a blue T-shirt with the word *"Muckraker"* sewn over the heart.

Jack said, "My oldest daughter sent the T-shirt to me."

LXIII
_____

Don't turn black!

Mlle. de Balloon

Barney and Maggi shared a terrible nightmare.

They dreamed that the candle burned down on New Year's Eve, when Maggi and Barney were deeply in love, and that they tumbled into a nightmare that plodded on and on taking one life they loved after another.

Quick and Quack were attacked by an animal while Buckeye was on his chain and unable to chase the intruder away. Barney couldn't tell Quick and Quack apart when they weren't walking together, so he didn't know which one's neck it was he wrung and broke because he or she was disembowled. The other one was punctured and torn under its feathers, but Barney was certain it had no great urge to live and felt imprisoned by every second of life Barney gave it by caring for it, and not breaking its neck, too. It died thankfully on the floor of the garage three days later.

Barney had no reverence for their bodies once they were dead. He threw them both in a clump of bushes in the woods and prayed that their spirits would be together.

Then Barney found Fearless-Kiss-Kiss dead on the ground under the bathroom window. He threw her away, too.

One day Buckeye dragged the skeleton of Quick, or Quack, with some feathers still stuck on it, into the yard in front of the red door.

One day Barney noticed from the upstairs window that something was misplaced about the inside of Happy's and Lucky's cage. He ran outside to see, and before he was halfway down the hill, he knew Happy and Lucky were gone. There was a hole in the wire door, about the size of a dog muzzle, and drops of fresh red blood and white rabbit fur on the ground. "Happy and Lucky are gone. Happy and Lucky are gone," he thought.

Barney and Maggi hunted the woods for the bodies or remains of their fur, but they didn't find any. Barney tried to think that Happy and Lucky escaped the jaws and were living in a hole together down in the woods, since there was no evidence to the contrary.

Maggi wanted to believe it, too, and they explained it that way to Kate.

Calico Cat got sick one day and struggled for breath and wouldn't

249

eat or drink. Barney and Maggi doctored him back to eating again, and then, while Barney was away in the mountains, trying to imagine his part of the book, Maggi found Calico breathing hard outside the red door. Maggi and Kate took Calico to the veterinarian, and Maggi was forced to make the decision that Calico must die. That night she called Barney and said, "One of our lifes left us today." Calico was a life they both loved.

The last stop before Heaven or Hell is *Baaaaawl-te-Muh!*

The railroad conductor

Stew was thin and relaxed in a yellow wool sweater in the living room of his home, and he wanted his portrait to be made before he was gone forever from the world.

I said, "Stew, you look good."

He grinned.

"You know the secret, Barney?"

"What?"

"Drugs."

It's your imagination that kills you.

*Stew Alsop, whose life left us
on May 26, 1974*

Kate said, "Finish writing . . . Kate write it . . . Maggi . . .
Maggi . . . Maggi. . . ."

And Maggi said to Barney, "I want to be with you."

Buckeye was asleep under their bed, and Kate said, "Funny
movie, eat popcorn."

And Barney, a man of few good words, now shook his shaving
cream can one hundred times each morning. It had something to do
with how much time he wanted he and Maggi to be together.

Among the people of the Washington Press
Corps included in this book are:

JOSEPH ALSOP, born October 11, 1910, Avon, Connecticut; at home.

STEWART ALSOP, born May 17, 1914, Avon, Connecticut; at home; died May 26, 1974.

JACK ANDERSON, born October 19, 1922, Long Beach, California; in hospital.

JOHNNY APPLE, born November 20, 1934, Akron, Ohio; in hospital.

BETTY BEALE, (Not divulged), Washington, D.C.; in hospital.

CARL BERNSTEIN, born February 14, 1944, Washington, D.C.; in hospital.

BEN BRADLEE, born August 26, 1921, Boston, Massachusetts; in hospital.

ART BUCHWALD, born October 20, 1925, Mt. Vernon, New York; at home.

MAGGI CASTELLOE, born October 14, 1938, Winterville, North Carolina; at home.

MAXINE CHESHIRE, born April 5, 1930, Harlan, Kentucky; at home.

CONNIE CHUNG, born August 20, 1947, Washington, D.C.; in hospital.

BARNEY COLLIER, born July 27, 1938, Detroit, Michigan; in hospital.

MEL ELFIN, born July 18, 1929, Brooklyn, New York; in hospital.

ROLAND EVANS, born April 28, 1921, White Marsh, Pennsylvania; at home.

SOMA GOLDEN, born August 27, 1939, Washington, D.C.; in hospital.

BERNARD KALB, born February 4 or 5, 1922, Bronx, New York; at home.

MARVIN KALB, born June 9, 1930, Bronx, New York; at home.

DOUGLAS KIKER, born January 7, 1930, Griffin, Georgia; at home.

THE REV. LESTER KINSOLVING, born December 18, 1927, New York, New York; in hospital.

CLEVE MATHEWS, born August 5, 1926, Valley Mills, Texas; at home.

CLARK MOLLENHOFF, born April 16, 1921, Burnside, Iowa; at home.

ROBERT NOVAK, born February 26, 1931, Joliet, Illinois; in hospital.

BOB PIERPOINT, born May 16, 1925, Redondo Beach, California; in hospital.

SALLY QUINN, born July 1, 1941, Savannah, Georgia; in hospital.

DAN RATHER, born October 31, 1931, Wharton, Texas; at home.

JAMES RESTON, born November 3, 1909, Clydebank, Scotland; at home.

HARRY ROSENFELD, born August 12, 1929, Berlin, Germany; at home.

CARL ROWAN, born August 11, 1925, Ravenscroft, Tennessee; at home.

ERIC SEVAREID, born November 26, 1912, Velva, North Dakota; at home.

EILEEN SHANAHAN, born February 29, 1924, Washington, D.C.; in hospital.

BILL SMALL, born September 20, 1926, Chicago, Illinois; in hospital.

LAWRENCE SPIVAK, born June 11, 1900, New York, New York; at home.
SUSAN STAMBERG, born September 7, 1938, Newark, New Jersey; in hospital.
HELEN THOMAS, born August 4, 1920, Winchester, Kentucky; at home.
SANDER VANOCUR, born January 8, 1928, Cleveland, Ohio; in hospital.
MIKE WATERS, born August 21, 1931, Buffalo, New York; in hospital.
BOB WOODWARD, born March 26, 1943, Geneva, Illinois; in hospital.